MY FATHER'S WAR STORIES

AS TOLD BY TOYS

✝

A CHILD'S HISTORY OF WORLD WAR II

ADVANCE COPY
Publication Date: May 6, 2019

TOM AHERN

My Father's War Stories, As Told By Toys: A Child's History of World War II by Tom Ahern

ISBN: 978-1-949790-02-3

eISBN: 978-1-949790-03-0

Layout and book design by Mark Givens

First Pelekinesis Printing 2019

For information: Pelekinesis, 112 Harvard Ave #65, Claremont, CA 91711 USA

Library of Congress Cataloging-in-Publication Data

www.pelekinesis.com

MY FATHER'S WAR STORIES

AS TOLD BY TOYS

by

TOM AHERN

For all the fathers

CONTENTS

APOLOGY

So wrong.
So long.

PROLOGUE

HE WAS BOTH A LOVING, LAUGHING FATHER AND A BULLY. It was common for his time and place, don't get me wrong. Then: men were fierce, frightening; determined to be nobody's fool. They despised anything different, such as women and of course buggerific boys.

Which led to conflict in *our* home. My mother put herself through college, earned a white-collar income *twice* his, and carried with confidence an intimidating title: business manager of (1st) a hospital; then of the daily newspaper, back when such mattered in every life and household. In retrospect, was mom a natural-born dominatrix? Not really given the times. Still, I do know this for a fact: she sprayed her disappointed opinion of him across her family, like a frightened skunk.

She was a suicide. Her mind killed her. My father did not. She made sure he got the blame, though.

Dad, Big Tom, was a factory worker. He also held a small elected office as our town's water commissioner. He won term after term. A few lawn signs did the trick back then. Honest, dependable, got the bills out on time.

Was there a special reason for Dad's dedicated public service? Financial desperation, if anything. If he stayed in office long enough, he knew, he'd earn a small pension forever. I imagine he figured, *You never have enough.* I think exactly the same way. I'm afraid. I'm anxious. I'm so old I should qualify as an antique. Like most my age, I can't sleep because the obvious options are worse than any zombie/vampire/rising dead/Millennials show I know.

Public office lifted Dad out of the puddle. But he was still an Irishman and combative. A race despised, he taught me early. Just one generation earlier employers had advertised with their jobs, *Irish need not apply!* A closet orphan. A veteran dogface shocked so far beyond fear that panic felt like relief. A man with no discernible goals or high expectations. He expected to live. He just needed to get through that, and he'd be OK. He was cursed with durability.

One of the nation's worst toxic waste spills occurred around a well site my Dad, as water commissioner, oversaw. The dirt turned the soil black around the town's pump house. He laughed when he told me. *There you go.* Another thing he often said, *Every politician's a crook.*

His war stories.

Dad's war stories: his best (only) legacy to me.

My humble (you can't *imagine* how humble) goal: the historical context to be anything but ordinary. Willing readers of history are a minority. And so: our future wanders like a drunk in a tank, heels tangled up in the pedals; story far to come.

My moral Rubicon was a plastic model by Revell of a US Army WWII Sherman tank.

My aunties saw no reason to buy the kit, though I milked my performance in their dusky front room. Beneath an afghan hand-knit by devoted, faithful fingers.

My father wanted me to get it. So Aunt Alice bought it before Dad. She made a point with that purchase a whining child had coerced from her.

It took decades of "family algebra" to figure out what she was saying. Part was just mean: "I can afford this nor can you, you failure." Mean, not meaningful. Not worth expending hate and energy on: similar throw-aways true inevitable in so many families.

I learned, though. It was all you had on earth sometimes: knifing your own family. It was the only clay deposit given you at birth, so you worked it if you needed to.

Irish lives—Irish-American lives, even more—are about the secrets. There's really nothing else. Facade and secrets.

EPILOGUE

Dad signaled me over to his hospital bed. We were alone in the middle of a busy ward.

His lower face wore the touch of a smile, all he could muster. His penis lolled beneath the hem of his abbreviated hospital gown, like a piece of lost mail. He was running on fumes.

"Tom," he croaked. At least he knew my name.

His crusted eyes looked terrified. Strangers raced past. I wore my best, well-tailored, fuck-everyone, circa copper-age, suit; ready for war in the courtroom. Nurses already mistook me for some doctor they should know.

"Getting old is hard," Dad reported. From where he was. Murmured. He turned away. Forever, though I didn't know it then.

I was now unfortunately the new first lieutenant in his life. He was reporting in. I was in charge of his comfort and his address on this entire earth, circa forever. And I knew: Dad didn't think much of first lieutenants, for good reason.

CHAPTER 1

THE VOICE IN MY HEAD

"THEY USED TO SAY, STAY WITH HIM, BOY, HE'S LUCKY."

Dad was telling me about a sergeant.

"He wouldn't dig a hole. Shell come in over here, he'd move over there. Shell'd come in over there, he'd move here. But he wouldn't dig that hole. He just wouldn't do it.

"And he was a hot rock.

"He was telling me one night how he was driving a truck out in Chicago. He said, 'I get into the city and these guys are right behind me in a big black car. Four of them.' And they were going to hijack his truck. 'I let them come up side of me right near a corner of a building, and I swung that truck and caught that car between the building, and I just pushed it right in. I never stopped. They must have all been dead. I pushed that car right against the building and squashed it right up.'

"Oh, a laugh ... he'd tell you some.

"But he didn't give a damn. Lot of times they'd pull the outfit back, he'd say, 'I think I'll go up to headquarters. See if I've lost my stripes.' They were always breaking him and giving them back to him."

Sergeant Lucky.

"He didn't take orders from anybody," my father insisted. The American Dream right there. "They just told him what they wanted, and he got it for them."

Management by results. Sure; best way to go.

"One day there we had a pillbox up in front of us," Dad said. "And the officers are in the house, and they got maps on the table. Sergeant's standing there listening to all the talk. And one of the officers turned around and he said something, and the sergeant said, 'You mean to say, I'm going to take that pillbox?'

"The officer said yeah.

"'Well,' the sergeant said, 'what the hell are you guys doing here? If I'm going to take it, I'm going to take it my way, not your way.' They said, 'You go right ahead and do anything you want.'

"And he took the pillbox.

"He got so he wouldn't lose men. He'd try to protect them. And they all knew it."

Lucky was a good man, in Dad's view. An admirable man: hard, canny, careful with the human flesh entrusted to him, insubordinate when it mattered, intolerant of shiftless rank. Army had a lot of that. Tolerant of his men, though.

Dad: "One night I was doing guard duty up in Germany, and I'm sitting out on the steps of this house. I take it for an hour, another guy takes it for an hour." The men on guard have a wristwatch they share back and forth, so they know when an hour's up. "And that's the way it goes until morning.

"The next morning the sergeant said, 'I'm really surprised to find out how much this watch gains in a night.' Well, everybody was cutting ten minutes off. They'd sit there probably for fifty minutes and say to hell with this, and they'd turn the clock." Advance the hands of the watch ten minutes. "He said, 'I can't figure out why.' He knew damn well what was happening."

"There's about fifteen of us in the cellar of this house. The whole top of it is blown out. There's a floor here, a door over there, but nothing around it. We're taking turns guarding. You go up the cellar steps, and you stay there with a rifle.

"It's pitch black and all of a sudden we heard *step, step, step* on the broken glass. I was on the top step, taking my turn, and the sergeant comes up and he whispers, 'There's somebody walking around the back of this house. If he comes to that door, shoot him.'

"Well, OK.

"So I turn, and I got the rifle pointed right at that door. The steps came, crunch, crunch ... and then they stopped. Then the first thing we knew, the steps retreated. Went *boom, boom,* back. And we didn't hear anymore.

"We had a two-way radio that we carried. Next day it came over the radio: this lieutenant in charge of the tanks was coming in to talk to us. We had tanks of each side of the houses. He'd be in about ten o'clock at night, when it got dark. OK.

"So he came in, and he and the sergeant are talking, and the lieutenant says, 'We're a-scared of the Germans coming up with a bazooka team to attack our tanks. What I'd like to do is have a couple of your men dig in on the sides of each tank.'

"The sergeant looked at him and said, 'Like hell. You want two men on each tank to dig in, you use your own men to do it. But you're not getting any of mine.' The sergeant said, 'By the way, were you the guy that was around here last night?' The lieutenant said, 'Yeah. But I couldn't find how to get into the house.' The sergeant said, 'Damn good you didn't. Because that guy there...'" Sergeant Lucky pointed at Tom Ahern, who in about 22 months' time back in the States would fill my mother's womb with his warm, wiggling surge and pass along all sorts of things, genetic and less defined. "'...was going to shoot you when you opened the door.'"

CHAPTER 2

THE SECRET OF LIFE PER SE

He HAD BEEN SHOVED INTO YET ANOTHER HUGE EVENT. First the Depression, now this, World War Two.

So when my father came back from the war, he had things to say. A hundred stories to tell with hardly a pause. He knew how to beat Hitler! And Hitler was a tough guy to beat.

I was born in 1947.

Three hundred and fifty-nine years to the day after the Spanish Armada's worst losses. A military birthday, if you knew where to look.

My father had a standard-issue peeled-potato Irish nose. It looked like a corpulent little fist shaking in a fierce face.

Fiercest at me.

I have that same nose now; as if every lazy thought I had, found the same place to hide, in front, where people could immediately see.

I'm not sure what came first in my emotional downfall: his anger, his contempt, his sad-eyed, bottomless disappointment in the curiosity that was his son. Or was it my mother jumping in to save me.

All five-foot-six of him, Tom Senior, scared me silly. I wished it was silly. He had the lungs of a steam whistle. He'd killed other men. Batted balls out of the park with ease, in our town. He had a soft center buried beneath the cast-iron lid. He could cry; I saw it a few times.

But.

He was reflexively contemptuous. Made fun of things first.

Bad for the loved ones, some of us. And a habit I picked up. Forgive me, anyone I have ever presumed to embrace as my own. Cheap contempt is my self-indulgent habit, indelible as a tattoo. Not his fault. I can do without. And I don't.

I was my mother's pretty boy. *Pretty boy:* like the parakeet that hung outside our one bathroom in a cage. Inhaled our odors. Never sang a song. Never saw direct sunlight. Scrabbled in his own brittle white worms of shit. Overfed. Depressed, I expect. I was.

Hazel was my mother. A type of birch, hazel was; and color, a kind of yellow brown. I was Hazel's sick child. Ding-toed. Asthmatic, in a house overrun by silverfish. Mummified on bad days, my chest seized up like sheet steel. Try to breathe through a pinhole sometime; that's how it felt.

My sister thought it was an act. She wanted me dead or discredited, on an *I was here first* principle. My father didn't believe my illness either. He never got sick, until he actually died.

Dad was an orphan. We figure his parents died sometime

around his tenth year on earth. Between one day and the next, gone of what was mislabeled in the press Spanish influenza.

The Spanish weren't the culprits. And this was not the kind of seasonal flu remedied today by over-the-counter medicines. This flu turned Caucasians a strange, never-before-witnessed color that was black-purple; and burst your lungs. At least it was fast. A few days of incredible suffering, untreatable, then you were dead.

We forget. Up to five percent of the world's human population perished in the flu pandemic between 1918 and 1920. In two years as many as 100 million people worldwide died, one in every eighteen? No one knows the final tally. World War One, the slaughterhouse to end all slaughterhouses, was a comparative piker: 19,000,000 killed maybe. Odd disease, too: the Spanish flu particularly favored the strong: young adults like Dad's parents, newcomers to the Boston slums, starting a better life outside Ireland. Mortuaries operated second, then third shifts. Among the Boston Irish, the dead went unwaked, a fiendish omission, the Irish as fixed on the rituals of death as the ancient Egyptians.

In his tenement, seven-year-old Thomas Francis Scanlon, *we think his patronymic was,* watched his parents sicken and die horribly, all in a week. He was a child. He could do nothing but tremble and run a few errands at the start. With the end, all the comfort and certainty in his world was extinguished. The parish priest came for the parents' remains, stuffed the boy's clothes in a sack, and spirited my father off. A quick mass for the dead—many dead—and that part of his life was done. He was official, a ward of the church.

We heard he had a brother. If so, the nuns separated

them: hard enough getting a family to adopt one beggared orphan, much less a pair.

"Orphan trains" headed west. They stopped at rural railroad stations, offering children for adoption en route, a boon for farm families in need of hands. My father, though, traveled exactly twelve miles to his new home, by trolley. To a church south of Boston, in the small town of Holbrook, Massachusetts. The faithful—mostly Irish, mostly female—perched on their pews as the priest, Father You-Will-Do-As-I-Say, made his assignments: "Mary O'Connor, you have room for one more unfortunate Catholic soul in your household, surely. These poor motherless fatherless children. Mrs. Ahern, an extra hand around the house...." It was a small, crowded house, curtained to twilight, with an ill husband, soon to die; but she raised no objection. Signaled little ... Thomas Francis, is it? Signaled him over. He genuflected as he passed the altar. Knew his church manners. His new mother, worn out, in her fifties, said her first words to him: "There's paper work, I dare say. Stick by me and don't get lost." He slipped into the pew, not quite touching her strange broad beam, the smell of soap a garland from her to him. Bearded St. Joseph, symbol of foster care for another's child, approving with a steady plaster eye, dandling on one robed arm an infant Jesus.

Dad studied St. Joseph's benign unsemitic gaze: the perfect husband, bland, inessential, good with his hands.

Then they were outside the church, down the wide granite steps. Granite was common, with the Quincy quarries so near. "Are you sick at all?" Young Thomas Francis didn't answer. Didn't realize yet that this stranger was talking to him. Walking for the first time the neighborhood where he would grow up, go to school, fight, play town ball, marry, raise kids of his own, get elected, and lose a wife: an inconceivable future as they crossed South Franklin Street, the town's main street, crossed the cobblestones and the trolley tracks, the trees losing their leaves.

"Pay attention. Are you sick?" A new mother speaking. *Yes, speaking to him.*

He trembled, "No, Mrs. Ahern."

Which was the wonder of it. He had a cast iron constitution. The gift of good health. Influenza couldn't touch him. Wondering himself, he would later boast that he never had measles, mumps, chicken pox, or any other childhood disease. When the Army tried to vaccinate him for smallpox, his immune system spit the vaccine out. This remarkable, all-weather immune system would make him a cranky patient late in life. He was so used to good health that he assumed his body would repair itself of anything, given enough time, coffee, and cigarettes.

Walking home that day from the church, his bare, cold hand wrapped in a stranger's, three blocks under a leafless canopy of tall trees, to a trim white house with black shutters, Dad adopted Tenet #1 of the scarred, the secret agents of the heart: remain amiable, but keep your emotions out of sight.

She ran a strict religious home and installed Dad there. Behind drawn curtains, in sub aqueous light, facing forbidding religious lithographs behind glass, a crucifix tacked above each bed.

The family was burdened by heart disease. The husband had passed young. Widow Ahern had two maiden daughters, Mary and Alice. Both were adults when Dad was dragged home like a pail. *These are your sisters.*

He loved it. He had a gun. He had woods. He hunted small game. He picked blueberries. He played tennis and baseball very well. He was tough and friendly. A likeable guy with dependable opinions.

My parents introduced me to my first dead body when I was six.

It was a big decision for them, discussed with the relatives: *Should a child go to a funeral?* They were afraid I wouldn't understand. *Why isn't that man breathing?* But I could see their pride, too. *Tommy's first funeral.* A social occasion. *How would he act?* In a large Scotch-Irish family, dead people in open caskets were no surprise. The oldest generation went, like a worn edge against a grinding wheel. The young had accidents. You behaved a certain way. Childishness was unwelcome.

I don't even remember which of my countless aunts or uncles it was who'd stumbled into the afterlife. But children have the curiosity of Elizabethans. I was excited, if in murmurs. I tiptoed up, at my father's urging. I kept my eyes fixed on the puckered taffeta lining of the lifted lid. I'd wondered about the smell. Bouquets cloyed the air; otherwise nothing. And then I looked down. The corpse's eyelids were shut. The face looked vaguely familiar. Very wrinkled. Very powdered. Very settled. A face so still it vibrated; maybe it was the molecules.

Now I knew.

Something. I wasn't sure then. Now I know: I'd been shown the end. A voice could have whispered into my waxy ear: "You have *now*, my fragile little nudgkin. This time you're standing in. And then you'll have *this*, three showings to anyone who remembers you exist. And between those two points in time you will have to fit in anything you want to do, anything you want to accomplish, anything you want to savor, anything you want to say. We pray it's for good, but that's not truly a requirement."

CHAPTER 3

MY DAD SAVES YOUR LIFE

MY FATHER TOLD ME:

When you see the car ahead flash its brake lights, immediately *hit your brakes as well.*

That's the big news. *I've just saved your life.*

Thanks to that lick of cautionary advice I've avoided how *many* accidents. You've just made back the price of this book, if you bought it. And assuming you value human life. Dad had an opinion on that. *We* valued human life; *we* being European transplants to America. North Africans did not (he admired their cutthroat ways). Asians did not (they baked their children in pies when times got tough, if the dogs were gone).

The injunction re: brake lights he barked at me one of the first times he allowed me to drive, on a sunny late morning leaving the church's expanded parking lot, under his supervision. He enjoyed teaching me to drive. I loved driving. But he was a nervous sort; mostly from the artillery barrages aimed at his head, my mother would have people believe. The family said he went to war with a head of black hair. He came back gray to his roots.

I am alive to write this, unmaimed, *not* in a wheelchair. Brusquely fed and one-third-cleaned by nursing home keepers, the most terrifying sight in modern America: *no hope* is the message sent.

All because he taught me defensive driving.

And from that lesson, I learned to be prepared.

People in automobiles are unpredictable. *Idiots*, a one-word summary of my father's opinion of his species. Said a thousand times. *And a smart person anticipates the worst.* From which flowed my father's really great lesson: *Life is hard.*

He said this repeatedly to me, to make a point when I was growing up. Life is hard. Just like you breathe oxygen: *Life is hard.* You drink water. *Life is hard.*

Harder than you think, he meant in my case. Harder than you could *ever* know, he told me, shaking his head. He could see I was ready to take everything for granted and become an ungrateful little snot (I did). I realized late what a cruel and terrifying creature I was when I set my mind to it. I made his life a living hell with free napalm. I was blessed, endowed, bred to have—take your pick—imagination. Great torturers have imaginations. Physical pain can be a start; bit graceless, though. Emotional pain is the luxury goods.

But you'll find out, he predicted with certainty. Desperately.

Followed by a small smug evil snort.

Someday somebody's going to wipe that grin off your face, my father would say. *I'll be cheering him on,* he implied. Me, too, I admitted. The man or woman who beats me to a pulp would be a hero. I had no use for me either. My father was right.

My father's life was a struggle, almost from the start. A done-to, not a doing-to; roadway, not wheel. He was a demographic flag raised on a hilltop.

His was the first generation of U.S. teenagers to stay in school instead of working. He graduated high school just in time for the Great Depression. A decade later, he finally got a job building ships for the Navy, which gave him the income to propose marriage. He was married June 19, 1941, six months before Pearl Harbor blew the U.S., like a dandelion, into the Second World War as a belligerent nation. Two years later he got drafted. He was in his thirties. For another two years he lived in barracks, tents, on the run, sleeping where you fell, to hear him tell it, in foxholes, in basements, in a field. Not a lucky life, by fancy standards.

Dad was the default soldier, a private in the Army infantry.

Leaning middle-aged, yet marching.

He drove trucks around France. Making deliveries, sightseeing. Until they needed more men at the front. That was different. He dug holes and bounced off the cold Belgian mud as German artillery shells screamed to earth. Horror opera. He warned me time and again, shaking his head. His hair was scraped cast iron. Life isn't all fun and games. He had the shell shock to prove it.

And yet.

When he spoke of his childhood, it was all fun and ballgames. And good friends. Hunting with a dog. He was an optimist and a pessimist and a fatalist, an angry and sentimental man who almost never got sick. That was the thing that amazed people about him. Everybody commented on his stout constitution.

He told me about the Army. Like Scheherazade, he loomed tales.

He *didn't* tell me, but I thought this was fascinating, he'd cared for his second mother while she lay bed bound. For years. The woman who had taken him in when he was seven and alone in the world. There was religious art in every room, beaming down a message of violent sacrifice for the hope of salvation. Under the stairs to the cramped second floor was the one tiny bathroom; his replacement mother slept right outside its door, the best place in the house for the old and dying.

In Dad's shoes, who *wouldn't* be jealous when my mother chose me and put him up on a shelf, with her unfashionable hats?

I don't know if they stopped having sex when I was born. There were no more children. Of course she was getting old for kids, stepping from her thirties into her forties.

CHAPTER 4

TOM AND HAZEL

THE MOST INFLUENTIAL ECONOMIST OF THE 20TH CENTURY, JOHN MAYNARD KEYNES, WHEN ASKED IF HE COULD RECALL ANYTHING ELSE LIKE THE GREAT DEPRESSION OF THE 1930S, SAID HE CERTAINLY COULD: "IT WAS CALLED THE DARK AGES, AND IT LASTED FOUR HUNDRED YEARS."

What Keynes referred to was the tempering of my father's generation. Part, anyway.

Dad remembered the Great Depression as a healthy time. "Nobody had a dime." But no one cared. You helped each other, he said. Faded laundry flapping on the line, a family goat, milk bottles clinking, the account at the grocery carried until you could pay.

Economies creaked to a standstill all over the globe. A young century ceased to be promising. William Manchester later wrote, reaching for the rear of the hall: "This was calamity howling on a cosmic scale...."

"And do you, Thomas Francis Scanlon Ahern...."

Scanlon? My father winced. The priest had to say that?

"...take this woman...." Hazel, his June bride, ready top

and bottom for delivery into Dad's trembling hands.

He heard the predictable whispers skitter through the front pew where three of Hazel's sisters sat, mostly in judgment *as the family was wont*; three short women with exceptionally pale skin and practical hair. A well-dusted St. Joseph looked down from a pedestal. Frank Smith witnessed for the groom; honest and plain. Hazel's sister, Philomena, a busy mouse, was the maid of honor. Five Presbyterian sisters altogether, counting Hazel, female splinters from a thick plank of Scottish mother. Nervous enough in a Catholic church, with the Pope's finger pointing this way and that. Even though most of them had their own Catholic husbands and had accepted Catholic baptisms for their babies, relinquished—as the Church of Rome demanded in exchange for its blessing on a "mixed" union—to an upbringing in "the One True Faith." *The One False Faith*, the McKays would insist if cornered. What did the Church of Rome ever do for Scotland except get us killed?

So: *Scanlon?*

The sisters' pew calculated. Hazel knew the story but hadn't told.

Tom Ahern *nee* Tom Scanlon. *Tom? Adopted? And he never said a thing.* They liked that. And didn't. He was tossed to the busybodies. Treasure for them. On the day of his wedding. The McKay sisters valued gossip more than heirloom pearls. Dad's big secret was O-U-T, *thanks to a fuckin' priest.*

It was hot enough to sweat. A rare perfumed scarf of cooler June air touched them. The priest continued to officiate, with a nice mahogany brogue. Like an actor. Succinct. Moving it along. There was another wedding right behind. The times. War was all over the news. A new draft had begun. People were racing to marry. Marriage might mean deferment, maybe not. A kid might anyway. Pearl Harbor wouldn't happen for another six months, the ants' nest not yet truly disturbed. But the clouds raced overhead.

So be it, Dad thought about the adoption thing. What was there to be ashamed of.

Thomas Francis SCANLON! Ahern straightened his spine and pushed out his golf ball chin as a challenge to the biddies, letting whatever it was—*fuck you! about to get laid any time I want!*—fall where it may.

In the same poorly ventilated church where an exhausted Mrs. Ahern, soon a widow, had accepted her duty 22 years earlier and adopted a boy in the name of the Lord Our Savior Jesus Christ, Thomas Francis *Scanlon* Ahern married Hazel Elizabeth McKay. She had turned 30 the year before. He was 32.

Hazel was not marrying her first choice. Her druthers had proved a recalcitrant groom.

If God indeed reads every thought and wish, then the Almighty knew the truth of this particular solemn ceremony: that Hazel was at the altar, already disappointed in her match. Still, it *was* marriage. Dad was semi-handsome; a dependable man, if you took the trouble. And Hazel could finally scratch her itch, the warm buzzing down below. Have sex of some sort, within the security of wedlock.

Twenty-one months later she gave birth to a girl they named Alice, after Dad's oldest sister, whom Mom despised.

In 1944 postcards arrived from Paris: "Just a line to let you know I'm fine. Hope you and the baby are the same. Seems years instead of months since I have been home. Is Alice walking yet? How is Tootsie doing?" Alice was Tootsie, all toes and go. A year and a half old.

On the back of a postcard of the Place Vendôme, he wrote, "In last few weeks I've seen an awful lot of France." The postcard showed a circumcised bronze-clad column poking the clouds. Dad sighed, "The square is really beautiful. I'd rather have our apartment." Despite the excitement, he yearned for the warm creature comforts of their home and his skinny wife with the wide hips, a fertile bowl.

My mother's life was more than halfway over when that postcard arrived, it would turn out (his was not). She'd won medals jumping horses. She'd been a ripping saxophone player in a female dance band. She had small feet, strong legs, not much bosom. She was smart enough to have skipped a grade and graduate a year early from Sumner High School, with the class of 1928. She was more ambitious than Dad probably realized. And a sex pistol. She had an instruction book for married women hidden in her lingerie drawer; boys snoop.

Tootsie wondered what they saw in each other.

Tootsie was an observant child. Much later, both our parents dead—all said, done and packed away—Alice called the marriage a mismatch. She claimed Mom had been much smarter than Dad. He worked in a factory. She was an executive. Tom bored Hazel, Alice decided. Worse, he knew it.

But he was a sentimental man, for all his elephant's hide.

Loyalty, maybe mere proximity, was supposed to be

enough. You stuck. You lasted. And that counted.

Not by a cannon shot.

My mother aimed one urgent precept at her daughter. I heard it many times in our starter G.I. home, scarcely larger than a tent. "Find yourself a rich man to marry," Mom's eyes blazed. "So you don't have to work." Take it literally if you want. I think she meant, *So you don't have to do the work of two.*

Understand: Hazel was one of five surviving sisters and two brothers. Her mother, Christine MacLeod, came from Prince Edward Island, a rough underarm of Canada. Offspring were all small shrubs, grown on rocky, unyielding soil. Hazel's father, John McKay, was a disappointing drunk. Human trash. He wagered their home in a poker game and lost. My mother was still in high school. The winner of the poker game brought the sheriff, to evict the McKays. The oldest sister, Doe, sped to the rescue. She was employed as a nurse in a state psychiatric facility. She lived in a small, ironclad room and saved her salary. In a few days, she bought a cheap house in Holbrook for the family to move to. With one condition: she forbade her father ever enter.

No one cared. He disappeared. Growing up I never heard him referenced once. Admirers of men? On my mother's side? No, they weren't. Certainly of no male past the age of puberty.

In 1929 Dad graduated high school. In October the stock market crashed. Whether it was symptomatic of a Great Depression already begun or a contributing cause, is debated.

He didn't attempt college; nor did the vast majority of American men then. He nursed his sick mother. He caddied in New Hampshire for the still rich during Great Depression summers. He sold shoes door to door. He took his turn, like three million others, building WPA roads and bridges.

Then the Nazis jumped Poland in 1939. All hell broke loose in Europe for the second time in twenty-five years. German submarines began bouncing torpedoes (the failure-to-detonate rate was high) off Britain's merchant fleet. Boats were in demand. American shipyards suddenly had business again, lots of it. The Fore River shipyard in Quincy hired Dad as an acetylene burner, building warships. He was in his late twenties. For the first time in his life, he was making steady money. Which meant he could afford to marry, given the inclination and a willing mate.

William Manchester: "For tens of millions the war boom was in fact a bonanza, a Depression dream come true.... In 1942 Washington was pumping three hundred million dollars a day into U.S. wallets and purses."

One amazing statistic: in just five years of pedal-to-the-metal war making, Washington outspent its previous 157 federal budgets combined.

With a war on, there was nothing much to buy, so people socked away their paychecks: $44 billion in wartime savings, burning a hole in America's pockets. Advertisers mused patriotically about all the things you could—and would!—own once Victory was assured and Freedom triumphed. New appliances. New miracle products. And mobility: brand new cars. U.S. automakers built just 139 new cars during the war. They would sell 6.7 million in 1950.

And when victory was declared: upward mobility. Uncle Sam was in a thankful mood. G.I. Loans would be available. Any serviceman could have the house, the family, the education and career he'd fought so hard for. Prosperity like you wouldn't believe was just around the corner. Business was ready to head off on an incredible tear: there were going to be uncountable billions of consumer dollars up for grabs, once the war was won.

I asked my father what the war meant to him, all told.

"It was quite a deal," he said. "'Course, it's one of those things. You know, you talk a lot about it and all that, but I don't think anybody would ever go through it again."

The American economy begged to differ.

Mr. and Mrs. Thomas Francis Ahern rented an apartment at 81 Brook Street, in Quincy, a couple of miles from the shipyard.

Alice—Tootsie—was born on March 15, 1943. Late in September that year, Dad's deferments ended. Operation Bolero, the build-up towards D-Day, was underway. To take on the Germans, the U.S. Army wanted 1.4 million men in England by May 1944.

Dad received his GREETING, the too-familiar order to report for induction. Draft board No. 31, Suffolk County, Mass. issued his. It declared: "Having submitted yourself to a local board composed of your neighbors for the purpose of determining your availability for training and service in the land or naval forces of the United States, you are hereby notified that you have now been selected for training and service therein."

He was told to show up for a physical exam at 6:45 in the morning. He was judged fit for duty, and sworn in on the spot. Then he was sent home for a couple of weeks to put his affairs in order.

Thanksgiving dinner that year he ate in boot camp, down in Alabama. While he was there, old Mrs. Ahern died. Dad got an emergency furlough to attend her funeral. When he returned to Alabama, another draftee had his bed. In the U.S. Army, now awakened, beds were in short supply. Germany, Italy and Japan had little idea what was headed their way.

In the U.S. Army nothing carried a stigma. Dad loved that part. "You had some tough nuts in the army," he said. "You might be friendly with a guy, and he might be the biggest gangster in Detroit." *And you know what? It didn't fucking matter.*

The army, it turned out, was the *ideal* place for an orphan terrified of wagging tongues.

An immense operation it was. Anonymous, pragmatic, cosmopolitan by default, fluid. Business-like. The U.S. Army was the antithesis of narrow, frowning small town life, where judgments lay like a layer of July dust on everything; opinions of you, your lifelong brand.

Historian Lee Kennett: "Unless a man had traveled extensively and done a great many different things in his life, the chances were that the Army presented him with a much broader sampling of humanity than he had ever encountered. [The] thirty-odd draftee divisions formed in 1942 and 1943"—Dad's year of induction—"were ethnic, cultural, and regional mélanges from the outset. As a result it was said you could find a soldier who spoke Italian just by shouting for one.... Within a division [with its 13,000 enlisted men] almost anything was possible. When the rabbi of the 88th Division needed an assistant, he sought a solder who was a Jew, could drive and service a jeep, type, sing, and play a portable organ. Within the division he found ten men with all those qualifications. This richness and variety impressed the soldiers themselves. A former New York bartender confided: 'I've seen all kinds of characters, but this place has got me doubled in spades.'"

Hanging in our bathroom, floodlighted by a setting sun, is a 1934 publicity photo of five Florida bathing beauties.

Dad would have been 23 or so. The younger women in the photograph would have been his age. Painted on their bare white backs, from one scapula to the other across their spines, are 1934's most optimistic economic indicators: newspaper classifieds, postal receipts, railroad traffic, office construction, and bank clearings. All up, up, up! *We hope you will believe and act accordingly.*

The message: not to worry. Things are improving. More rapidly than you know. Trust us.

We bought the photo on our first trip to Paris, my wife, Simone, and I. From a news bureau. Fairy-dusted with desire to find a new picture to be in. Her French father had died the year before, of a mad cancer that bowled through his body in just a few months. Weeks before we'd landed in Orly, *my* father had died; "the man who never got sick" was finally sick of everything; swept like trash into a nursing home. I earned next to nothing as an unwanted consultant; we lived month to month off Simone's income.

We saw the bathing beauties in a window on a narrow street a block from the Seine. We were walking back from Notre Dame; we'd lit memorial candles for our dead fathers. One candle for each man, 10 francs each, lit in memory of love. Forgiveness. Absence. Regret. Stupefaction.

The photo is Hamlet's skull, a memento mori, a reminder

each day as I brush my teeth and shave away the blur that there was a time when my parents were much younger than I am now. In 1934, my conception would still be a few minutes of pleasure 13 years in the future. The photo reminds me: that yesterday's crisis is yesterday's crisis. Each morning I look at that photo and think: these are people who found death unimaginable. And now they are dead. Get on with your life. Do something worth doing.

CHAPTER 5

BOOT CAMP

"THE FIRST DAY WE WERE UP AT DEVENS, THEY THREW ALL THE UNIFORMS AND EVERYTHING AT YOU." Fort Devens was a military reservation and assembly point in Ayer, Massachusetts, outside of Boston. "Had this fellow with me, Bill Ryan. Bill Ryan was a tobacco salesman. But he had an uncle in the shoe business.

"Well, there's an expression they have just in shoe factories. They have names for different sizes. They never say 'C.' They say 'Charlie.' Or 'D.' They say 'David.' When Bill Ryan came through in line, he said to the sergeant who was handing out the shoes, 'I take an eight and a half Charlie.' The sergeant says to himself, 'Oh, here's a wise guy.' He turns around and gives Ryan an eight.

"The next morning, Ryan said, 'I can't get my feet into these shoes. He gave me the wrong size.' I said, 'Go on sick leave. Get a slip from the doctor.'

"OK, he goes on sick leave. He went over to where they were handing out shoes. There's two sergeants standing there talking. He tries to tell them about his shoes. They don't even listen. One says to the other, 'Had your coffee yet?' And they leave. So he comes back crying, 'They won't change the shoes!' I said, 'Come on, I'll take you over.'

"There was a corporal there. I said to the kid, 'Do us a favor, will you?' He said, 'What's that?' I said, 'Change this guy's shoes. He doesn't wear this size.' Corporal said, 'What size does he wear?'

"So Bill Ryan got a new pair of shoes. I said, 'See, all you've got to do is talk to people. If you're reasonable, they'll go along with you.'"

Lesson #3 from my father.

Watch for brake lights. Life is hard. Talk reasonably.

In 1939, there were 227,000 active U.S. troops. The population of a medium-sized state capital. And none too crackerjack. *Time* magazine dismissed them: "The U.S. Army looked like a few nice boys with BB guns." The German army that same year had 98 divisions, marshaling 1.5 million well-trained men.

In 1939 Hitler overran Poland in 28 days and reinvented warfare.

There was a brief pause. The following spring, German mechanized troops took Denmark, as fast as they could drive. Norway came under Nazi control, in a basket delivered by traitors. Germany's armored fist then punched into Allied forces whose leaders thought they were fighting a "Phony War." The Netherlands, Belgium, France surrendered. In just six weeks the Germans were standing at the English Channel, getting their toes wet. The British went home from Dunkirk in anything that would float. A disgraced yet heroic exit.

Now the alarms were ringing, even in an isolationist U.S.A.

In 1940, Congress enacted a limited draft.

Then Pearl Harbor tied a rocket to our tails. Things went crazy.

By the beginning of 1944, eight million U.S. soldiers were training or already deployed. The U.S. Army ground forces had 179 camps and training centers scattered across the country, equipping millions of civilians for new jobs firing artillery, shooting down airplanes, sending messages, rumbling ahead in tanks, executing feats of engineering prowess, manning machine gun nests, advancing on orders, treating wounds, policing, handling financial matters, scaling mountains, and clerking supplies (my father).

One Army facility worked on the atomic bomb. Four facilities devoted themselves to war-dog training. Presumably, the canine assignment of choice was the Cat Island War Dog Center in Gulfport, Mississippi.

"Bill knew his way around," my father said. "The night before we were to board the train, we went over to headquarters. Because Bill knew a sergeant over there.

"Bill said, 'Where are we going?'" To the sergeant.

Fort Devens was a collection center. They sorted you out and put a uniform on you. Devens was step two in the manufacturing process; step one was being healthy enough to pass your physical. Boot camp training happened someplace else, someplace warm enough to operate year round.

"'Gee,' the sergeant said. 'I can't tell you that! It's a military secret!'"

"'Ah,' said Bill. 'Don't give me that baloney. We'll keep it to ourselves. You just tell us where we're going.'" The sergeant relented. It wasn't much of a secret anyway. 'You're going down to Fort McClellan, down in Alabama.'

Fort McClellan was a medium-sized infantry "Branch Immaterial" Replacement Training Center. It was named for Major General George B. McClellan. He stiffened the Army of the Potomac into a formidable force during the American Civil War. But he couldn't win a battle. He preferred preparation over engagement. He didn't want to be the last man standing. He wanted to be the last 1,000,000 men standing. President Lincoln dismissed him. Spurned, McClellan ran for the presidency against Lincoln in 1864, promising to end the war by negotiating with the Confederacy. He lost the election, too.

Fort McClellan was an assembly line for cannon, mine, and bullet fodder. Bomb fodder, too, except the Allies now owned the skies. The camp could process 24,000 inductees at a gulp. It downed 21 gulps altogether: a half-million men marched through Fort McClellan during World War Two. Fort McClellan was the express lane for combat. It's where you learned to point and shoot. There was even a camp within a camp, where 3,000 German and Italian prisoners liked to paint nostalgic murals.

My father: "The next day we board the train. I end up in a car up front, and about four cars down is Ryan. Next thing I know there's a guy coming through the train hollering 'Ahern!' at the top of his lungs. And me, Mickey the Dunce, I say, 'Right here!' He said, 'You're on K.P. Get back to the kitchen car. You got any friends?' So I said, 'Yeah. His name is Bill Ryan.' He said, 'I'll find him.' So I get back to the kitchen car, and the next thing I know, in walks Bill. And he looks at me and says, 'I should have known.'

"Anyway, it turned out to be a good deal. 'Cause these

guys were riding in coaches, two men to a seat. Six hundred men on the train. You have to sleep sitting up. But in the kitchen car, they had these long tables, so we could lay down on those and snooze. On top of that, every station we stopped, the Red Cross or some outfit was there to hand you oranges and all this junk. We got our pick of everything, because we brought it into the kitchen cars.

"We were on that train three nights and four days, and Bill said to me, 'You know, this mess sergeant's got a racket going.' 'Oh,' I said, 'he does?'

"Bill said, 'He goes through the cars with his hat in his hand, telling the G.I.s on the train that *these guys are doing all your work while all you got to do is sit here and eat*, and he's passing the hat around, and he's collecting plenty of money.'

"Course, all the guys were loaded with cash. They just came from home. Bill said, 'We're going to break this up.

"'You're going to take that half of the train, and I'm going to take this half. And we're going to start collecting.'

"So we went through the train, the two of us. And we got ourselves about a hundred and fifty dollars between the two of us. The sergeant went through the train the next day with his hat in his hand and got nothing. Everybody's saying, *I gave at the office*."

Nor did their personal military secret go to waste.

"Bill said, 'Guess what's going on? They're making bets on where we're going. We'll put in for Fort McClellan. A buck apiece.' I said OK. So we went in, and we found the guys that were handling the money, and sure enough, we won that. About a hundred bucks each, I think it was."

Historian Geoffrey Perret: "There is a story that may have been apocryphal, but could just as easily be true. At an induction center a milling crowd of draftees excitedly gossiped and wisecracked. They had just had their chests tapped, stuck out their tongues, urinated into bottles and had their teeth examined like horses at auction.

"A grizzled master sergeant forced his way from the back of the room to the front, to where a dais stood. As he pushed his way forward he pleaded, 'Gentlemen, gentlemen ... calm down ... let's have some quiet here, please ... be quiet, gentlemen.' As the uproar ebbed to a low drone, a captain entered the room, went to the dais and administered the oath.

"The moment he left, the room erupted in excited chatter once more. The master sergeant went to the dais, no longer a humble supplicant. 'Shut up, goddammit!' he roared. 'You men are now members of the United States Army!'"

John Ellis asserted: "Individual training had three main purposes: to rid the conscript of civilian preconceptions about his 'rights' and personal freedom; to familiarize him with the weapons that he was likely to have to operate...; and to give him some experience of the noise and confusion of actual combat. Armies succeeded best in the first of these tasks.... From the first moment he joined up the recruit was constantly made aware that his only role as an individual was to obey orders and sublimate his personality to the better functioning of the unit as a whole."

"The first day in McClellan we had a formation," said Dad. "This sergeant, he's pacing back and forth. Big tall guy. And the first words out of his mouth, he said, 'I hate draftees.' Bill Ryan was standing in back of me, and he hollers out, 'What's the matter, Sarge? Couldn't you get a job in civilian life?'

"Oh, boy! One o'clock in the morning this sergeant is calling 'Ryan!' at the top of his lungs. For a detail. Oh, he made Ryan's life miserable for a week or so.

"But that didn't bother Ryan one bit. When he quit, Bill went right down to his office and said, 'What's the matter, Sarge? Haven't you got any more details for me?' They became the best of friends. Out drinking together nights and everything else, him and Bill."

"OK, Ryan, I give up. What will it take to break you?"

"You could start, Sarge, with a shot of something."

Dad entered a new, revised U.S. Army. A different geometry.

Historian Shelby L. Stanton: "The 'square' four-regiment division ... of World War I was discarded as not mobile or flexible enough for modern conditions. On 1 January 1939 the new triangular infantry division emerged.... It reflected certain attributes of the German divisional structure and was premised on the association of all its elements, from squad to regiment, in three's." Squads were the smallest divisional element. Squads were an easily directed tactical unit comprising maybe sixteen men. Regiments were the largest divisional components: 3,000 enlisted men and officers. "Ideally it was envisioned that a given element would fix the enemy"—grab the enemy by the nose—"while another maneuvered against him and the third acted as a reserve." The man behind this revolution in doctrine was George C. Marshall, who took over the Infantry School at Camp Benning, Georgia in 1927.

Marshall was a restless innovator.

Geoffrey Perret: "Marshall saw in Benning more than a chance to remake the infantry. Here was a once-in-a-century opportunity to remake the entire Army.... Marshall intended to change the way officers *thought* about fighting. In the present Army there were cut-and-dried answers to almost every problem. In the Army he envisaged, there would be clear answers to almost nothing."

Better training became Marshall's obsession. That, and getting across one idea: expect battle to be bewildering.

Marshall revolutionized adult education. Perret: "He forced instructors to shorten their lectures.... When it was objected that he was asking too much in demanding a twenty-minute lecture covering the whole Civil War, he stood up and did it himself in five minutes. In this, and every lecture on military history, he demanded an emphasis on the confusion of battle, stressing the faulty information on which commanders had to act."

Marshall stumped for simplicity above all. Simple orders, simple maps, simple tactics. "How else could tens of thousands of reserve officers and millions of draftees be expected to handle them? Marshall had Benning teach exactly one tactic—the holding attack. It could be taught in less than five minutes."

Ironically, Marshall's arrived at his ideas because, after

World War One, he thought another European war highly unlikely. He predicted instead a war at home: "Our Army is most likely to operate on the American Continent and mobility is especially necessary under all probable conditions of warfare in this theater." He streamlined divisions to make them easier to transport. Wrong continent, right guess.

Certainly, the training at Benning seemed to promise U.S. officers a better shot at victory than the training handed out in the British army. There, when the war opened, colonels required that their combat officers learn how to dine properly, receiving instruction for a wide-ranging, many-course selection of knives, forks, and spoons.

Front-line-bound officers in the British army got full training in which glass to use for four kinds of alcohol, the anticipated pour at an average evening meal among the civilized classes. Presumably, British officers would soon be confronting the enemy *en table*, fighting the Jerries over seconds of pork roast. If good manners were bullets, the Brits would be deadly.

Dad *en table*: "The first week or so we were in camp, we had a mess sergeant. And he was a stinker! He'd put out big bowls of string beans, big bowls of mashed potatoes, and everybody's going into it with their own fork or spoon or whatever.

"So this guy says, 'Hey. Where's the spoons for these dishes?' The sergeant, a big tough guy, he said, 'You're not home now. You're in the Army.' All this baloney. So we had to do the best we could. This went on for about a week.

"And, all of a sudden one night, we're just about ready to eat, when in walks a major. And of course when an officer walks in, somebody hollers 'Attention!' Everybody stood up. He said, 'Sit down, fellows. Sit down.' He walked along, looking at the tables.

"All of a sudden he let a bellow out of him, 'Where's the spoons for these dishes?' Well, the sergeant, he come rushing out of the kitchen with a bundle of spoons. Dropped half of them on his way out, he was in such a hurry. But after that we had spoons in those dishes."

But that wasn't the end of it.

"One night I'm on guard duty. I walk a certain section. I meet this guy up here, and I meet a guy down there. Back and forth, back and forth. For an hour. So this guy comes down, and he starts talking to me. He says, 'Guess what's going on at the mess hall! The mess sergeant is up there, and he's got a bunch of his friends, and he's cooking them steaks and everything, and they're all half drunk!'

"'Well,' I said, 'report them. Get the officer of the guard down here.'

"We all had a whistle, and everybody blew their whistles. Beep, beep, beep, right down the line to guard headquarters. So the lieutenant comes walking. 'What's the matter, fellows?' This kid told him, and the lieutenant went right up to the mess hall. Two days later, the mess sergeant's on the boat. They got rid of him." On the boat: headed for a war zone. Not good.

George C. Marshall called General Lesley James McNair "the brains of the Army."

McNair was the Army's chief trainer and Marshall's right-hand man.

McNair packed a slide rule as a sidearm, but preached

slaughter. He instructed his citizen-soldier draftees, "We must hate with every fiber of our being. We must lust for battle; our object in life must be to kill."[1]

Training to hate proceeded along conventional lines: demonize and dehumanize. The Germans were cruel, barbaric, robotic monsters of war. Sadists by nature and preference. Even so, the Japanese were far, far worse. Not even human. Not really.

Racism became a weapon of mass destruction, at least in the Pacific. Allied propaganda variously characterized the Japanese as angry sheep, rats, mad dogs, rattlesnakes, lice, ants or cockroaches stirred from their nests, wildcats, terrified cattle, and jackals. "Without question," as John W. Dower recounts in *War Without Mercy*, "the most common caricature of the Japanese by Westerners...was the monkey or ape." Anything but capable, well-led men enacting their government's policies. A creature less evolved. Frustrated U.S. journalists, watching Japanese armies chew up the maps, demeaned them as "apes in khaki." And Western cartoonists depicted Japanese assault infantry swinging in full combat gear through the jungle—by their tails.

Even the diplomats were undiplomatic. A total war, including words. Mr. Dower: "Sir Alexander Cadogan, the influential permanent undersecretary of the British Foreign Office, routinely referred" to the Japanese as "beastly little monkeys." Cadogan's other favorite description: "yellow dwarf slaves." Altogether, not unlike the flying monkeys

---

[1.] McNair's personal lust for battle prematurely ended his contribution to the war effort. In 1944 he became the highest ranking American officer ever killed in action, an honor of a sort, when he strayed too near the front lines on an inspection. It was a day famed in the annals of military irony, and a day when the insufficiency of air-ground coordination was bared. McNair was blown to bits by an American bomb that fell short.

who did the dirty work for the Wicked Witch in the Wizard of Oz, which had opened three years earlier. It was a handy mental reference. Everyone knew the film.

Sir Alexander's vantage surely suffered a hard knock, of course, when an inept and unprepared British establishment surrendered Singapore to his monkeys a few months later, on February 15, 1942. Almost without a fight. Monkeys eat crumpets just fine.

The subhuman Japanese, so visibly different, might invite extermination. But the average G.I.—so polls would show—felt little deep hatred for the German soldier during the war.

After, when news of the death camps became commonly known, a permanent stink attached to Germany, a country that could allow such a thing. *Who were these monsters?* Even so, complicit civilians and their political masters smelled far worse than the common soldier, whose reputation for blind obedience and competence preceded him. When the German soldier took cover behind the stock excuse, "I was just following orders," it actually sounded plausible. Von Clausewitz and Bismarck had shaped a German military that was the envy of the ruthless: they got results on the battlefield. If you had the ends, they had the means.

Not everyone was fooled. *LIFE* photographer Robert Capa thought they were nasty whiner-schnitzels: "The Germans are the meanest bastards. They are the meanest during an operation, and afterward they all have a cousin in Philadelphia." After you've captured them. "That is what I like about the French. They do not have cousins in Philadelphia."

The pace of training was quick: three months and you were done with basic. They handed you off to your next assignment. Ready to kill or be killed.

Dad: "Boot camp was rough for about a month, because they had you going, morning, noon and night. You never knew when you were going to be called out. They had you so you were leg-weary; you could hardly move.

"And then this guy wrote a letter to the Secretary of War! Complaining about all the things they were doing to him and his buddies."

My father was part of the great democratic citizen army. Questioning authority was seen as a symptom of good mental health.

"And the first thing we knew, the captain of our outfit, he called the whole company together, and he had the letter. Seems like the Secretary of War wrote back, and the captain had to send eight copies stating why he thought that man complained. Right off the bat he told the cadre, the sergeants and corporals, 'You lay off that company.' And he's up there in front of us saying, 'Fellows, if I can do anything for you, let me know! But, please, don't write another letter like this!' That put the kibosh on all the extra work, see. That stopped everything right in its tracks."

Military urban myth.

What I learned later was, Dad mixed his first-person accounts liberally with the stories he'd heard. He was doing what good storytellers do: entertain at all costs. No foul.

Dad could have done the training faster, but his mother's funeral set him back a few weeks.

"I started in Company C. But when I got back from the furlough, they put me in Company D, and that's how I bumped into Carswell. I had the bed next to him."

It was a nice piece of luck. They were old for inductees, each in their early thirties and starting families. Carswell was a farmer from Illinois. The two became buddies.

Alabama was like another country, oddly tilted.

"Carswell and I used to go into the next town, Anniston, and have our breakfast on Sunday mornings at a hotel there. They had all colored waiters." In Alabama, blacks could serve you food. But they couldn't eat with you, which was fine with my father. Generally speaking, he had "no use for them." *Them* being anyone "colored." It was a common attitude among immigrant Irish, who had gone to war with clubs and fists to take jobs away from blacks at ports of entry like New Orleans.

The U.S. military was segregated in every branch of the service, with almost no opportunity for advancement if your skin was black. Henry Stimson, the same Secretary of War who cared so much about a complainer in Company D, insisted that black units be led by white officers. His decision rested on this assessment: "Leadership is not imbedded in the negro race yet." At least he said yet, the patronizing SOB. Black G.I.s reported the unique humiliation of being refused service at the same Southern lunch counters where German POWs sat joking and eating their meals.

"In those days," Dad pointed out, "they were still put on the back of the bus, and the railroad stations were like cut in half. One side said, 'Colored.' The other side said, 'White.' You've heard of 'nigger heaven?' The theaters down there had that. They had a back stairway that led right up to the balcony. And that's where all the colored went. And you'd see those Southerners, the men, civilians, walking down the sidewalk. A colored guy comes along, he'd step into the gutter till the white guy went by." Dad smiled knowingly; a happy remembrance for him. "They had them well-trained, don't think they didn't." You are what you are. Your times are what they are. No excuses.

Dad appreciated the coercive power of a caste system. He told me about the signs in store windows around Boston, "No Irish need apply." That was his context. He believed society hated you until proven acceptable.

Anniston, Alabama was a good-sized town of maybe 25 thousand people. It was hill country.

"They had pool halls all over the place. They'd come in with all kinds of old wrecks, all kinds of old cars, all covered with that red mud. And the women would go shopping. And if there was a man along, he'd go over to the pool hall.

"Some of the people were pretty good," Dad recollected.

"One Saturday night we were in town, and this woman invited about ten of us to her house. And she had a regular luncheon for us. Everybody's from around Boston, and they were talking schools. And one guy was saying, 'Well, the colleges up in the Eastern part of the country are way ahead of these colleges you have down South.'

"Which didn't set right with her at all.

"'No,' she argued that the colleges down there were just as good as the ones up around Boston. But finally they said, 'Your boy goes to college, doesn't he?' And she said, 'Yes.' They said, 'What college does he go to?'"

A full smug stop. Dad proud.

"'Harvard,'" she admitted. She was probably Pork Queen 1925.

Dad was content. The home team won at that dinner table.

Harvard was a team, an academic team. Our brains beat your brains. North vs. south.

Stories jumped from his tongue like crickets. Gouts of water.

I'd hoist my small, skinny self up on a kitchen stool, hoping to prime the pump again, to fill my life with his stories, that had guns and heroes and strong, tired men doing the right things: "Dad, tell me about the time...."

"You had to laugh...." Was his ritual opening. Light snort. Shake his head once.

He'd tell about the time they put a length of rope between the sheets of a trainee terrified of snakes. And the boy died of fright. Right there. As his toes touched a giving, dry coil in the dark, thick Alabama night.

A man's home is his castle. Dad was a household king with two thrones. His living room easy chair, with the ashtray stand next to it. And a stool at our narrow kitchen counter, where he could see the television in the living room if he turned a few degrees. He told most of his stories at the counter. The kitchen was the color of a shaved honeycomb bleeding. The cabinets and walls were made of knotty pine, darkening with smoke and cooking grease. Watched by a thousand black eyes.

The snake prank happened "while I was there," Dad claimed, a giveaway that the tale was something he'd heard about, but not witnessed. Most training centers were in the pestilential South. Snakes were supposed to be common as roots, and Northerners were used to walking without looking where they stepped. "What may have originated as a scare story told a trainee," said folklorist Richard Dorson, who ran across this boot camp myth, "grew into a legend associated with nearly every training camp in the United States."

Same for the guy, he's driving along late at night and sees two headlights coming at him. Says Dad. So far apart this guy figures they can't possibly be on the same vehicle. He says to himself, they must be two motorcycles riding side by side. So the guy decides to have some fun with them and drive between them.

Dad smacks his lips. Except it's not two motorcycles, it's a tank retriever, this huge, special truck the Army uses for transporting wounded tanks. The guy drives between the two lights.

Bang.

"He never knew what hit him."

The German soldier was viewed as a warrior of destiny, avenging the injustices of a previous world war. His only future—his nation's only future—was combat, he was told from childhood. He was treated harshly because the task was large, and he had to be durable. He was, by all accounts, the toughest, best-trained, most professional soldier fighting, irresistible in small unit tactics, resourceful, pugnacious by doctrine, never beaten, always counterattacking.

In a poll conducted during World War Two, three out of four Americans agreed that the draft board should call up single women *before* fathers. Before.

That's how much family meant to the national myth. The fathers should stay home, as the bedrock. *Unwed girls* can take on the Germans.

Nice poll. The Army had no intention of marching women to the front.

When the country ran out of bachelors, they called up men like Thomas Francis Ahern Number One, a father since March of that year. Inducted October 4, 1943.

He'd be in the armed services two years, one month, and twenty-one days. He loved babies. His daughter was just six months old on his induction. He called her "Tootsie." He fell in love long distance, via a couple of phone calls and some postcards. He wouldn't see Tootsie for two years.

My mother marveled.

Dad went to war with a flourishing head of thick, black, wavy hair.

He came back his hair turning white, fishing-line-filament white.

The German military surrendered first on May 7 and again on May 8. On May 25, 1945, my father appears in a snapshot in Germany, with two other soldiers. There's a canal in the background. Nothing looks blown up. On the back of the photo, he penciled a note: "Can you see my white hair on the sides." It's just beginning to turn. In a photograph taken a few years later, the sides of his hair are as powdery as a barrister's wig. He's sitting on the floor. He looks like a small, gentle man with a pie-pan face, snuggled between his two children on Christmas morning, unsure what any of it means, or how he escaped, but happy enough.

We assumed we knew why his hair color had changed: the horrors of war. Like seeing a ghost, only on an industrial scale. White from too many artillery shells passing overhead, sucking the color right out of him.

But I think there was more to it than that.

I think, while he was overseas, he saw death and disfigurement in wholesale lots. He hugged mud for comfort through mind-shattering bombardments. He lost any delusions of immortality.

Which is an old man's thought. He grew old before his time, with hair to match: doomsday hair. He had been a realist, thanks to an orphan's uncertainties and the Great Depression.

Now he was a fatalist, too.

CHAPTER 6

ENGLAND

"I SEE ENGLAND. I see France. I see Judy's underpants." That jibe, I believe, first developed some small desire in me to visit France.

A country that was mostly about female undergarments was the country for me.

Aboard my father's convoy, transporting him from American shores to England:

"You never saw so many boats in your whole life. As far as you could see: boats.

"Then one day!

"The sun is out. Nice day. Everybody's up on deck. It was a big English liner. Twenty thousand troops on this one boat." Rounded up to the nearest ten grand. It was sailing past the tub my father was consigned to. The actual record was 15,028 troops aboard the *Queen Elizabeth*, virtually the entire U.S. 1st Infantry Division. With two fast British liners, the *Queen Elizabeth* and the *Queen Mary*, the Allies transported about 420,000 U.S. troops to England, a quarter of the total, in just 37 trips. The Queens usually traveled alone, their 28.5 knot speed their chief protection against submarines.

"We had a couple of destroyers with us. All of a sudden one of these destroyers starts cutting circles in front of us, and there's the cans"—depth charges—"coming off it like crazy. And every time they explode underneath, it's just like you took a hammer and hit the side of the boat. What a bang! Oh, boy, I'm telling you. We were scared. 'Cause they had orders: if any boat gets hit with a torpedo, the other boats keep right on going. They don't stop and pick up anybody."

Tense.

Picturesque. German submarines never sank a single U.S. troop ship headed for Europe. Certainly not now. Had Dad only known, by 1944 German torpedoes weren't a serious threat. Wolf packs no longer feasted for days on thinly defended convoys. Only 18 months earlier, U-boat captains had toasted the "happy times," sinking shipping faster than it could be built.

Those times were gone.

Numerous improvements in antisubmarine warfare had turned the tables. A dozen U-boats a month were blasted to the bottom, never to rise again. Going to sea in a U-boat had become a 70% guarantee of dying in uniform.

Finally, most German submarines stayed in port, pumping bilge, too valuable to risk, awaiting some technical miracle that would make them dangerous, elusive as eels again.

"I landed at Liverpool about four months before the D-Day invasion. And while we were there, we got the tetanus shot." Combat-related preventive medicine: tetanus-inducing bacilli are usually introduced through a wound. Lockjaw. "So being A," *Ahern*, "I was the first one in line. I come out of there and I'm telling you, I thought my arm would drop off. Boy, did that hurt. And they're all hollering at me, 'How is it?' And I'm hollering back, 'Just like water. Nothing to it.' I said to myself, 'Wait till you get it.'"

Wartime England was down to the thins.

"They gave us a day off, and we went into Sheffield." Sheffield is a manufacturing town. It makes cutlery. Robin Hood's long-gone Sherwood Forest is nearby.

"We walked around, another fellow and myself. It got around noontime. We're walking by, and there's a little tea garden there. So we walked in, and there's a couple of tables sitting there in the yard. We sat down, and this woman came out and she's talking to us: 'Well, I haven't got much. But I could give you a couple of eggs, some bread, and a cup of tea.' So we said OK. We sat there and she brought it out, and she mixed up a little salad. He was eating the salad and I said to him, 'Do you know what you're eating?' He said, 'No.' I said, 'You're eating grass.' She had mixed grass with lettuce."

Dad admired the island's beautiful roses. He admired the resilience of the Brits.

"England was in tough shape. I don't know what the hell they'd have done if it wasn't for the U.S. The people that lived there, they'd show you the marks on the buildings were the German fighters come right down the streets, spraying the whole place with machine-gun bullets. Nothing to stop them. They said, 'Nobody realizes—unless you were over here during the start of that deal—how close we were to surrendering.' They said, 'We had nothing.' They lost all their guns at Dunkirk. They had about one machine gun for every mile of beach. And they had telephone poles across the roads. Which wouldn't have stopped a band of Boy Scouts. They were in awful shape.

"But, when this country got in there,"—the U.S.—"holy smoke!"

Historian Geoffrey Perret: "There had never been a supply operation like this one. The number of separate items Sears, Roebuck and Company supplied to its customers was approximately 100,000. (The Army's) Service of Supply had to acquire and distribute nearly 3 million. More than 100,000 men were arriving every month, plus 500,000 tons of supplies and thousands upon thousands of vehicles. Desperate quartermasters finally had to admit defeat and lined British roads with trucks, bombs and crated rations."

Dad: "They had ammunition piled up between the houses so that it looked like another house. They even had a roof on the ammunition. So if you were in a plane going over, you'd think it was another house.

"One day there, I was on a truck with another guy, we were going up for some supplies for our outfit, and they had trucks parked wheel to wheel right along this road we were using, and we clocked that. They were wheel to wheel. Anything from a three-quarter ton truck right up to the big wreckers that they had to pull in tanks. We clocked that for twenty-eight solid miles. Nothing but trucks, wheel to wheel.

"They used to say, If it wasn't for the barrage balloons holding it up, England would have sunk beneath the weight of everything the Americans brought over."

Geoffrey Perret again. "The popular idea that the Army simply blasted its way to victory, like a rich kid buying his way through life, was wrong ... flesh and blood made good the failures of production and planning."

Some planners calculated that the U.S. was one hundred divisions short—1.5 million men—of a decisive margin of victory.

So they piled on the firepower instead.

"The American Army in the European Theater of Operations had a combination of fire power, mobility and armored might never before seen in warfare," wrote Lt. Col. Randolph Leigh in 1945. He'd been there.

Dad described how the infantry advanced; that was indicative. "They walk, and all they do is fire ahead of them. Fire. Put another clip in. Fire. Keep firing. So there's only grass, say, still ahead of them. They still fire. Fifteen thousand men and tanks, and the whole works, boy, they make a mess, don't think they don't. That's all they do, the infantry. They just go, puh-whitt, boom, boom, boom, boom. Put in another clip, boom, boom, boom. They're firing ahead of them all the time. Anything in front of them is dead."

Dad's M1 Garand rifle held a clip of eight .30 caliber cartridges. As fast as he pulled the trigger, the rifle fired, 40 rounds a minute on average, five clips, pouring out into the wild blue yonder.

Walk and shoot. Walk and shoot.

Army tactics directed the application of force; in this case, massed firepower aimed forward. Marksmanship was not the point, at all: *Fill the air with destruction* was. Create a killing zone so lethal, the enemy must retire, its flesh and morale overwhelmed by your flying metal. The bullet was a sharply pointed missile as long as your little finger. It was designed to do as much damage as possible to human flesh. Tests showed that the .30 caliber cartridge kept going when other bullets quit, putting big holes in things quite far away.

Perret: "The M1 was a brilliant weapon [that] gave the U.S. forces unquestionable superiority in the field." Dad was familiar with guns, and he admired the M1.

It scared some. Dad: "I'm laying there, I'm on a target two hundred yards out. And I'm firing away like crazy. On the rifle range. I look at this guy laying down side of me about a yard away. I look at him, here's the tears rolling down his face. I said, 'What's the matter with you?' 'I never shot a gun in my life!' he's hollering. He was from New York City."

In those days, being from a big city meant you *didn't* know about guns.

"Course that M1 meant nothing to me," said Dad. "Because I was used to a shotgun. Shotgun's got more kick than that M1 ever had." Dad killed his man with an M1. It was an easy-going gun, in his opinion.

My father's Army was meant to be a nasty, biting beast.

Behind the bite was a bucket brigade of noncombatant support, despite the Army's "avowed aim...to make killers of you all."

John Ellis: "One source went so far as to compute that about 18 men were needed in the supply services to keep one rifleman firing." Usually, my father was one of the 18. A supply clerk in the Signal Corps. But he was also a qualified Army sharpshooter, and sometimes they dropped him in the mud or the basement of a blasted out house. The Signal Corps was in charge of communications and was never far from the front.

There were always advocates of a harder, leaner Army.

All thorn.

But the advocates of a softer, more convenient, more "citizen friendly" Army prevailed. On paper, America's teeth-to-tail (fighting-to-support) ratio inside the European theater dictated that there be one Services of Supply soldier (like my father)—forwarding ammunition, fuel, food, clothing, medical care, entertainment, information, mail—for every two men in combat. On paper, two-thirds of the U.S. troops on European soil during World War Two were armed and quite dangerous.

The truth started with a sixty percent discount. John Ellis redid the math and more accurately estimated that "only between a fifth and a quarter of any army's paper strength was actually involved in the shooting war." Imagine something like a wolf's head on a cow's body.

It was an Army abundantly supplied with the necessities of war. Though not every day. On August 29, 1944, U.S. General George S. Patton, Jr. found his thrust across France abruptly curbed when his precious daily ration of gas for his Sherman tanks went to other, "more pressing" fronts.

In Patton's unforgiving judgment, this was "the momentous error of the war." At that point, his Third Army was rolling over German units like a speeding truck over dithering squirrels. He intended to push on—and in his hard, contemptuous opinion, save G.I. lives—before enemy resistance got organized.

Finally, still unsupplied but unwilling to give up his advance, Patton ordered his commanders to continue driving "until the tanks stopped, and then get out and walk."

It was an Army supplied with some of the comforts of home.

Starting with boot camp. "Congress made it clear that this generation of draftees was to be looked after kindly," said Geoffrey Perret, "with well-heated barracks, modern toilets and showers, ample bed space and well-run mess halls. Camp streets were curved, to relieve the monotony. Buildings were painted to make them more attractive." Lee Kennett described an unmilitary love of soft living: "If the Army were to enjoy the full support of the government and the American public, it would have to accommodate itself to the citizen-soldier and make his stay in the ranks if not enjoyable, at least as bearable as possible. (His) various needs would have to be supplied, his wants anticipated, whether they be on-post tailor shops or portable showers— and such things did not make for a lean army."

The British were simply agape.

In their war, you rationed the air if you could and wiped your tail clean on a meager three sheets of toilet paper a day. Expecting a bare larder in Europe, Americans shipped over whatever they needed. Bum wipes: each G.I. received twenty-two and a half sheets a day.

And floating toward victory in the holds of U.S. convoys: not just munitions, but countless vital crates of Coca-Cola. Psychologists explained the significance: "Any symbol or representation of (his) culture ... assumes exaggerated value (for the G.I. abroad). A visitor from home, sports scores, moving pictures, American food or drinks are extraordinarily important for maintaining morale in expeditionary forces."

A sentimental concern for the G.I's well-being—

expressed in material plenty and throw-away surpluses—lifted morale, the Army believed. It even proved our side was right.

Lt. Col. Randolph Leigh, wrote a summary of the Allies' supply-side victory in 1945, under the title *48 Million Tons to Eisenhower*, with charts like "The Best-Fed Army" that boastfully compared American chow to German and to Brit (who got the least to eat). Our chief enemy and our chief ally got mostly potatoes to eat. G.I.s had nutritious servings of citrus, dairy and meat.

"The Germans had, in effect, admitted the instability of their economic-military machine in their prewar slogan 'Guns or Butter,'" Leigh concluded. "The United States proved that it could handle both the economic and the military sides of war by the actual and ample deliveries to our armies of guns and butter both."

The French were fascinated.

François Bertin: "For the newly-liberated French people, (G.I.s) were a source of surprise and astonishment. Their relaxed, even athletic, appearance, their lithe silent way of moving, and the luxuries displayed by a young wealthy army were quickly to become symbols of the return of Freedom. There can be few people who do not remember the 'Nescafé' instant coffee, sachets of soluble lemonade, fruit pastilles, bars of vitamin-filled chocolate, sticks of chewing gum, and packets of four cigarettes that smiling GIs would toss ….as they drove through towns and villages. More than the cannons, rifles and tanks, it is this picture that was to remain in the memory of all those for whom the Liberation represented the high point of their existence. Even the cigarettes had a whiff of freedom."

The English were more reserved. Though not by much. They'd gone too long *without* to resist the temptations offered by the 1.5 million U.S. servicemen with access— through post exchanges and doting families—to otherwise unobtainable luxuries like scented soap.

"The English, they couldn't understand these G.I.s." Dad recalled the clash of cultures. "And, of course, every G.I. over in England, they're all millionaires, they're all driving Cadillacs when they're home. They'd give them all that baloney. One guy there, he was getting silk stockings from home. So he'd go out with a girl, and he'd give her one stocking. She'd have to go out with him again to get the other one." *Go with him again* meaning *fuck him.*

Or maybe the English understood all too well.

My father: "One day I said to this guy, 'Let's go to the movies. We'll spend the afternoon.' He said, 'I've got a date.'

"OK. Well, I get almost to the movie, and he's behind me. I said. 'Hey, what happened to you. I thought you had a date.' He said, 'She went off with another G.I.'

"We're standing in line to get into the theater, and who comes up in back of him?

"I said, 'Look at your girl.' He turned around, and there she's got a big colored guy with her; yeah." Mental shake of the head. Outrageous behavior, in Dad's view. He looked down on the whole business. "Of course, they got away with that." Over there. Among the naive Brits. Where many had never seen a person with darkly pigmented skin. A bumpkin in a pub would be told a black man was an American Indian and believe it.

The English held a different view. For them, the put-upon blacks were a welcome relief. In *Rich Relations: The*

American Occupation of Britain 1942-1945, David Reynolds quotes from a letter penned in 1943 by a Englishwoman with typical opinions. "Everybody here adores the negro troops," she wrote, "all the girls go to their dances, but nobody likes the white Americans. They swagger around as if they were the only people fighting this war, they all get so drunk and look so untidy while the negroes are very polite, much smarter and everybody's pets."

Pets wasn't right, either, of course. But at least it was friendly. And tolerant.

Dad thought he had the final word. "After the war was over, the people in England turned against them, the colored." He insisted that familiarity bred contempt in the end. *It would have to* was his sub-message.

He expected me to be a racist. Not in the here and now—there weren't enough blacks in our world to matter, three or four families in our entire *small* small town. But as a way of correctly knowing the world, where the value of some people is naturally and repeatedly and demonstrably less—or more—than the value of others.

His casual racism appalled me. It seemed so stupid and unfair. Malicious. Diseased. And it was in me. He put it in me. And I wanted it out. His racism appalled my sister, too. But she laughed at it. He was ignorant, was all. And after college, a safe distance away, she got down to the business of dating outside her race.

"One night I'm on guard duty, right in front of the mess hall. And, of course, over there when it got dark, it got real dark. There's not a light anywhere. So I'm standing in front of the main door to the mess hall, and along comes this bobby.

"I can hear him, but I can't see him. It's that black. And he knows I'm there, so going by he says, 'Hi, soldier.' I said, 'Hi.' We talked a little bit. I said, 'When you come back from your rounds, we'll have a cup of coffee.'

"Well, they loved that, because they weren't getting too much, the English people.

"So he came back, and we go in the mess hall, and this damn mess sergeant, he had to leave a pot of coffee for the guards." It was required. "But instead of leaving like a loaf of bread or something, he left a few crusts on the table, and all his bread was up in a glass case with a padlock on it.

"This bobby said to me, 'I guess he didn't leave much for you.' I said, 'Maybe not. But we'll get it.' I just took the butt of my rifle, and I went, *boom!*, and I broke that goddamn case all to pieces.

"Pull out a fresh loaf of bread, sat there eating.

"You know the next day not a word was said. I thought sure as hell they were going to court-martial me. Nobody said boo."

CHAPTER 7

SEX WITH MOM

I got my first sex education (little did I know) from my father's tales of wartime England.

"Another night I was on guard duty down at this motor pool on the outskirts of Swindon.

"About six o'clock at night I see all these G.I.s coming down with girls on their arms. Everybody's got a couple of blankets with them.

"They come up to me, and they said, 'When do you go off?'

"I said, 'Another hour.' They said, 'We're going to use the ambulances.'

"We had about twenty-five ambulances.

"I said, 'Go ahead. I don't care.'

"So in they went. They said, 'What time do you come on in the morning?'

"I said, 'Six o'clock.' 'Well,' they said, 'when you come on, wake us up.'

"I said, 'I better wake you up. The officer of the guard will be here at seven. And you boys better be out of here before that.'

"So the next morning I walk around the ambulances, pounding on them with the gun. 'Come on, get out of there.' They all trooped out, and off they went."

What I learned: men hung out with women in ambulances, and Dad woke everybody up in the morning.

I couldn't imagine what was going on behind those closed doors painted olive drab with a big red cross in a white circle *so you could see it clearly*.

I couldn't imagine the thumps and the clumsiness in the dark. Shared cigarettes. A bottle. Two sipping mouths, wet and ready. Cloth moving from decency, moving north and south of the waist. Becoming a curtain. And a hand through the curtain. I didn't know anything about hands. Not consciously. Not with a sense of shame.

My entire sex life until the third grade was with my mother.

Until I was probably five, my mother took me into her bath to wash me clean.

We sat there naked together in the warm, soapy water. I loved to stick my head beneath the surface and blow bubbles. She had breasts I don't remember. Her thin waist was ringed with gray bath water. But I could see the black spot like a baby's head between her submerged thighs.

She was lightly holding my tiny prick, wondering if I would get hard. Curious maybe to see if all boys were sexual creatures, as the articles and books insisted. My mother was forever looking in books for explanations. And she was a semi-modern woman.

I loved it. I couldn't imagine anything more pleasant than

having my mother touch me there, where it felt especially good. I smiled. She smiled. I reached out my small and delicate hand, breaking the soapy surface of the waist-high water, and touched her tummy. I giggled. She looked plainly at me, without the glasses she wore almost every waking minute. Her eyes searching for focus. And my finger skated down her bread-white skin, smash into the bath water, skidding into her bush, through the underbrush, releasing a cloud of champagne bubbles. Poking between the skinny pink rails of her....

?

I didn't have a name for it. I didn't have a name for it on me either, except mine was different and bare. And hurt at least once every bath because soap got inside the tip. Hers was a spot where everything changed. An inexpressibly intriguing undersea place. A bearded invitation, one-quarter open. The dark pine bathroom door was closed, and I could hear the radio playing in the kitchen, where my father sat with his beer. I pressed my finger in gently, just to the first little joint.

It was where her smile came from.

"That's enough, Tommy." She shifted and squeaked, wet rubber flesh—and not much of it—against vitreous enamel. The tub was as big as an ocean, the biggest thing in a tiny bathroom in a very small house.

She splashed me lightly to get my attention. We went back to the once-a-week world of washing. It was Saturday night, and you had to smell presentable for church the next morning.

Dwight David Eisenhower, President of the United States, waved right at me; and I became one of my father's stories.

Ike singled me out for recognition from the hundreds lining a windy street in Newport, Rhode Island, where he made his summer White House in 1957. Eisenhower, whose smiling face hung like a benevolent, second moon over America, whose bald head seemed to guarantee: no lies, no secrets, what you see is what you get. A career general who hated warmongers. Who popularized the term "military-industrial complex" and warned the country to beware it. Ike: the hero of D-Day (to American eyes), the managing executive credited (in America) with Victory in Europe. All symbol and a mile wide: tough but fair, unpretentious; at ease, the consensus builder, the daddy-figure subordinate generals like Montgomery and Patton dared to criticize because he wouldn't go gooey for their schemes.

Looked me right in the eye, man to boy. Or so my father insisted.

Dad knew Eisenhower's reputation for working a crowd. They'd served together in Europe during the Second World War, Eisenhower at the very top, Dad in the great linoleum floor: a private in the infantry.

"What state are you from, son?"

And some 19-year-old paratrooper about to jump into enemy-held France would reply: "Kansas, sir!" And Eisenhower would say, shaking hands, leaping down from his five-star general's pedestal: "I'm from Kansas, too!" He looked everyone in the eye. *That's what good leaders did*, according to Dad.

We stood on the curb, part of a hedge of waving hands and flags, a foursome: Dad, Mom, my sister Alice, me. "Tommy, wave! Here he comes!" I cranked up my ten-year-old hand as President Eisenhower, *my* president, the one I pledged allegiance to each and every school day morning, exited a navy base, afloat in the back of a gleaming Chrysler limo bossed with diplomat's chrome, an ink-black mobile throne crunching the gravel in bloated whitewalls. On his way to a round of golf. The most powerful man on earth, had he had ambitions that way. He didn't look the type.

He smiled. And I waved back in the raw cold, until my arm grew tired and my hand curled like a fat, happy little leaf.

Aunt Alice was Dad's oldest sister.

She smelled like stardust and wore a red fox throw, as soft as water; that ended in two narrow faces with dark glass eyes, like cunning advisors draped at her ear.

With dead foxes circling her fluted neck, Aunty Alice seemed wise and regal. I loved all my aunts, the seven or eight I saw regularly, all gifted doters. But Aunt Alice was my favorite. She smelled rich. She looked elegant. She had thin long, smooth legs under long silk skirts.

I was happier when she was around. She elevated me. Light flowed from her.

One day she said I looked *exactly* like my father. She meant a family resemblance.

I was eight. I took her literally. I knew that people who looked alike were called twins. Therefore, my father and I were twins. At our next show-and-tell in elementary school, I took my turn in front of my class to say that I had a twin.

I held up a crinkled snapshot of a much older man. I said that this was him.

I was about to be instantly glamorous. I would be, to the

amazement of my friends and peers, the first twin in our school.

My teacher, warming her bottom on the radiator, asked to see the photo. Which showed a bunch of men posing in full-length military overcoats, aboard a troop ship.

She asked, "Which one?" The big clock over the door clicked away metronomically, like a screw being tightened by precise half turns. I enthusiastically pointed to one of the men, not the tallest, and said, *That's my dad*. My teacher didn't understand. I explained that my dad was my twin. The class waited to hear her verdict. Maybe I was right. In the third grade, it was all new. Anything was possible.

Mrs. MacIntyre smiled inconclusively. She liked to call me *Bright Eyes*, which meant I was special. Now she leaned down and whispered: "You know—you *do* know?—that your father can't be your twin." Soft. Not inaudible.

I was deboned. Branded by embarrassment. *In this small classroom in this small town*. My skin smoking. I sat down with nothing to say—FOREVER. Desperate for a time machine. *We have the same name*, I begged silently in my own defense, at my tiny desk. *Thomas Francis Ahern?* I am a *Junior!* That has to make us the same.

My dad and I even looked the same. Everyone said so. Just at different times.

Aunt Alice was the glamour-puss of the family.

She was unmarried, a devout and jealous Catholic, a tall bag of bones in good clothes. She always drove a new car. My mother considered Aunt Alice a prima donna and didn't like her. But I did. Hopelessly. She was an angel dispensing gifts and treats, steeped in perfume, her lap a place of privilege. Her lap should have had its own embassy and Marine guards.

She lived with her equally maiden sister, Mary, in their dead mother's house. They took in my teenage cousin Jackie when his parents died suddenly a few months apart. Jackie had a narrow rat's face and suppurating pimples. He was a declared cynic and atheist. He complained about everything, in a scratchy, sarcastic voice; and kept a stack of *Playboys* within easy reach, defying his aunts' saturated piety.

They were saints. Jackie proved it. On one wall in the dark living room hung a depiction of the Last Supper; on another the Nativity of Jesus. Like a medical illustration in a frame, there was a bleeding heart crowned with thorns. And a crucifix warded each bed (except Jackie's), a small bronze tortured figure pinned to a walnut-stained cross. My aunts said nightly prayers on their knees, forearms pressed into the bedspreads. Jackie spent his nights in the next room, silently stiffening tissues with his discarded seed.

Aunt Alice must have whispered complex prayers. For years, she had been the soft-centered secret "second wife" of her married boss, a fuel-oil dealer. Always his, never his. Each workday stung her heart with tiny arrows.

I was in the kitchen, lurking.

Aunt Alice was in the living room. My father was on the couch. Smoking a Camel cigarette with a quarter-inch pinky of ash, the smoke from Aladdin's lamp winding out of it, looking for a wish to grant.

My wish: I had rigged one of Dad's cigarettes to explode. So far nothing had happened. It was only a matter of time. If the trick worked at all. He inhaled deeply, the way soldiers did. Blew a smoke ring that lassoed his index finger. He took another hot puff.

BANG!

Quick and sharp, sounding like a shot.

Actually BAH-BOOM! if you heard it in slow motion. Because your life had suddenly ground to a halt. Which mine *had* just then. For the first time I experienced a pregnant pause. A pause about to give birth to something unexpected. But monstrously familiar. I was shocked silly, trembling with horror. This was MUCH LOUDER than I'd imagined when I'd doctored the cigarette Dad would eventually tap out of his pack. The joke-store explosive had looked like a small white thorn, not a dangerous bomb.

My aunt sat very still. Dad was a wax figure, with an odd half-raised smile. The mutilated stub of his cigarette was still gripped in his lips. The noise had slapped everyone rigid. In the air, drifted quiet flakes of paper and threads of smoke.

"It worked," I announced, entering into view. I claimed the attitude of a scientist conducting an experiment, hoping that would keep me safe. *Sorry. Oops. Sometimes happens. Just testing the effects of sticking a piece of dynamite between your teeth. Lot to learn.* Because I knew that I had stepped into a tub of shit unbelievably deep. I knew Dad's temper: it was a frightening black rage that tore parts of your self-confidence away like suds in a wind. He could not tolerate sudden loud noises. They turned his nervous system into an instantaneous six-alarm fire. The war, we figured; all those artillery shells falling on him. The exploding cigarette, though, had a paradoxical effect.

Maybe he was relieved he wasn't hurt. Instead of anger, he froze. Then his hand rose toward his face and retrieved the cigarette's remains. He looked at it benignly. The thing was far too short and shattered to relight. He flipped it into the ashtray.

Aunt Alice wore a hat with a veil. She sat in her chair like she might be dented. I couldn't see her expression behind the fine black lace.

I wasn't sure what to do.

Maybe he assumed his cigarette had malfunctioned. Dad, the domestic fool: *Damndest thing. Cigarette blew up in my face. Never heard of that before.* But it was too late. I already had the momentum up to confess. "I'm sorry, Dad. I didn't know that would happen."

The half-smile didn't change. "OK."

He wasn't putting two and two together; his mind was off hunting foxholes to hide in. I cleared out, while he was still too dazed to ask incriminating questions: *What was I thinking of? Why had I restarted his war?* How cruel was that?

Sundays I dressed like a replica of a well-raised boy. In a striped tie that meant nothing to any exclusive group; best slacks ironed by my mother; and a jacket that was never cleaned, I wore it so seldom. Eventually I just outgrew the dirt.

I had my Sunday sentry post: a window in the living room overlooking our short, steep driveway. Beside that window, there was a chair with an embroidered seat where I perched and peered through the café curtains.

Each Sunday it was the same. I sat in the living room

on my chair. I watched my mother open the kitchen door behind me. I heard her heels scrape down our few back stairs. Saw her reappear, below my watcher's window, outside in the driveway. Miraculously. My mother was capable of miracles. Protestant miracles. The Catholic kind were a magic show: lots of showy paint and mind control. Protestant miracles were more practical: installing an air conditioner in my bedroom to control my asthma. My father smiled when I stopped breathing. He didn't know what to do: physical weakness scared him. My sister resented the air conditioner, which was a luxury. In her opinion, my asthma was a scam, a bid for attention. Which she'd *never* stoop to in our struggle for parental attention. And she'd love some privacy, "while I'm listing things that could change around here." Every young girl craves privacy. And I was a boy: I wanted to see anything that had to do with girls.

In later years, my mother faced two transportation choices each Sunday.

#1: She would drive the family car, which otherwise she rarely touched. Or #2: Walk next door to borrow my Aunt Doe's sober mint-green economy sedan. A car so plain no manufacturer claimed it; it just was.

Sundays, my mother disappeared for a couple of hours. Gone to the pagans. Into a mystery ordained by her mixed marriage, she the waterside Protestant, he the plow-footed Catholic, together in the same union. The Roman Church had once righteously burned people for much less.

If the nuns told true, my miracle mom would still fry in the skillet of the afterlife.

Because in the Catholic version of what comes next, the

ignorant, the apostate, were tinder.

Shaking their heads, clicking with disapproval and menace, the nuns who taught us our catechism in the church basement on Saturday mornings told us outright that Protestants, the children who were our schoolmates, my mother, for pity's sake, were damned. An eternity on the barbecue for all the Martin Luther's buggering offspawn.

Mother didn't have a regular church. Come Sunday morning, anything Protestant would do. There was plenty of choice. Methodists. Presbyterians. Protestant Protestants, in their nondescript bungalow. The Baptists up the street from our house; of modest means, not mad as hatters. They owned a concrete foundation and a roof, nothing in between, all they could afford. The town had no upper crust. Even Holbrook's Episcopalians were poor. Somewhere, the Lutherans had a place. My mother was a small, fierce woman packed in an iron girdle. She sampled. Spirited her ears from minister to minister. Staring at strangers' necks. Their boils and collars. Dropping her coins in different plates. Buying hope, I think. Hoping to buy hope, anyway, by the Sunday lot. And plain talk. With maybe a sprinkle of inspiration on top.

Finally, if you had no imagination, there were the Congregationalists, next to town hall.

Their church seemed semi-official, a branch of government. Its needle-sharp steeple rose through the elms, as if planted at the same time here at the highest point in town, and grown with them, aiming for a clear shot at the sun.

A sign under glass outside on the lawn announced the sermon, in white letters pressed into black. The town's lawyer worshipped there. The town's non-denominational Boy Scout troop met in its basement and practiced being trustworthy, loyal, helpful, friendly, courteous, kind, obedient, cheerful, thrifty, brave, clean, reverent and heterosexual.

What Dad noticed about French churches as he tramped across World War Two: "You go into these churches: no heat. Never *did* have any heat. And you can see everybody's breath. And instead of pews they have chairs. They have a small chair and a big chair. You sit in the high chair, and you kneel on the low chair."

Catholics expect to kneel. Thanks to this early training they can be naturals when it comes to oral sex.

"Well, the churches that aren't cathedrals, that are out in the towns and that, they only have one chair," Dad reported. "Because they can't afford both, I guess. So what happens? Every time it comes to kneel down, everybody turns their chair around. And you hear all this scraping. Because it's all marble or brick floors. But they have no heat in anything.

"One little country church we went into, about ten of us one day.

"We were just in the vicinity and somebody said, Let's go over and see that church over there. We walk in, and the place is filled with people. Mass is just about to start. And the first thing we know, out comes all these people around the altar, and they've all got horns. And instead of an organ, they're playing the church music on their horns.

"Well, the first thing you know, you hear a giggle here, and a giggle there.

"The guys, you know, they're getting a laugh out of it. They've never seen anything like it. So the priest, when he saw ten of us sitting there, he changed the whole thing over, and he started to thank us in English, for saving the country."

My father, my sister, and I went to St. Joseph's Catholic church, to listen to Latin and a shrill choir, the sopranos lifting our hairs, the organ massaging our feet.

We were inside an ark.

St. Joseph's dark, board pews creaked and sawed during the long Latin mass.

If this were a forkful of purgatory, think what hell must be like. Numerous Catholic bottoms shifted weight; pelvic bones poked muscle. A week of dust rose from Sunday clothes. There was no ventilation. The doors were shut against sin and temptation. I stared at the criss-crossing shoulder straps beneath girls' white blouses and tried not to faint.

To no avail. Even at my confirmation I ended up on St. Joseph's granite front steps, with my head between my knees, a nun at my side.

My father bathed once a week. My mother claimed he had an aversion to water. I never saw him swim. By Sunday—bath night for the whole family—he was ripe. Sitting next to him in the pew I smelled the same odor every week: the smell of cheese hidden in some pocket.

War veteran and historian William Manchester: "...lying in a muddy foxhole while the enemy tried to hit him with bombs, tanks, grenades, bullets, flamethrowers, booby traps and HE (high explosive) and phosphorescent shells, a man looked like a tramp. His behavior was often uncivilized. He moved his bowels in full view of his peers, many of whom took a critical interest in his performance. He was foul-mouthed ... had been wet so long that his combat jacket was disintegrating and sometimes he smelled vile. Most of all he was tired. Some men took years to recover from that weariness. Some never did."

I loved my mother for her noises.

In the early evening, she'd return by bus from work. I would hear the sound of a massive motor vectoring in to idle by the curb, then the sigh of heavy brakes. Like a monster resigned to giving up its prey. Behind the curtains. Through the windows and clapboards. Sometimes almost in front of the house, sometimes a bit farther, depending on when she'd pulled the cord to signal the driver to stop. That unmistakable auditory cue, the slowing engine, a signal I heard thousands of times, no matter where I was in our small, stick-built house. "Mom's home!" Even if I didn't say it aloud. And each time my heart flooded with love and hope and a complex form of anticipation. And I was rescued and complete for another day.

To this day, my happiest hour is still between 5 and 6 p.m., the time when she'd step down onto the sidewalk and the bus would Doppler off to finish its route, followed by her high heels, sharp, hard, regular on the asphalt driveway, the determined sound of shotgun shells racked home, coming my way, aimed right at my heart. *Blow me to pieces, Mom!*

My father I loved for his high smell of rubber.

After the war he took a job at Avon Sole, a small factory half in our hometown and half in the next town over. He worked there until he retired, which is exactly what was expected: you found your job and stayed with it until the law moved you out, and you were too old to do much but die. Bugs made a living, birds made a living, Dad made a living. Five days a week, for a quarter century, from 7 a.m. until 3:30 p.m., he ran a machine that calendered rubber, pressing it into thin sheets for shoe soles. Every workday afternoon he came home and took a well-deserved nap. His work clothes smelled of rubber: powdery, warm, like a mechanical herb.

The best toy you ever get is sex. Unless you're a Catholic.

I went to hell pretty early.

After bath time with my mother, it was entirely other boys for a while. Which was sex, but generic. Playing "doctor," "captured spy," a few hands of strip poker when adults weren't around. Excuses to pull down each other's pants. In the basement, in a canning shed, in a derelict car. Poke and prod. Sometimes eagerly, sometimes ashamed. Looking for answers. *Desperate* for answers. Because girls hadn't been invented yet. And curiosity was burning a hole in my brain.

Ejaculation was never the point. We were pre-pubescent. Dry holes.

What we shared was a clinical interest in erogenous secrets. The frail little circumcised cocks we flicked and "tortured" during our games were a substitute. Touching generated a little electricity, a faint muzz at best.

But pricks were too familiar, a ludicrous body-double for a girl's private stuff. A girl had *twice* the potential of any boy, *two* erogenous zones—the things on her chest and the question mark between her legs.

Whatever was there, we knew for sure it wasn't a penis. It was some other name never spoken. A name we never heard. Something else. Shadowy, unimaginable. A machine. Something they owned that we didn't. Something they offered for our inspection. In their own time. Maybe. My sister was no help. She avoided me. I called her a slut, just to have something bad to say. I didn't know what the word meant. The marriage manual buried beneath my mother's scarves dealt with sex in a single paragraph, without pictures. My parents were having unillustrated, one-paragraph sex.

The boys debated: *Would any girl remove her clothes for us?*

No one *we* knew. We didn't play with girls much anyway. Or they didn't play with us.

We craved a solution to our sex mystery.

We gorged on rumors. Fantasies. At night you'd dream something up and next day you'd tell your friends. Holbrook Grove was the tough part of town. Around a flooded meadow, a thin disk of water so richly polluted it was only safe to touch in skates, weatherized cottages sagged into the weeds and dirt. Holbrook Grove was where greasers lived, tough guys with unpleasant ducktail haircuts. *They had a gang,* someone heard. Initiates were led blindfolded deep into the woods. *Where you handed over your clothes.* You had to find your way home naked. We imagined lots of different girls jumping to join up.

The other sworn truth was this:

Behind the high school, deep in the woods, past the part that everyone knew, there was a swing in a clearing. Outlaw girls rode that swing. Twisting on the seat, kicking leaves that had fallen from second-growth trees. While their thuggish boyfriends sat their blue-jeaned asses on stone walls built by once-upon-a-time farmers to keep their cattle honest.

The girl swung. The circle of boys smoked. Punched each other on the arm.

And designated which article of clothing she should remove next. No one had seen this activity. But it happened.

We haunted the woods, hunting for that swing. Up faint wagon trails. Past the parts that everyone knew. Because the woods were where people took off their clothes. Because the woods were ours and lawless, beyond observation and supervision. Feral. Where we could be naked ourselves and expose our flesh to the air, forced, *as humiliated spies,* to wear our underpants on our heads.

Billy Burstein was my first and best lover. He tied me to trees, he pulled down my pants, he stuck his dick in my mouth. Boys were available. Girls were not. Any crotch in a storm.

CHAPTER 8

MY THIRD LEG

IN JUNIOR HIGH SCHOOL I GOT AN ERECTION THAT WOULDN'T QUIT.

My joint went up like a derrick and stayed up, surprising me a little. I had something new to hang on to. Ready to pump. I don't think it surprised my teachers, though. Common enough phenomenon. Danger pay? Accidental boy semen splash?

I played with my penis constantly. I had nothing better to do.

I remember myself, hand in pocket, walking across our junior high school gym, knocking my tough little boner back and forth in my underwear like a switch that wasn't connected to anything. Like a skittle. I was the drum major in a one-penis parade, always on the march.

Then one afternoon a miracle happened.

I was home alone. The curtains drawn because my Aunt Doe who lived next door was a peeker, maybe. I got up on my father's bed. And lay face down, fully clothed, balanced on my erect and soft hard warm tingly penis.

I rocked slowly, listening to some music in my head.

My inconvenient little pocket log melted like a stick of

butter in a hot pan. It filled with water, a slug of it. Command central was sending urgent memos: *feels good!*

And I came.

Splash.

Cum came.

I'm sharing.

That was my very first time. Without warning. A couple of quiet jerks on Dad's lonesome bed, and I was done.

And petrified.

No barks of joy from this boy. *On the contrary.* My parents were not always gentle with mistakes. I was sure I'd snapped something vital. Some internal organ. *Sorry, Mom, Dad, while you were out I broke my body. Down there.* It felt like my crotch had a runny nose. I had a funny taste in my mouth.

I peeked in my underwear expecting to see a bright bloom of blood. Scrambled tissue. I knew my parents would be mad if I had to do the hospital again.

But there was nothing. Just wet.

I touched it: clear wet. A film where I usually had pee stains. *Thank you, thank you, thank you.* The miracle was, something strange and unexpected had splashed out of me; and yet I wasn't physically hurt. *I'd survived intact!*

And I wouldn't have to tell (!).

My parents never delivered a sex lecture.

It was better that way. I'd learn it one way or another, like they did.

And that way they would *not* have to conquer the flaming

barricades of their embarrassment.

So I knew nothing. At all. In any fashion. About the birds and the devil bees. In our family they didn't exist. *We don't talk about such things,* you could certainly hear that coming from my mother's mouth. But even *that* was never said.

We lived by certain standards. And we didn't talk about sex.

I called my sister a slut; I must have been in the sixth grade. "You don't know what that means," my father said. "Don't ever call someone that." My mother was frowning nearby.

I had no idea what sex was. Did you *have* sex? Did you *touch* sex?

And yet. Upstairs in my bedroom, masturbation had become my imaginary friend, visiting once, sometimes *twice* a day.

I'd become a stalker. Of me. I craved the feel of my hard, soft, smooth, downy-haired penis, a lean and prominently circumcised thing.

There was a rule: You needed a scene to masturbate to.

Jack and Jill illustrated a deck of cards in my mind. Each card was a separate, brief, looping fantasy. Black and white, like our television. Jumpy, scratchy, almost silent. Writhing. Looping over and over. Like private-label porn films. Now freezing. Freezing.

I envisioned naked girls. Boys, too. The crotch was the thing. The boys had all their parts. The girls had soft-focus blurs between their legs, a patch of fog I couldn't penetrate. No atoms. No facts. Or sometimes I imagined them smooth like dolls. Unpunctured.

I ejaculated frantically. I plunged deeper into shame after every time, like falling into a pit of earthworms. A blackboard of check marks kept track. Every sin was a rung on a ladder down. Down to rest. I built longer and longer ladders. I was already months down from the surface of the earth. I pumped out gallons of *stuff*, jism, painting my sheets stiff. Innocence was gone. Shame was in my bloodstream. I'd been infected in the basement of St. Joseph's Holy Roman Catholic church. I sank into depravity, an immature 12-year-old overdosing on hormones, already with a perpetual booking *in my name* at the center of the earth, where hell turned like clothes in a clothes dryer.

I couldn't confess to a priest, which could have reversed my damnation. It was too embarrassing. The confession simply wouldn't leave my mouth.

In the dictionary I hunted down words like "teat." Which is the nipple, not the whole breast. It would be years before I actually saw a breast, and stared at it like a beagle's nose, admiring its parts. Even little nipple hairs. Astonishing: like wires of gold pushed from the earth.

I was trying to build a girl out of words I'd read. To confirm the reality of *anything* that definitely had to do with a girl's sexual features. This was my first professional research project, "professional" meaning that something's at stake. I can recommend this form of sex education. It's a vocabulary builder. But I couldn't find all the pieces. No matter how many words I knew, they never added up to a naked girl.

In junior high school I got a new set of friends. I stopped hanging out with younger kids, and started hanging out with kids my own age. We found a few dirty magazines by the side of the road. It was a treasure hunt. Sex was strewn along the back roads. I walked for miles hoping to run across more discarded porn or a busted bra or a used condom hanging from a twig by the side of the road. Putting together a sex education from trash. One random clue at a time. In the thorns and rhododendron, there hung one day a pennant of soft, dry white latex, a little droopy in the tip. I didn't know how condoms worked. But I knew that a condom dusted with road dirt had been in contact with a woman's bare crotch. Somehow. My new friends said so, and they knew all the things that I didn't know. That condom had been where I so desperately prayed to go.

Then there was the "You are evil" episode.

At age thirteen I believed that my father could read my thoughts. I expected it. In the family car while he drove, I cringed in one corner of the front seat, trying not to think at all. And I would recall that, yes, I had masturbated again last night after a furious battle with my feeble-witted efforts at self-control. Efforts that snapped like a soda straw. Then I would remember the scene I fantasized with Jack or Jill, or Jack *and* Jill.

Right then Dad would turn his head from the steering wheel. He'd look at me strangely. And I would *know*. I didn't think it was something special, necessarily. I was willing to bet that fathers just naturally read thoughts; part of the job.

He and I were driving north, into New Hampshire, to our piss-poor summer house near Lake Winnipesaukee. I was in my corner, deeper than ever. Staring at him with my pimpled, angry face. I couldn't look at him anymore. I looked out the window instead. The ride to New

Hampshire was boring to the point of death.

The trees by the fields whipped in the wind. It was a sailing day. Strong winds shook the trees like pompoms.

Then those same tree breaks bent down and judged me. I heard them saying, *You are evil.* I fully agreed. Our second-hand Chevrolet or Pontiac or Buick or Oldsmobile sizzled north on the two-lane tar. Never a new model. I didn't understand that. Advertising told me it was my right to have a new car like the happy people, the good people.

Open fields whipped by. Another field of trees bent. And pointed toward me in the speeding car. With their branches. Passing it along, field to field, like barking dogs spreading the alarm.

You are evil.

I heard the trees in my head, their voices, spoken with their leaves.

And my heart broke. I fully agreed. I *fully* agreed. I was condemned to eternal damnation in the razor-sharp fires of hell. And I knew what *eternal* meant. Like driving through New Hampshire, only longer. Judged by the forest. Judged by everything that moved.

Only longer.

On the topic of shame.

I've felt ashamed forever. It's just there, like a second, small beating heart. Misshapen, like a tumor. An affliction.

I can't blame it all on my Catholic training, either. Everyone has a "them." Some way to pin the tail on the donkey. The Catholic church is my "them." Of course, their sophisticated form of child abuse and brainwashing didn't help. I mean, *really*: instilling the concept of hell in a child.

I was just bad at the things people told me to be good at.

I was bad at keeping my hands off myself and biddable playmates.

I was good at keeping score. The score was god everything, me not a damn thing. Except an eternity of unimaginable pain. I became an agnostic: *couldn't prove the existence of*. Then an atheist: *none at all*. In self-defense.

I wasn't really an atheist. I believed in god. Look around you. Plant your eyes. God was a wonderful accident I was privileged to witness until my senses dimmed. God was my brain and all the things it attached to.

I just didn't believe in humans. They were liars. Self-serving and delusional. I couldn't believe they'd gotten any of this right.

Life was a seven-part series: you were born, you went to school, you got a job, you got married, you had kids, you retired, you died. A soap opera your relatives watched, and only to criticize. I was ashamed of not being a better person. Everyone else in my family was perfect.

There were seven kinds of casualties you were exposed to in the U.S. Army: death, wounds, injury, sickness, internment, capture, or missing in action. Dad talked about putting one foot in front of another, when people were trying to stop your advance.

"Our outfit was what they call a 'spearhead' division. We went in first. We'd go in and take a town, and then these two divisions—the first and the ninth—would come in on the sides, all through the fields and everything. The first and the ninth divisions were considered the varsity of the First Army.

"We had gotten into this German town. We'd started off with a battalion of tanks, which is about forty-two tanks. When we got into the town, all we had left was two.

"The squad I was in had sixteen men in it. We got into the town and had seven men left. The sergeant was one of them; he was lucky." Death was casual, occurring by chance. That's what *casual* meant, in the military context: something bad that happened by chance.

Lieutenants were disposable.

In my father's stories, looies never lasted long enough to have a name. Sergeants were cautious, blue collar, trustworthy in combat; they could save your life. Lieutenants were management. Outsiders, segregated by rank and education, "90-day wonders," forever suggesting foolish things that might get you killed.

There was a smell about them, the odor of impending death: in U.S. infantry divisions fighting in Europe, second lieutenants were three times more likely to end up casualties than most other troops. Only ordinary riflemen—who made up just 11% of a division's total complement—died more often.

Dad: "We had a lieutenant, he came into the town with us. And there was a church steeple. And up in that church, up in the belfry, was a German sharpshooter. He got the lieutenant right off the bat. We called in the artillery and had the top of the church knocked to pieces."

Snipers came in all sizes. Kids were good at it. Small, easy to conceal, good eyesight. Biddable. "One of the squad moved around and found this kid, twelve years old, in a hole with a rifle. The guy come up behind him and got the kid out of the hole and brought him in. So the sergeant come down the street, and this guy said, 'Come here.' Sergeant walked over. The guy said, 'Here's the kid that killed Ed.' Sergeant said, 'Him?'

"Guy said, 'Yup.'

"Sergeant didn't say anything. He always carried a forty-five. He pulled that forty-five out and, boom, right into the kid. This captain come running down the street. He said, 'You can't do that!' The sergeant looked at him. He said, 'Bring him back.' That's all that was said."

Matty was my longest-running hometown sweetheart.

We met in a well-worn middle school. My father had graduated high school in the same building. He'd played tennis on the same asphalt courts where Matty and I chatted during recess.

Matty was extraordinarily gentle, sweet, and biddable. We entered adolescence together and practiced on each other. She was my transition sex object: I was moving from boy genitalia to a girl's, I hoped and prayed. More mysterious than the Virgin Birth was what a girl had *down there*. I became a heterosexual-in-training with Matty. She learned how to set limits with boys who were all paws. She starred in most of my wet dreams, though occasionally I gave her a rest. In truth or stereotype, she was the usual good Catholic girl. Modest. Tentative.

She was the first girl I seriously cared about. Where my heart did the talking. Where I burned and cried and hated to be separated from her.

Matty was perfect for a selfish, insecure kid who craved attention.

She was kind. Safe. Limpid. Nothing harsh nor nasty

lurked in her. Patient and enduring. Smiling. Unpredatory. Perky and self-deprecating. Earnest. Broad faced. A basketball player. Our class secretary for four years, with no effort to rise higher. Popular without being *popular*. Even her hairdo was cheerful. Her breath smelled of apple blossoms. Of course, *you cynics,* she was secretly troubled. She *had* her suicide attempt. But much later, after high school.

I secretly gave Matty a monogrammed gold ring of my father's he'd worn during the war, 14 karat. I begged him to let me wear it because we shared the same initials: TFA. I was Thomas Francis Ahern, Jr. He agreed. In truth, I wanted to give it to her; it was the only precious thing I could get my hands on.

By convention in our whispering world, presenting Matty with that ring meant she and I were "going steady": the first step on a long, doubtful road that might ultimately lead to marriage. Such things could run on tracks in our small town. We had no knowledge of the outside world beyond the sports teams we contested against, in our small-squad league; that, plus television. By accepting the ring and hanging it privately on a gold-plated chain under her blouse (and not telling her parents), Matty acknowledged her total commitment to me.

As I had desired. I was a pimply little squirt, a mouth breather with a slack jaw, stunted by asthma. I scowled a lot. I'd been sinning since the age of five, at least in thought: I knew I was as ugly as gargoyle. I was surprised—amazed—when someone liked me.

I gave Matty the ring just before we entered high school.

To keep her loyal more than anything else.

High school was going to be dangerous.

CHAPTER 9

HOW WHITE PEOPLE WON THE WAR

"WE CAME INTO OMAHA BEACH ON A BIG FREIGHTER."
This was a few weeks after D-Day. Omaha Beach was one of two U.S. landing zones in Normandy. This small gravel beach had seen the roughest action of the invasion. But that was long over. Now the troops were pouring in.

"And we had an ordnance outfit on the boat with us, all colored." ("Ordnance responsibility extended to 'everything that rolls, shoots, is shot, or is dropped from the air,'" explains the paperback *48 Million Tons to Eisenhower*, published in 1945.)

Dad told me: "It was getting dark. These colored guys, they are taking all the beds. I'm wrapped up in a blanket, sitting on the deck. The first thing we knew, all this ack-ack opened up; and they're filling the sky. And you can hear the German planes, and they're dropping bombs. Holy smoke! We didn't know that the Germans bombed that harbor every night. Of course, it was my first experience. All you can do is sit there and hope that one of those bombs doesn't hit that ship. Which it didn't.

"But these colored guys, they went crazy. We had a gangway, and it accommodated two people. They were going up it three abreast, yelling. All I could think of was pigs. Screeching, the way a pig squeals.

"Well, of course, all these ninety-millimeter guns that they had on shore shooting at these planes, they carry big shells. And what goes up has got to come down. All of a sudden, these big hunks of metal start hitting the deck of that ship. Well, brother, those colored guys came down just the same way they went up: three abreast, screaming."

The Allies invaded on June 6, 1944. The next day their supplies began hitting the beaches. In staggering quantities. Ten days after D-Day, 81,000 vehicles and more than a half million troops had crossed the sands, headed toward the fighting. That was just the beginning.

Dad described his stay in Normandy: "I had a Frenchman with me. He was a Canadian. And we got along pretty good, the pair of us. And he could talk the old language." This was a G.I. of French-Canadian ancestry.

The nights were soft, almost warm, within sound of the breakers along the coast if the cicadas ever shut up. "We rolled up in a couple of blankets in a field there, and about seven in the morning, he woke me and said, *'Breakfast?'*

"I said, Where the hell are you going to get breakfast up here?

"*'Come with me.'*

"There was a big farmhouse, you could see the roof of it over in the woods. We rapped on the door, and this farmer came out, and Frenchie started talking." The farmer was beside himself. "Oh, he greeted us with open arms. We walk in there, in that big old kitchen. He put big pitchers of milk on the table, his wife was cooking eggs, and big loaves of bread. We had a breakfast, I'm telling you!

"And he was telling us about the invasion." On D-Day, the first Allied invasion forces that jammed their heels into French soil were American and British airborne troops, a mix of parachutists and glider-mounted infantry. They dropped inside enemy lines in the dark hours before dawn, to block German reserves from coming up and reinforcing the beaches.

"The farmer said, *'I don't know what woke me up, but I walked out, and I could see these round shapes coming down from the sky. I said to myself,* This is the invasion.

"'I went back in the house, and about half an hour later, there's a rap on the door. I open the door, and there's this German lieutenant, and he's got about fifteen soldiers around him. And he wants to know if I've seen any American G.I.s. I told him no.

"'The Germans walked out of the yard here, onto the street, and they no more than hit the street and a machine gun opened up and wiped them right out. They didn't have a chance to run or anything else.' Who was it? Two paratroopers." I knew the punch line. Dad had told these blood-curdling tales since I was an infant. Still my arm hairs stiffened. "Wiped the whole fifteen of them right out."

But wait. There's more.

"One day, Frenchie and myself we were walking through this town, and all of a sudden this civilian came out, and he's yammering like mad. And I said to Frenchie, What's the matter? He says, *'There's a dead German up there in a barn. Come on, we'll take a look.'* So we walk into the barn. Sure enough, there's a German soldier there with his throat cut. So pretty soon, along comes this paratrooper. We said, *'Dead German up in that barn there, with his throat cut.'* He said, *'I know, I cut it this morning.'* He was walking along like he was delivering papers. Sure. Nothing to it."

In Normandy, more than two dozen contending divisions were hemmed up along the coast. The dead were even underfoot. An Allied colonel wrote, "The sight that fascinated me most was a corpse of a German soldier in a roadway.... It had been run over by so many tracked vehicles that it was ironed flat like a figure in a comic strip—really—absolutely flat, the arms of its grey uniform at right angles to its pressed and flattened coat. Its black boots and the legs that were in them were just as flat and thin as if they had been cut from a sheet of dirty cardboard."

Liberation was particularly sweet for Dad's farmer, it would turn out.

"That night Frenchie went back to the farmhouse to play cribbage with the old man.

"He came back and said, 'You know what? They haven't had any sugar for four years.'

"I said, 'What the hell's on these trucks?'" The field was full of supply trucks. "We started slitting these cardboard boxes with knives, and we found these big boxes of lump sugar. So what'd we do? Got a bag, we're dumping in sugar.

"When he went over that night to play cribbage with the old farmer, he must have had twenty pounds of lump sugar in a bag.

"So the next morning I said, 'How'd they like the sugar?' 'Oh God,' he said, *'I could have had the house. They're tickled to death!'"*

Almost two months past D-Day, Allied generals were measuring progress yard by frustrating yard. The German entrenchment across the base of the Norman peninsula was sealed tight as a vacuum jar. Inside the jar: nearly one million Allied troops bumping elbows, more than 300,000 vehicles churning the roads and dairy pastures into thigh-deep mud. You didn't walk; you waded.

Americans had occupied the city Saint-Lô by July 18. Saint-Lô was a transportation hub. It had been a favorite furlough destination for German occupation troops. That place was gone. Saint-Lô now had "the sad privilege of having earned the title of Capital of Ruins," the Michelin guide laments. "By ... the day the town was liberated, only the battered towers of the Collegiate Church of Our Lady and a few outlying houses remained standing."

Outside the city limits, a German hard crust still held. The hoped-for breakout of American armor stalled.

Six stalemated days later, "the forward infantry of Panzer Lehr Division, manning the front opposite the Americans west of Saint-Lô, reported that the enemy were leaving their positions and retiring ... without apparent reason." The Germans, who had little respect yet for this particular enemy, wondered if the Americans were giving up.

U.S. First Army commander Omar Bradley had a plan.

He would treat bombers like artillery, only bigger, *much much bigger*: a massive aerial attack in a very concentrated area, to turn the earth over and kill everything on the face of it, to blow a hole in the German lines.

Then, plan said, American ground forces would pour through, the dam broke, into the uninterrupted French countryside, get out into much better tank country, where the Allies could take their killer dogs off the leash. Paris, the symbolic prize, beckoned.

"Shortly afterwards [German outposts] reported the

approach of heavy bomber formations...."

John Keegan relates that during the next two days, "Flying Fortresses in hundreds upon hundreds ... dump(ed) their enormous bomb loads on and behind German positions. The effect was catastrophic."

"It was on a Saturday morning. And all of a sudden we hear this ungodly noise. They threw two thousand bombers at Saint-Lô. There was something like five hundred fighters with them, protecting them. I was watching the planes go over my head. We were five miles back," Dad said, "and the ground was shaking under us just like an earthquake.

"These planes went in, with a lead plane and say six planes, like a duck formation. The lead plane dropped smoke bombs. And then you were supposed to bomb in between the smoke."

Remember McNair? For what happened next, military lexicographers have a euphonious, almost soothing term: "amicicide." Killing friends. Accidental, ironic, alas. Friendly fire. It happened on day one, when bombs dropped short killed 25 G.I.s. No one thought it would happen twice.

Day one had been a *minor* mistake. Overcast weather cancelled the attack mid-flight. A few bombers didn't get the message and came in anyway.

Day two the weather cleared. The attack was on, full tear.

The planes dropped a total of 3,950 tons of high explosives. It's hard how to describe that quantity in a way you can appreciate. These are words; words on the page make no noise. Sure, it sounds like a pretty big amount: almost 4,000 tons. It's actually a change in the human condition for those on the receiving end. Nervous systems explode.

George Wilson, a newly arrived American lieutenant on the scene, said: "The rush of air from the blasts gave us a good push, even though we were a half mile away. The destructive power of those thousands of five-hundred-pound bombs overwhelmed the senses."

"When they bombed Saint-Lô," Dad said, "they blew a path through it something like five miles wide and two miles long."

Almost 18,000 bombs fell. Imagine a dynamite-packed car engine falling from the sky. Now imagine 18,000 such car engines falling and exploding as they hit, churning every foot of ground, filling the air with flying razor-sharp metal casing fragments, subsonic wickering steel. The Americans remarked on how lazy the ordinance looked tumbling down and how confidently and slowly the planes flew. The Allies owned the skies. "I don't understand how any of (the Germans) even survived," Lt. Wilson wondered. "Bomb craters big enough to swallow a jeep were so close together in some areas it was difficult for our tank drivers to zigzag through."

Keegan quotes Panzer Lehr commander, Major General Fritz Bayerlein: "...back and forth the bomb carpets were laid, artillery positions were wiped out, tanks overturned and buried, infantry positions flattened and all roads and tracks destroyed. By midday the entire area resembled a moon landscape, with the bomb craters touching rim to rim.... The shock effect on the troops was indescribable. Several of my men went mad and rushed around in the open until they were cut down by [bomb] splinters."

Panzer Lehr was not an easily rattled formation. They did not ordinarily run around like madmen. "The strongest armored division in the German army," Keegan rates it.

"Perhaps the best." These were Nazi bad boys, a well-armed, disciplined, ideologically hardened gang capable of living off raindrops and maggots.

But even Panzer Lehr had never seen anything like this: carpets of bombs landing unobstructed—with every watch tick: twenty bombs a second—in one extended blast that flipped entire fields. "The planes kept coming over as if on a conveyor belt," reported the grief-stricken Bayerlein. About 1,000 of his men died, "and at least 70 per cent of my troops were knocked out—dead, wounded, crazed or numbed."

"What Germans were still alive were so shaky they couldn't hold a gun," Dad said. "You couldn't believe the noise. You couldn't distinguish an individual motor. It was just one continuous roar."

Sixty tanks were promised to Bayerlein as reinforcements. Five made it through.

Confronted with a hold-or-die directive from his superior, Bayerlein countered: "Out in front every one *is* holding out. *Every* one. My grenadiers and my engineers and my tank crews—they're all holding their ground. Not a single man is leaving his post. They are lying silent in their foxholes for they are dead. You may report to the Field-Marshal that the Panzer Lehr Division is annihilated."

The Brits called the phenomenon "creepback."

War correspondent Ernie Pyle, the G.I.'s Boswell, "Old Indestructible" (turned out later he wasn't), happened to be at Saint-Lô reporting from the front lines when the bombing began on day two.

"As we watched, there crept into our consciousness a

realization that windrows of exploding bombs were easing back toward us, flight by flight, instead of gradually forward, as the plan called for. Then we were horrified by the suspicion that these machines, high in the sky and completely detached from us, were aiming their bombs at the smokeline on the ground, and a gentle breeze was drifting the smokeline back over us! An indescribable kind of panic comes over you at such times. We stood tensed in muscle and frozen in intellect, watching each flight approach and pass over us, feeling trapped and completely helpless."

Dad said, "And what they didn't realize, after the first few flights of planes went in and dropped their bombs, these smoke bombs that the leading plane was dropping, the smoke was drifting back to our lines." He was remembering news accounts like Ernie Pyle's.

General Leslie J. McNair, the operations genius who had trained the U.S. Army, happened to be on the front line that day, in a foxhole. Geoffrey Perret: "McNair believed ardently that to understand what was going on, you had to get close to it."

"The first thing you know," said Dad, "they were bombing their own men. McNair got killed up there. As one guy said, 'Here was a stone wall, and I don't know which side of it to jump on.'"

Still.

From Saint-Lô, the Allied fighting mass erupted into open country, hurling the enemy back. By August 25th, Paris was liberated. By mid-September, almost all German troops were pushed off French soil.

Not counting the million buried in it.

It happened that fast. Bottled up for seven weeks and then, *boom!* The Allies bust out.

At a price, though: each month, 15,000 G.I.s dead, 50,000 others wounded. The odometer on casualties was spinning wildly. Headquarters started moving supply clerks like my father into the line. The U.S. Army even decided to let negroes fight, an experiment that the white majority expected to fail.

According to a study conducted by senior Army officers, "The negro is cheerful, loyal and usually uncomplaining if reasonably well fed." A slightly different species, of course.

In the European Theater, it was a white man's fight. Racially pure Nazis vs. the Allies. Fighting over the headwaters of the white man's world. Or in the Far East, white against yellow, fighting over the white man's spoils.

John Morton Blum: "The battle for freedom, as the Allies fought it, did not promise freedom for dark peoples. That anomaly especially troubled American blacks, and whites, too, in the case of the British in India. Though only a few black fanatics sympathized with the Nazis—for Hitler was so patently a racist that the prospect of his triumph threatened disaster—many blacks felt some affinity for the Japanese, even after Pearl Harbor, and few informed blacks had unequivocal enthusiasm for Great Britain."

Although the U.S. government increased its hiring of blacks (reluctantly), the Army—innovative in so many other ways—was opposed to social experimentation. Blum: "When in 1940 blacks began to enlist, which they did at a rate 60 percent above their proportion of the population, the Army assigned them almost exclusively to segregated units and trained them almost entirely for noncombatant tasks as laborers, stevedores, and servants."

"They didn't train colored troops." Dad said. "They drafted them. But when they found out what they had, they couldn't do anything with them. They were all in transportation. It was the only thing they were good for."

Bigotry was gospel in the military.

"At the end of it," my father recalled, "Eisenhower tried to put like one colored guy with about fourteen white [infantrymen]. Even that, I don't think, worked out. I never bumped into it myself. But according to the talk, they'd run, take off.

"And they'd tell you they'd take off." He pretended amazement. "They didn't mince any words. As quick as the lead starts to fly, boy, they took off."

"The ... 761st Tank Battalion (an all-black unit)...fought across Europe with Patton for an unheard-of duration—six straight months without relief—capturing or liberating more than 30 major towns along the way," Ann Banks told *New York Times Sunday Magazine* readers in 1995. Fifty years after VE day, she hoped to set the record straight once and for all on the question of "colored guys" in combat.

Johnnie Stevens, a platoon sergeant with the 761st, told her: "I was drafted in June 1942, and they took me to Fort Benning, Georgia. At the time, they were taking I.Q.'s on black guys to see if they could qualify to do technical things that had to do with tanks.

"It didn't make any difference to me where I went, but I didn't want to drive trucks. I didn't want to load materials and stuff. I'm going to give it to you straight. I didn't want to wait on the white boys. We completed our advanced training in Texas. But there was no intention of sending this black outfit into combat. It was a big show for the public. Then General Patton came into the picture. He was on an inspection tour and watched how we handled tanks, how we fired guns. Patton said: 'I like them. I want them.' That's how we ended up in the Third Army. They called us Patton's Pets and Eleanor's Niggers.

"When we landed in France, we went directly into combat. All I remember is fighting and killing and freezing and starving and fighting and killing. We mostly spearheaded. The Maginot line, the Siegfried line, the Ardennes Forest, Battle of the Bulge.

"A lot of people asked us: 'Why did you guys earn such a record? Why did you chalk up so many kills? With all the hatred and segregation, why would you fight like you did?'

"I lost a tank on Hill 309 in France. We were in support of the 26th Infantry, a Yankee division, meaning they were white. We fought well with them guys. They liked us, we liked them, and most of them said they liked our support better than the white tankers because we took care of them.

"I led the attack that morning. My tank was hit by a round from a German 88. I used the ejection seat to dismount. When I hit the ground I had a bullet hole in the chest. I had shrapnel sticking out the left side of my head. My leg was bleeding. My right hand had shrapnel in it. There was a white infantry sergeant over by the embankment. He and I had got to know each other pretty good in a couple of days of combat, and he yells, 'Sergeant, you hear me?' I said, 'Yeah— I'm hit hard as hell, man.'

"The Germans ... were raking the field with machine gun fire. They didn't intend for us to get out because tankers kill too many people. The sergeant crawled over and gave me a hand." The short of it: Stevens lived, the white infantry sergeant got shot—and died right there—helping Stevens to safety.

According to U.S. Army records: serving under Patton were two tank battalions with the official designation "colored." Both fought right through to the German surrender and stayed in Germany a year thereafter on Occupation duties.

Dad: "Patton, he had a battalion of tanks, and they were all colored crews. Oh, they were the toughest boys on the earth, to hear them tell it. But they got close to the German lines, and the Germans opened up on them, and when they did, those tanks just turned around and headed right back. A battalion: something like forty-five tanks. Patton said, 'Don't you dare give me any more colored crews. I don't want them.'"

Maybe. Patton was a prick. In his own words, "I inspected and made a talk to the 761st Tank Battalion." This was the first colored battalion to arrive, in late October 1944. "A good many of the lieutenants and some of the captains had been my sergeants in the 9th and 10th Cavalry. Individually they were good soldiers, but I expressed my belief at that time, and have never found the necessity of changing it, that a colored soldier cannot think fast enough to fight in armor."

Patton had a lot of ready opinions about his fellow man.

He was shocked by the Nazi death camps. But he didn't blame the Germans for bestializing their victims. He blamed the Jews for giving in. In his mind, their abjectness stripped them of their rank as humans. He believed in breeding.

Well-bred people did not grovel. "The Jews ... are lower than animals. My personal opinion is that no people could have sunk to the level of degradation these have reached in the short space of four years." At the close of the war, Patton confided to his wife his preference in foreigners: "The Germans are the only decent people in Europe. The trouble-makers must be the Jews...."

CHAPTER 10

FRUITS OF HIS LABORS

IN 1947, THE YEAR MATTY AND I SLID ONTO THIS EARTH, THE WAR WAS TWO YEARS DONE.

And *gone*.

General Electric ran full-page ads announcing the technological wonder of "electronic television," a communications meteor soon to be slamming into the human race and changing everything.

R.J. Reynolds Tobacco had health news, reporting that in "a recent Nationwide survey: More Doctors Smoke Camels than any other cigarette." So, *see*....

I was born August 3rd.

The next day, as it happened, *Life* magazine ran a cover feature on "Renaissance Venice: Fourth in a series on the history of Western culture." America was looking outward. Confidently. Eagerly. During the war, newspapers had carried campaign maps by the thousands. U.S. readers got a refresher course in world geography. Radio news broadcast events taking place far away, in places with exotic names; you could hear the difference. The far away became familiar. The U.S., introspective during the Depression, was curious now about the world at large. Education was on a rampage.

Life readers wanted to know more about what they'd fought for, this Western civilization they'd ostensibly saved.

Had the long encounter with death provoked a nation-wide lust for life, too?

American bedrooms were *sizzling*. Bed boards beat the walls like tom-toms, *have a child, have a child, have a child;* and Baby Boom nests filled. And would continue filling for another 15 years.

The immediate big problem? Making more nests.

In 1949, William J. Levitt opened a modest sales office on Long Island and found more than a thousand couples lined up that first sunny morning to buy his basic four-room house. On a 1,500-acre ex-potato field 17,500 homes would sprout, assembled by efficiency experts.

In his prime, Levitt was a hero who did something about the housing shortage. But each home was exactly like its neighbor (it was the fastest way to build). The day you were allowed to hang your wash (Mondays) was written into the deed. Levittowns became a synonym for excess conformity—tasteless, stultifying, if not really sinister. The first houses came in just one two-color paint scheme. And the families came in "just Caucasian": until the 1960s, occupancy restrictions applied.

My parent's personal little grass shack was a Cape Cod-style house built in 1950, in the same small town where they had both grown up. The 1944 G.I. Bill, enacted to help millions of returning vets get a leg up, helped things along with a low-cost mortgage.

The house contained two bedrooms, a living room, a knotty pine kitchen, and one bath; with an unfinished basement, tree trunks serving as posts; and an attic infested by silverfish. Bugs like aluminum toenail clippings shooting for the cracks when the lights blazed on. No garage yet. The place was soundly and snugly constructed on a tiny parcel of land my maternal grandmother had given my parents as a wedding gift. We had nine flowering shrubs as landscaping. A house, a driveway, a patio: it made a neat, little package.

Friday nights we ate no meat, following the Catholic taboo.

It was a small sacrifice to remind you, via a kick to the tripes, that *they* nailed Christ, Guineas and Jews, to a cross on Friday, *you unworthy, ungrateful cretin.* Under dark clouds and lightning, in the company of thieves, taunted, abandoned by a father who *could* have, if he'd chosen, beat up any other father *forever IN HELL:* you did not *fuck* with god almighty and his only begotten son, whatever the fuck *begotten* meant. I sure didn't know.

Except this time. This time you *could* fuck with god's son.

Once a week in commemoration we ate no meat. I had a favorite Friday meal: ruler-straight fish sticks floating in a puddle of baked beans and ketchup.

Tasty to this day. And a reminder.

After supper on Fridays, I would walk the mile to Matty's house.

Friday was our night, too.

Matty lived with her mama bear, papa bear, brother cubby, sister cubby, herself, in their equally starter home, one of two dozen built in a sand pit.

Holbrook was a town of glacial remnants. Cape Cod was the picturesque version, with waves and beaches. Holbrook had the overgrown version: sand under a skin of lightly-rooted trees, easy for bulldozers to clear. A patch of a town among many similar patches. It is now exurbia, a small nexus on a wire of convenience stores and strip development. When Dad was a boy, you could still hunt there. Trolleys and radios were the communications technologies of the day. He rode a trolley to work, if there was any work. He heard and imagined baseball games and boxing matches, the drama properly scaled to a human brain.

Matty's family was typical of new suburbanites. They'd left behind, with no regrets that I ever heard, apartments in Boston's ethnic neighborhoods: Irish, French, Italian, Jewish, Polish. The typical project house in Holbrook probably wasn't much bigger than a triple-decker apartment. But it had a yard with its own fence. That made a distinct difference. You could have a dog. You could hang laundry in the open air and barbecue meat on your Weber, invented 1951. The neighbors lived next door, instead of underfoot or overhead. That made a difference.

In the suburbs, you had a little more psychological elbowroom. *Lebensraum,* the same thing Hitler shouted about and went to war over. Hitler wanted Poland and the Soviet Union. Immigrants to America wanted suburbs inside a generation. Urban for them meant crowded, dirty, loud, nasty, dangerous. Suburban meant space, neat, private, predictable, safe.

I walked to Matty's house in the late summer sun, on dusty, unpaved roads. In the winter I walked from streetlight to infrequent streetlight, through otherwise dark neighborhoods. Sometimes I ran, just for the pleasure of moving faster. Or giving dogs the slip. I was a soon-to-be track star. I could outrun a dog in a distance sprint; and if I couldn't, I'd learned the trick of becoming BIG. Truth? *Real* truth? I would have crawled bare-naked through leeches to take my place at her kitchen table, given the rewards she had on offer.

I was an early adolescent heterosexual male. She was an early adolescent heterosexual female. She was a flower. I was a bee.

She'd allow me—not invite me, but allow me—to play with her breasts for a few hours. Out of sight. Beneath two layers of cloth, her cotton blouse and her unrevealing brassiere.

It was my beginner hetero sex.

While I was fumbling her mamms, her family watched TV in the living room a few yards away. I could hear the laughter, theirs and the canned stuff. Blue light shook in the little corridor between the two rooms. I was always amazed that Matty's father left us alone. I was a gargoyle. A demon stare. A selfish heart. *He should* know *my intentions were selfish.*

My target each Friday: her top button.

We sat, Matty and I.

Knees touched under a corner of the table.

We passed the time with gossip and school news, shifting in her family's vinyl-and-chrome chairs. Overhead, a harsh fluorescent halo shined. Mood lighting? Then the mood was surgery: no gradations, no shadows. Locker-room glare.

On hard seats.

We talked at first. Then I'd lean forward, hold her chin on the tips of my fingers, and kiss her soft, dissolving lips. Inhale her sweet exhalations. The real evening, for me, had begun.

Matty played basketball; an athlete. Yet everything about her was soft. Once we began kissing, I couldn't stop. Kissing led to touching. Touching was where I wanted to be. My fingers had eyes. I hastily undid her blouse, for easier access. The route: over her blouse, inside her blouse, under her bra, unhooking her bra so it fell away in front, clearing the way for insertion. Her breasts had the density of unbaked dough. Her nipples were never erect. These were surreptitious gropings, all my hands on deck beneath her plaid or white shirt.

She wasn't trying to be sexy. She was trying to be good.

She would *never* let me see her breasts. I wasn't all that sure she *had* nipples, or how nipples fit into the overall picture, girls being mostly large swaths of terra incognita. I had nipples, of course. But my nipples were obsolete. My nipples were uncalled for, pointless, *and maybe that was the point*. Unlike Matty's, my nipples weren't glue strips for a boy's blind touch.

Joe never intruded, without an announcing cough.

A knowing gentleman.

Ten p.m. was my curfew, though. Exotically late. He drove me home each week.

Joe was a stumpy, cheerful man, with a new car: a white Ford Falcon without chrome, the cheapest model sold. Economy cars were new on the market. The Falcon was styled like a gym sock. Detroit didn't want anyone too crazy about the look.

Matty and I climbed into the back seat and silently, desperately necked. Tongues like stalks of celery, our chapped lips touching all the way home; bruised lips, hard against the teeth. More breast fondling on the ride. Her blouse bunched out of her pants. Her sensible bra like the map of the world. Beneath, her heart. The sense of her. The woman built atop the girl.

Joe took the longest way possible. He was a sweet guy. He didn't take offense that I was touching his daughter. He wanted Matty to be happy. A happy female would be a nice addition.

His wife was agoraphobic. She never left the house. A few small windows, occluded by curtains and shades, pierced her mind-made prison. Out back she viewed a scuffed, sloping, sun-burnt yard out back. Out front a small sagging lawn. They owned no trees. No garage. The driveway was a small rectangular lick of asphalt. Life came to *her*, if at all. And not much did. The neighbors soon learned. Her children brought in the mail when they came home from school, that legendary place. Her husband hung out the damp laundry in the evening, telling neighbors it was *his* chore.

Joe in Heaven, an interview: *I don't know if I made Matty happy. I hope so. She turned out real good, by anybody's standards.* Matty liked me. She trusted me, which made me just slightly better than I really was. I never did do with her what boys always want to do. When she got pregnant, it wasn't by me. There she got lucky.

Matty was an Irish-American fertility goddess. Eggs dangled from her vaginal lips, daring all comers. The first male inside, he knocked her up. It was her first swive; her clean white undies, a forlorn ankle bracelet; thighs the texture and shade of a Guinness properly poured; bundled down on some drunken weekend, in some filthy college fraternity.

Here's the thing.

Had I *been* the father, she would have raised the child alone and lived a small life. Abortion then was illegal. Who knew where you got such a thing.

Didn't happen.

Instead, the man who tossed the match inside Matty's combustible thighs, married her. To add insult to injury he was ambitious. Became rich and famous. Occasionally, yes, she was bored, to judge from her phone calls; which were always breathless.

But she was launched. Instead of dropped. Chutes and ladders.

She was on a ladder that led, finally, *admittedly*, to the A list. In Washington, D.C.'s political society. White House-level A list. *See what I'm saying?* Things change.

I banged my knuckles bloody—a little bloody—on the seams of our poured concrete basement. I don't know why. I was unhappy. It felt good. Sauce on despair. Pain was more interesting than anger. A little pain, anyway. It never got very far. No broken bones.

I was horny 190% of the time. That might explain it. Hormones fired through me like 16-inch guns. Just as the battleship U.S.S. Massachusetts, which my dad helped weld together in Quincy's Fore River, lofted one-ton projectiles into Casablanca harbor. Wreckage! In my life, too. I give thanks to Catholic guilt.

A high-voltage transmission line ended in my whittled penis. Hormones made my fingers dance! Clench! Trying to grasp a larger world. The air above my bed vibrated. My fingertips cast into the night like fishing lines, past the planets, trying to hug *something*. Something comprehensible. Growth. Or my soul. It felt universal, whatever it was.

Dried semen starched the fronts of my underwear. I had a new team color: *Protein yellow*. Masturbation rubbed me raw. Like walking into a series of fence posts. I ached with the need to think about sex. And not just any kind.

Dirty sex. *Nasty* sex. *Unromantic* sex.

Each day I jerked my chicken. On good days, twice.

Oh, my Catholic soul, I wanted to stop. Desperately. And then desperately gave in each time the point was raised. I shoveled sand in front of a cresting river: sex kept bursting through, flooding the town, chasing all the nice people out. Once a day. More than once. I walked around, a part-time human. An imposter in my own house. A sinner who didn't dare reveal himself. How could I tell my mother, father, or my parish priest, some circuit stranger who spoke to me through a sliding grill, that I'd had an active sex life since at least the third grade? That I'd sucked a boy's prick? That I'd looked *forward* to sucking a boy's prick, just to see? (Like sucking your own boneless finger, it turned out. Tasteless and without condiments that day.) That I fantasized about naked girls in boxcars? Naked girls and their naked mothers? The church told me I was doomed. Unless I spoke. Confessing made the difference. Confessing saved you.

I couldn't.

Confession was a place where I lied about my sins, inventing what I considered a plausible assortment of minor transgressions: *I'd been disrespectful, I'd used the Lord's name in vain, I'd said bad things to my sister* (that *was* the truth). Wallpaper sins. Misdemeanors.

My father must have thought at times it was snowing sheets of paper.

In less than a year, six BILLION leaflets were dropped on German targets, a MILLION EACH NIGHT when weather permitted, all of them urging surrender against insurmountable odds, making the case that it was pointless to die.

During the last year of the European war, the Allies' propaganda air force—a special arm—dropped four thousand non-lethal bombs each month, spilling safe conduct passes, alternative daily newspapers reporting "the real war" to German civilians, weekly newspapers published by the American Army for German soldiers, "How to save yourself" flyers, and warnings.

Delivery was most reliable via the T-1 propaganda bomb, a cardboard container with a barometric fuse. The bomb casing self-destructed at 2,000 feet, casting its contents to the winds of war and chance.

It made quite a mess. Daniel Lerner, Sykewar's leading chronicler: "On the ground the paper from each bomb made a pattern covering an area of between one-half and one mile square." Psychological warfare—Sykewar—was a major, though debated, component of the European battle. The "Standing Directive for Psychological Warfare" issued by Supreme Headquarters Allied Expeditionary Force (SHAEF), cautions sensibly that "Psychological Warfare is not a magic substitute for physical battle, but an auxiliary to it. By attacking the fighting morale of the enemy, it aims at: (a) reducing the cost of the physical battle, and (b) rendering the enemy easier to handle after the surrender."

The same directive probes the mind (and heart) of the German soldier: "The habit of uncritical obedience to authority, rather than any ruthless enforcement of discipline from above, remains the strongest factor in German morale today."

Two hundred years of conditioning crouched inside each German uniform: passed down from Frederick the Great, King of Prussia, who fielded Europe's best-led, best-disciplined, most self-sacrificing rabble armies. Dr. Herbert Rosinski, a German refugee and military scholar, writing during World War II: "The Prussian officer was the iron rivet which bound these heterogeneous and doubtful elements into the solid body of a blindly obedient machine; his control over his men was expected to be such as to enable him to lead them forward even under the heaviest fire."

SHAEF acknowledged the enemy's determination: "The average German's conviction that the best life is the soldier's life, plus the social fact that the highest calling in Germany is the soldier's calling, constitutes a great source of strength.

"Added to this the German soldier, and often the non-German soldier serving in the Wehrmacht [i.e., the German Army], is convinced:–

"(a) that he is privileged to be serving in the finest army in the world, permeated with a code of soldierly honor which rules him and his officers alike;

"(b) that the Wehrmacht is the embodiment of the highest physical and spiritual attainments of German culture;

"(c) that the Wehrmacht is therefore the *nonpolitical* guardian of the future of the German race;

"(d) that, as a fighting machine, German 'quality' can *probably* succeed in throwing back both Anglo-American and Russian 'quantity.'

"Thousands of officers ... and tens of thousands of NCO's [non-commissioned officers such as sergeants] have signed on not simply for the duration, but for periods varying from 7-14 years, or longer, and are fighting not only to preserve the German Army as a war machine, but as a means of livelihood."

The war, as a consequence, was tough to call, even in 1944 and '45.

Dad: lavishly supplied, fighting in someone else's garden, skeptical of authority vs. the proud Kraut: a potato a day, fighting for the Fatherland, worshipping command and control.

Both scarred by the Great Depression, both quite aware that war put cash in their pockets.

Allied senior strategists with wings for brains predicted that the round-the-clock terror bombing of civilian centers would bring about the psychological collapse of Germany.

At night the Brits, bent on revenge, flew their "bomber streams", a tidal flush of 600 planes an hour ordering "Bombs away!" over a single spot.

While the day belonged to the Yanks, by their own choice. American bombardiers liked to see their targets clearly, claiming that their top-secret Norden bombsight was so accurate it could "drop a bomb in a pickle barrel" from

20,000 feet. They wished. Time-Life: "The very notion of precision bombing appealed to the American psyche: it summoned up the old frontier pride in marksmanship."

Engines at dawn meant blue skies for Britain. "A clear dawn has a new clarion—the deep and throbbing roar of hundreds of planes, outward bound.... As their roar fades with them, another rises until things on the kitchen mantelshelf tinkle and rattle as they catch the vibration...." A thousand bombers at a time lifted off from English airfields, headed for a few square miles of urban Germany. Cities turned into Heinie roasts. In one ten-day-long British raid on Hamburg, 50,000 civilians died when incendiary bombs ignited a firestorm so hot it set the asphalt streets ablaze and reached below ground, to incinerate those crowded into shelters. "Hamburg has been Hamburgered!" shrieked the British press.

There was method to the madness, though even the method itself was mad. Unfounded theory gone to war. Without any real evidence to support the prejudice, British high command concluded that German spirits were brittle; and that a loss of residence would be the "hardest trial to bear" for the German civilian and worker. Bomb them out of house and home.

Orders from the British Air Ministry authorized unrestricted attacks, scrapping what had been far too optimistically called "precision" bombing and adopting "area" bombing instead, the blanket destruction of entire communities. Indiscriminate killing. "The primary object of your operations should now be focused on the morale of the enemy civil population and in particular, of the industrial workers." The war against Germany's lunch buckets was declared.

British mathematicians estimated that one bomber, over a lifetime of service (an average fourteen hazardous missions), could "dehouse" 4,000 to 8,000 Germans. Dehouse sounded like delouse, which was just about right. With determination, the calculators calculated, British bomber crews might ultimately blast a third of the German population into the streets, and decide the war from the air. "Bombing wins the war!" they hoped the headlines would ultimately read. And the punch line was, The ground forces would have little left to do except sweep up the pieces. The British liked the idea of saving a bit on the ground; they didn't have that many soldiers left.

Lord Cherwell, Winston Churchill's most trusted scientific advisor, forecast with utmost confidence that area bombing would "break the spirit of the people."

If anything, area bombing hardened Germany for the final days.

The honest, statistical truth: while Allied bombing intensified steadily, German industrial capacity soared, setting new records, it seemed, every month.

During December of 1943, Germany built 700 fighters. The worst air assaults ever unleashed soon followed. Allied bombs damaged half the aircraft plants in Germany. The net result? Monthly aircraft production rose almost 300%: just five months later, in April of 1944, 2,000 Axis fighters rolled off the newly decentralized production lines. (Of course, finding pilots and fuel would be another story.)

The amazing thing was how many cows died in the bombing.

Ninety percent of the British bombs landed more than five miles from their target. And the Americans crews, with their Deadeye Dick bombsight, did only slightly better.

While the ground was still smoking, a clear-sighted young U.S. economist tramped around, weighing the impact of American high altitude bombing. "There was a saying in 1945: We made a major onslaught on German agriculture," John Kenneth Galbraith related, concluding his report: "Strategic bombing was designed to destroy the industrial base of the enemy and the morale of its people. It did neither."

Still, the air barons weren't completely wrong. Allied bomber fleets *did* help to win the war, by making things easier for the Soviets. Air historian Walter J. Boyne: "(Nazi Armament Minister) Albert Speer called (the day-and-night bombing of Germany) the unrecognized second front, as it diverted 2 million men, 30 percent of the gun output, 20 percent of the heavy ammunition, 50 percent of electronic equipment, and 33 percent of optical equipment to antiaircraft units. Perhaps most important, 75 percent of the vital dual-purpose 88-mm guns were diverted to antiaircraft duty from their primary task of killing tanks on the Eastern Front."

Last word goes to Dad: "Some of those towns over in Germany were nothing but rubble. Building after building, nothing but a pile of brick. You imagine two thousand bombers going over in one crack. And when they dropped those bombs.... Boy, I don't know how anybody could stand it."

Truth was, for all the sad, sweeping death brought to bear

on our species, for all the intensity of national movements, war was an effect, not a cause.

World War Two had a purpose; and the purpose was to build a new and improved society in which economic depression would be stared down and an upward spiral of prosperity, justice, education (for anyone could see that that was needed), material improvement and scientific advancement would give little old me a better life than my mom and dad.

And, of course, it would all be expressed by symbols. It would *have* to be, if everyone were to understand. Symbols: like a good education, a nice house, a car with fins, discriminating taste, and anything else the monkeys of Madison Avenue could make us crave.

CHAPTER 11

WHEN IRRELEVANCE BLOOMS

IT WAS SUMMER. I ran along South Franklin Street, pelting home in the sandy gutter of Holbrook's main drag. A car pulled up next to me. I ignored it.

I was in training. Cross-country season started in a few weeks, when school opened. This was the fastest part of my run. On the last half mile toward home I'd sprint, my feet ripping up distance. I couldn't believe my own speed. I pushed myself faster and faster. Couldn't find the limit, there was always more. More strength, more oxygen, more kick. Nothing to think about. Happy. Grinding past sections of sparkling granite curb. My legs spinning so fast they were wheels.

"Hey, Tom," Linda called in her low, laughing voice. She leaned out the car window, looking her sunglasses. She had an interesting, haughty face. Linda played first clarinet the band. I played first trumpet. I was a junior; she was a senior, a year older. Which put her on a different shelf, out of reach. She had adult thoughts. Some guy was driving. He was smiling, she was smiling. Big smiles. I didn't slow down, so they rolled alongside at a crawl.

Linda leaned out the window of the car. Saying something I didn't catch. Teasing me. The guy probably felt sorry for me. I was some kid. Senior girls didn't talk to junior boys, except maybe to say hi and gather some worship on the cheap. I didn't know what to say. I had a vocabulary. I had thoughts. They were on the moon was all, right this moment. I tried to run even faster, faster than physics allowed. Now I just wanted to impress her. If I couldn't find words to talk to her like a real person.

Panic. Torture. "Got to finish this!" Big gasp. Which was totally faked. I was never out of breath when I ran. Lungs like dirigibles.

"OK," she waved. Her grin got even bigger, an invitation. Then she turned away to make some joke to the guy, and the car effortlessly sped off. I slowed. Counting trees. Coasted past the Hannigans. They were rough. Past the house where my childhood baby sitter once lived. Past the little store and Henry's gas station, with a cozy of grease and oil. Past the next-door neighbors we never said much to. I walked up the little rise of our driveway. At the top I stopped and waited as my breathing rate clicked down.

Linda was flirting with me, I realized. A senior was flirting with a junior. Something remarkable and curious had just happened.

Hanging in our house was a poem by Sam Walter Foss, probably a gift for a wedding shower:

Let me live in my house by the side of the road

Where the race of men go by;

They are good, they are bad, they are weak, they are strong,

Wise, foolish—so am I.

Then why should I sit in the scorner's seat,

Or hurl the cynic's ban?

Let me live in my house by the side of the road

And be a friend of man.

Dad agreed with that poem straight down the line, I think. He had a humble nature. He didn't see life much as worth getting excited over. Mere people weren't all that special or amazing. Some were lucky. Some were smart. Life is hard, for everyone except maybe the rich; he didn't know much about them. He had a sweet "live and let live" outlook I wish I'd swallowed more of.

I thought he was a racist.

I thought that being a racist made him stupid.

Because racism was stupid, in my hardened, quick-draw opinion.

I was proud of my unerring logic. I'd learn some context later. When intellectual humility swept out assurance.

His prejudices were typical of his class, ethnicity, and race: white, working-class, Irish-American. Fuck you if you think that needs an excuse. Irish immigrants fought the blacks in America since the potato famine, for hard jobs: whatever a strong, willing back could manage. Violently. Underhandedly. "The colored" were natural enemies. The Irish might be nothing. But at least they were *white*. Pasty white. Unhealthy white. Against black or red hair.

I grew up in a mildly racist household. I didn't see it that way. The black kids in my class were just other kids. They acted just like us. No, you would never invite them home, because your parents wouldn't understand and would definitely misbehave. In the yearbook's *Senior Superlatives*, we voted one black guy Class Comedian, we voted a black girl and a guy Best Dancers. Black always swept the entertainment categories, though the other categories weren't closed. If I hated blacks, it was a coincidence, nothing personal. They were more popular than me, like dozens of others. I hated all of them. I hated anyone could hold an ordinary conversation, basically. I was neurotically tongue-tied. Plus I was jerking off in my head about 90% of my waking time, which was exhausting.

Once I judged Dad stupid, he and I had no future. I became intolerant of his opinion. Wouldn't even listen: fingers in my ears, singing loudly. *Familiarity breeds contempt* is a sentiment first realized at home.

"I was parked up in Germany waiting to come home," Dad said.

"And these trains would come through. German trains. And there'd be people hanging off the sides of them, even off the engine. And do you know what all those people were doing?" A rhetorical question was his number one trick for building suspense. He would stare at me. If it was Friday, and he was having his one beer of the week, he'd work this moment by grabbing a sip. I liked to watch the foam tear into faces and mouths sliding down the inside of his glass. I loved the salty smell of it tickling inside my nose. I always asked for a sip. If my mother was there, she'd say, "Just a sip." That settled it. He'd pour half a swallow into a separate glass. I'd nod. He'd continue, with the answer. "They were going from town to town trying to get something to eat."

One day up in occupied Germany they caught this German civilian stealing a G.I.'s pet puppy. "You know what he was going to do?" Dad asked. *Yeah, I knew.* "Eat the dog," He looked at me as if to say, *How do you like them apples?* This is what white people could sink to, his moral said: Eating dogs. I didn't like dogs. Barking annoyed me. People could eat a lot more dogs; I'd support the effort.

He was 70, no longer clear-eyed. Yellow-eyed actually. His generation would be dying soon. Was dying. The audiotape silently turned behind its tiny plastic window, recording his stories: his eyewitness account of a vast event, the Second World War; and a small life tossed by it, like a tin can in a tornado.

"That's how bad off they were." Dad snorted through his blow hole. "You'd be going through the line for your dinner. You'd come out, and you'd have your little tray, and you'd have probably a little meat on it, a little potato, a little string bean."

German civilians would beg for the trays.

"They would take anything you had on your tray. Drop it in their tin cup. Coffee? In that went, too. When they got through, all they were eating was garbage. Oh, yeah, they were a mess over there, no doubt about it."

I imagine it was nice to feel rich for a change. Representative of the United States, with all sorts of wealth; *fuck the Great Depression.* And stick Europe's nose in its own fallen status. We're the emigrants come back to straighten things out in the old country. Where people had nothing better to do than slaughter each other by the millions, same old shit.

"That war never should have gone that long," Dad said. What sights he must have seen. I'm thinking of that Jerry run over by tanks until he was flat and corrugated as cardboard. "Hitler, being a fanatic, waited to the last minute. That war should have been declared over almost a year before it was. Hitler wouldn't let them stop. They were defeated, they were licked. He let them ruin Germany rather than give up."

Very near the end, Reich propaganda minister Joseph Goebbels, keeper of the party line, wrote: "Now that everything is in ruins, we are forced to rebuild Europe. In the past, private possessions tied us to bourgeois restraint. Now the bombs, instead of killing all Europeans, have only smashed the prison walls which held them captive... In trying to destroy Europe's future, the enemy has succeeded in smashing its past; and with that everything old and outworn has gone... Thus we say a melancholy farewell to a past which will never return. A world is going down but we all retain a firm faith that a new world will arise from the ashes."

No shit. This was a guy who plumped against Communism.

He wouldn't see the new, next world that, indeed, did rise. Neither would his family. Less than two months later, as the battle for Berlin raged aboveground, Goebbels and his wife, hiding in the Führer's bunker, poisoned their six children.

Battle?

Call it what it was: a demolition. Starring a vast lost number of assaulting Soviet troops. A million armed Slavs against evil. Great stone buildings atomized, reduced to gravel. You could hide and fight in rubble; not in gravel.

Goebbels' wife, Magda, made her peace: "Our splendid concept is perishing and with it goes everything beautiful, admirable, noble and good that I have known in my life. The world which will succeed the Führer and National Socialism is not worth living in...."

She drank off her glass of poison.

Goebbels shot himself.

The next day Fortress Berlin surrendered to Soviet forces. Six days later the war in Europe ended with a signature on a document. The last man in uniform, turn out the lights.

I was hugely flattered. An older girl.

"Let's take a walk," Linda turned me around, and we headed back inside the school. It was Saturday afternoon, crudding toward dark. Winter up next. "Want a ride?" she asked me, as he walked toward the classroom end of the building. I was in my band uniform, no overcoat, a cold walk home. She had a new driver's license and her father's car for the afternoon. I'd spied it in the lot. "Come *on*. I'll drive you after."

After what?

One set of doors eased shut behind us. We clacked down the four steps to the cafeteria. The corridor was quiet, the floor tiles symmetrically polished. Behind the door to the girls' locker room, far away, a shower ran. Something fell and echoed. We came to the cafeteria with its wall of windows. Bare autumn trees. The grass was long and rich, plastered down like hair, double green from a cold, wet fall. Familiar. The cross-country course I set records on passed right by this window. I could see the trail.

The security barrier was down: a wire gate cut off the classroom and administrative wing from the public part of the high school. We stopped and peered through, into the darkness. We were both in uniform, sky blue wool with white stripes. The jackets boasted epaulets and braids, the hats white vinyl bills.

She looked like a military dictator, teenage version. I looked like an undernourished doorman, teenage version. Our mud-specked white bucks tapped toe to toe.

"Don't you want to kiss me?" she said. Impatient. A test.

She backed against the gate, to get me started. I leaned down. Linda's head tilted back, smiling, eyes closed. Her officer's cap flipped to the floor. Her fine chestnut hair swung free like music. I pushed my fingers through it for the first time. It weighed nothing. Tasted her saliva, as pure as mineral water. The fine fragrance of burning lust from my every pore.

Everything from the planets on down reduced *to my lips kissing her lips.*

I asked her 35 years later what she remembered.

Linda remembered kissing.

Witness: The view from the other side.

Girls remember from the waist up. I didn't punch into her during our high school thing. She was a Fort Knox virgin: no entrance, no way. *Anyway:* psychology, sense memories. Horny little guys like me remember from the waist down: *Exactly* how far I got, every stitch I put behind my questing fingers.

One certain night.

Sometimes we had her sister's car. Her father's car was bigger. More room for the horizontal. Radio playing instead of conversation. Stations of the cross: hugging, kissing, hand to her well-basketed breast, so small it was hard to detect beneath her clothes. Another song.

My fingers. The eyes of the blind. Determined. Focused. Looking in the dark. Recording. Making notes. Each thing a first.

Thigh. Stockings. Bare, cold flesh. Row after row of panty ruffles, flouncing the entrance to everything I cared about. Tracing the elastic with my knuckles.

Her legs locked my hand, trapped in a giant, indomitable *clam*. I could feel her bones pressing my wrist. Here, my furthest point of advance on Linda's senior class thighs: and *still outside the sideshow tent*. Inside, beneath the Big Top: *The Greatest Mystery on the Face of the Earth,* a Woman's Crotch. *What Would It Be?*

The clam relinquished my hand, with a grouchy warning.

She was saving it for college. Understandable. Back then, virginity was an asset.

Here's what goes into my Linda box, to be buried at some future date:

My lust, her romantic absorption in other males, the band hat.

Thirty years later—30 years later—we met at the Orlando airport.

Why not? Being heterosexual sucks sometimes. I was *still* so obsessed with her as a sex object, as the object of my pure desire; her cunt smelling of cigarette smoke, I liked that; that I couldn't talk to her ... in anything but cartoon voices.

She replied with the same conversational devices she'd

used as an 18-year old: off-center questions, challenging flirtation.

I admired her. We were at a varnished plank table inside Uncle Mike's or some other local chain seafood joint. Uncle Mike's was perfect and three-quarters empty.

Linda has processed an OK collection of males: the trumpeter in the BSO, the Yaqui Indian with an MIT Ph.D. My problem?

At 55, Linda looked unnervingly like my sister. Linda at 18 was hips and angles pointing toward some interesting frontiers. At 55, the shifting sands of time had buried those landmarks. And she now looked like my closest surviving relative. Intimacy would have seemed like incest. Or bad piano; my fingers utterly out of practice.

So, with a stake driven through my shoulder muscle and a pounding tension headache, having not cheated[2] *even if that had been on the menu*, I boarded a plane for Australia, where I was due to meet my wife. Linda: aloha. Or whatever Massachusettsians *turned* Floridians say.

[2.] Facto: 103% of married men do not consider it infidelity when they sleep with a former girlfriend. It's more like a reunion.

CHAPTER 12

ADULTS LIKE ME

M Y FATHER: "THE GERMANS SAID, 'HOW CAN YOU FIGURE OUT THESE AMERICANS WHEN THEY DON'T KNOW WHAT THEY'RE DOING THEMSELVES?'

"And half of it was true," he agreed. "After the war was over, they took a bunch of us up to German headquarters, up in Bavaria.

"There was one house set in a pine grove, and in that house was an elevator, and you went down in this elevator... why, it was beautiful. Nice corridors. All tile. Ceilings and everything. And off the corridor was all these different offices. Nobody knew it was there.

"One of the things they showed us in German headquarters was a radio message the Germans got hold of from the Americans. They couldn't decipher it. It was two Sioux Indians talking their own language over the radio.

"As I say, a lot of things happened over there. They couldn't figure out the Americans at all.

"And course one thing about the G.I.s, you always got a brain in the crowd. No matter how dumb they looked, you always got a brain.

"And the G.I.s operated just as well without an officer as

they did with them. Half of the officers weren't any good to you anyway. They were just as scared as you were; that bar on their shoulder didn't make a damn bit of difference when you were up on a front line.

"Well, the Germans were just the opposite. They relied on their officers. So much so that if you knocked off their officers, nine times out of ten, they'd give up. They didn't know what to do. They couldn't take control themselves.

"Because their military way, why an officer could line up a bunch of German soldiers and go right along and slap everybody across the face; and they wouldn't move a muscle. That was their bringing up as far as military went. The officer was the law."

Pulitzer Prize-winning author Barbara Tuchman traces this oh-so-German reverence for command back to the second half of the nineteenth century, when the military received credit for unifying the country and making it prosperous: "(The German Army's) authority and prestige grew with every year, its officers were creatures of ineffable arrogance, above the law, who inspired an almost superstitious worship in the public. German ladies stepped off the sidewalk to let an officer pass."

Matty reclined on my sagging boy's bed. Supine and still. I knelt beside her. The washroom scent of Ivory Soap went up my nose. Her usual perfume. She'd scrubbed.

My hand recognized destiny and reached for the zipper on her shorts. Matty didn't object or interfere. Her eyes peeked at me from beneath her bangs. *Today was the day. All other days had not been.* For the first time, I was confident that my advances would work. She sighed. My eyes about to be amazed. Clinically close. About to see something that I'd never seen in the morning light, the object of my devotion and obsession. The hair-upholstered entry and exit between bleach white thighs. Skinny-dipping in her pond. Joan's I'd fucked. Barbara's I'd jammed my fingers into many times, wet or dry. Matty's never.

I placed my hands lightly at her waist.

With slipping fingers, unbuttoned her. Once or twice we'd gone this far before. She'd always said no to more.

This time Matty let me unzip her. She was a virgin still, I knew that. A virgin even to a boy's touch and sight. Today was firsts. I was the first boy to tug on her zipper. The first to know with her that special anticipation: that sex was a sure thing in the next few minutes. There was no fight left in her. Catholic girls could give up so beautifully. The shame and the guilt extruding from every pore.

I was her first sexual intimacy, and she wanted me to do it. Matty rocked on the bed. So horny. Under the Ivory Soap there was heat. *Take the mystery out of it. I want to get on with life.* I was somebody she liked and trusted. I certainly wasn't some stranger. I'd been sticking my fingers under her clothes for years. I'd wanted to stick my fingers inside *her*. Feel the warm squeeze of her womb.

Matty didn't say anything. She stared at me, her head in the blades of morning light slanting through the wooden shutters. I could just feel Aunt Doe's face pressed against my second-floor window, trying to see in. Her cataracts were like fried egg whites, just as opaque.

Up close Matty had brown copper eyes with rolled lashes. We kissed. I tasted the light fear acid on her breath. My hand slid into her open shorts, tight on her belly. I moved down. She lifted her bottom, to give me clearance. The final accommodation. Go. Yes. I felt honored. True luminous joy.

I shimmied her shorts down her legs. Matty's long athletic legs were firm as pincushions and scratchy with shaved hair. Her tight shorts bunched on her tennis shoes, still bound to her feet. I was beginning to go insane with lust; and I admit, I *yanked* her shorts away.

Patience.

Matty took guppy breaths.

My head swiveled like a microscope toward her waist. There, her next-to-last secret revealed. Matty's panties. I'd always wanted to see Matty's panties. More maybe than what was underneath. The religious cloth. Veil of a virgin. White cotton, full-waisted, washed thin. Almost a rag. Three-in-a-package underwear. A garment that draped the most intimate, forbidden, alluring—to me—bit of real estate on her. *Behind the curtain, the big mystery.* Glowing in the weak morning light, somewhere between 9:30 and 11:00 a.m.

Slightly puffed in the crotch where her pelt stretched the fabric.

Not a shadow of her brown hair visible, not a curl outside the gusset.

That was a moment to stop and appreciate for several years.

One more comment:

Catholic cunt smelled different.

Could smell of warm caramel. Or poison bait.

You just didn't know until knuckles went missing.

My mother wanted to know, *What was Matty's method?*

Matty, I'd gossiped, tried to commit suicide in her college dorm room. Without success. Straight to infirmary.

Sleeping pills, I said. I had the whole story. Matty called me beforehand, crazy.

What went wrong with the attempt? Mom asked. *Why isn't she dead?* I didn't realize that my mother was conducting research; evaluating her options. Was she *that* depressed? *That* anxious? *That* realistic about the potential for an aging human in a sub prime marriage?

A.

If you wish to succeed at suicide, do *not* call an old boyfriend and threaten to kill yourself. And, *two*, don't be popular; then attempt suicide with your door invitingly open *inside* a crowded dormitory. Matty never got past the shallow-breathing stage.

The source of her despair?

My mother didn't ask. Every despair is unique, alone, and without comparison.

I don't think she took Matty's failed attempt too seriously, after she learned the details. It was symbolic. Silly. What a teenager does. Not what a grown woman with determination, like Hazel Ahern, business executive, does. She gets the job *done*.

Being half-pregnant, a joke. Being suicidal: do it. Get it done.

I borrowed the family car and drove up to see Matty at college.

To talk to her about her troubles. And maybe have sex.

It was that same November. UMass Amherst was a brutally cold and graceless winter campus. I picked Matty up. We drove and parked on a neglected back road, beside a pinched, frozen farmer's field. She had bundled up.

I couldn't believe Matty was telling me this story. Like she'd been kidnapped by aliens and returned. It went like this:

Matty had had sex and smoked a cigarette. Finally. At the age of 20.

She had gone to visit this guy. From our high school.

She told me that he'd made her drink booze. And smoke cigarettes in some frat house while everyone listened to loud music.

Matty was crying now.

He wanted her to have sex. And she did that, too.

Now she was bawling beside me on the front seat and yelling, "Hit me! Hit me!"

She wanted to be punished.

She wanted me to slap her face.

No.

She tried again.

I said no again.

It never occurred to me to spank her bottom, which might have done us both some good.

That day in my bedroom, on the hot second floor above a field noisy with insect empire building, I saw Matty's tangled web for the first time.

Her panties were on the floor, like a handkerchief.

Her pussy was in plain view, breakfast on a hot plate.

I touched her timidly between the legs. Rapping on a doorframe. *Knock, knock.* No idea where to start. *Don't scare her. We've come this far.* Neat, new, soft brown fur. Matty had an unfucked cunt; her lips folded in.

She shuddered. Her first shudder was for me. Just to set the micro-record straight. Total surrender to her biological instincts.

I wanted to put my penis in her so bad that I forgot to take off my clothes. I hoisted myself on top of her. We were piled like manikins on the eroded narrow bed. As soon as my penis was between us, under pressure, I came in a spurt. Instantly. A few meek grunts. A pelvic jerk. Like a water balloon broke in my pocket. Just knowing I could come inside her, I came. In my pants.

I wouldn't own a condom for another quarter century.

That *particular* premature ejaculation near my 19th birthday saved me from an almost certain fate for which I was magnificently unequipped: fatherhood.

CHAPTER 13

ONE THING I FORGOT TO MENTION

THAT SUMMER DAY, OUR PREADOLESCENT MINDS WERE IN THE GUTTER. As usual.

Since you found things in the gutter: secrets, explanations, things lost and overlooked by adult eyes a foot higher in the air and focused on other aspects of what was coming. The gutters were thrown-open treasure chests for young socio-anthropologist-sex researchers like Eddie and me were.

Eddie and I were an odd couple. Endomorphic and ectomorphic. Me, Jack Spratt, knew no fat; Eddie knew no lean. And he had knocked me cold in the third grade, because we fancied the same girl who didn't know our names.

We were dirty young things now, though. A pair of us. I was tame compared to him. Eddie was an early pregnancy waiting to happen.[3]

[3.] You won't see him again. So let me skip ahead: goes to private high school, accepts football scholarship to second-tier college, inadequate to that task, knocks up high school friend one weekend, drops out, marries her, joins the Marines, discharged, second child soon follows first (printing on the condom packaging too small). Final act, for me and I think many others: Eddie becomes insurance agent, holds reunion parties so he can sell policies to his high school classmates. Decades later? He's doing okay; divorced.

Eddie and I were in Brockton: the city next door, a 25-minute bus ride away.

Brockton had a downtown about five blocks long. One block fronted a parking plaza. The plaza climbed a hill. The city's high school filled the crest. On the hill cars parked at an angle, facing meters, all, except the slight criminals, ticking.

Eddie and I walked past a filling station on the hill.

A uniformed attendant was pumping gas. *Whatever you're seeing,* it wasn't like that then. There was no self-serve. There were no credit cards. There were gas station attendants. Pull in, and you faced men in uniform.

Eddie and I walked past the station, with its vacant concrete aprons.

A gust of dollar bills kissed our sneakers: money blowing down the street like candy wrappers. Tumbling in a hot August wind.

"Get it!"

We each chased down two or three singles, soft with grease. "It's dirty!" Eddie was finicky. "I'll take it," I offered and stuck out my hand. He shoved his wad in his shorts. Even a dollar was a fortune. Now I realize the cash probably blew from the filling station, yanked from some pocket during a fast transaction; but I didn't then.

And so Eddie and I went home richer, believing that the city was a place where cash drifted through the streets. I don't remember whether I reported this good fortune to my family. If I did, they let me keep the money that time; because I wasn't warned off.

If I close my eyes, I see my boy's cold hand placing a

folded bowtie of money down on the blotter of her desk. She worked at a daily newspaper as the business manager. I knew how to find her, up the back stairs from an alley. There was the Virgin Mary; and above her was my mother.

I was so happy. Finders keepers, losers weepers; how many times you hear that? "Mom, I found five dollars." Said with a beaming, adoring smile. I was amazed: money had fluttered into my hand, like a trusting butterfly. Those words changed my life, though.

Certainly, the next words fired from my mother's tongue did.

"Where did you get this?" she demanded immediately. She held up the crushed five-dollar bill in her skinny white fingers. She never had much blood in her.

"I found it."

"Did you steal this?"

We were in Greenland: terra incognita. I heard my old, honorable life slip away in an instant. I stood—not very tall—accused of theft. "No, Mommy, I didn't. Honest, I didn't."

Next thing I knew we were out the door, into the alley. She had my hand and was charging ahead. It was cold, early November. "I'll show you," I pleaded. I had found the money peeking from a drift of wet leaves in the gutter in front of the high school.

She took me to Kresge's, a five-and-dime store near the bus station. "Which cashier was it?" her awful face asked. "Who did you steal it from?" We went the length of the store, past the candy, past linens, past the toys, past the pets and light bulbs, out the side door. If not the five-and-dime, then where? Did I steal it from the bakers? She sometimes took me there to buy an éclair. "I found it in front of the high school," I pleaded. It was just a block away.

We didn't bother to go look. On the bus home, my mother sat on another seat. She wouldn't have anything to do with me. I was a thief.

She told my father everything. During supper, I got the silent treatment from him, and a headshake from my sister, Alice.

I went up to my room, and I heard them talking in the living room. Eventually my mother called me down. She sat in the best chair and my father backed her up. I wept, wishing the day had never started, that money didn't grow on trees and fall into gutters. Wondering what I could say that would convince these people I was innocent.

My mother wanted me to return the money myself. I pleaded with them that there was no one to return it to. "Was it the toy department?" she demanded. What was the point? The idea of going to the store terrified me; the shame would kill me. My bones melted; my internal organs hardened; my growth stopped right then.

My parents waited. I begged them to believe me. "I didn't steal the money. I found it!" I had. I had found it. And it was cursed. And now my confidence was torn up. I was no match for my mother's contempt. Gone, too, the will to fight.

They sent me upstairs to bed. But first Mom brought me close and looked into what she now saw as liar's eyes, her hazel-colored eyes seeking some special deep truth hidden in my hazel-colored eyes. "We still don't believe you," she said softly, just so I'd know. That was it. I was dead. Not just to my church, now to my sainted mother. My first death was knowing I was evil. My second death was now: knowing my mother no longer trusted me, and I couldn't convince her she was wrong. There is a theory that trauma stops you from breathing deep for the rest of your life. Your shoulders harden into rebar. You hunch from that trauma forward, until they try to straighten you in a casket.

If so, this was my day.

She was 47, the Age of Skepticism. And immortal in my eyes.

She had nine years left. Mom's date of death: January 12. Of suicide: she carried out her very secret New Year's resolution. Age: 56 years, plus a month and 20 days.

My father wouldn't admit how my mother had died, at least not to me. He insisted that she'd suffered a heart attack, and he told me that. In his story, my mother raises the garage door, starts the car, drives him to work, then returns home and parks in the garage, leaving the car running. She gets out to lower the garage door even though she's headed for work herself in a few minutes, and, boom, her heart gives out. She collapses to the floor, and suffocates from the exhaust, unable to help herself. A very miserable, pathetic death.

Socially acceptable, though. Better than suicide for those concerned: the scandalized marriage, the mad and tainted family, the disapproving Catholic church.

Protect the living.

Maybe even slip the story by the life insurance company. (Didn't fly. The death certificate was frank.)

If there's a trick to remembering dreams, I don't have

it. You wake up and that was nice, *whatever* it was fading offstage.

Not this time: I remembered the rescue dream. Every detail. Waken just as a horse stamps its iron toe into your temple ... same as you've stepped on countless insects to crush their pith ... and you'll know. I woke up, my rescue dream vivid as the news.

A fire truck idles in the middle of my hometown's only major intersection. It's early spring. Sodden, bruised lawns. Sand covers the streets.

The truck's ladder extends much higher than the wires. On the top steps, far up in the air, stands my mother, in her nightclothes. She plans to jump.

First I consult with the firemen. The machinery roars; we put our heads together to talk. "Shouldn't you use something else for the wheels?" I shout. A log chocks the front tires. The truck keeps bucking forward dangerously.

I take the log, rest it on my shoulder, start to climb the ladder.

"Are you sure you want to do this?" I ask my mother when I reach the top. "Isn't this a nice log?" I say, hoping she'll agree. I'm holding my log like a baby.

She laughs.

And I awake, knowing one thing for certain: *Timing* is *everything*.

Without too much adjustment in the mundane facts of that January morning when she was 56 and I was 20, I might have entered the garage while inside she was gassing herself; and shut off the car. I might have stopped her, had I known what her game was. It wasn't her first suicide attempt, after all. But I wasn't in on the secret; my family didn't want me to know. My father and my sister hoped to "protect" me. From what? *Well....* From their opinions, I guess. Instead, oblivious, a late riser on winter break from college, I scurried past the Ahern one-car garage *slash* death chamber to fetch the mail in my pajamas, becoming a son who let his mother die and her involuntary co-conspirator.

Thanks, everyone; well done. That was death number three.

You died, too. Just so you know.

As kids playing war, fighting our men over lawn terrain, arguing who shot who from behind a blade of grass, the tank was a clincher: a crushing blow capable of driving everyone before its bone-grinding, guts-squishing tracks. Its cannon spouted flaming gouts. Automatic weapons bristled in every direction. It was, as advertised, a fortress on morass-subduing treads, almost unstoppable in its half-foot-thick armor.

And in real combat, a well-deployed tank, protected by infantry, could deliver remarkable punishment to the enemy's doorstep. Tanks were also sitting ducks. We didn't know that part.

Under fire, they were almost blind.

American tank drivers watched where they were going through an aperture the size of a mail slot. A buttoned-up Sherman—the primary Allied tank—was a 42-ton ignoramus. A German soldier could stand next to it and no one inside would be the wiser unless Fritz banged on the hull with a hammer.

A German soldier (or, toward the end, a German woman

or child) armed with a lightweight, disposable Panzer-faust—a cheap, simple, short-range weapon capable of punching a hole in any tank of its time—could brew up a Sherman with one quick shot. And the aviation-fueled Shermans were remarkably apt to burn. Troops nicknamed them "Ronsons," after a heavily advertised cigarette lighter that claimed to light first time. It was grim humor, pushing aside an unthinkable reality.

Nat Frankel: "A tank, you see, had four gas inlets, and each one was filled with high octane. If any of those four were hit, the whole machine would go up.... At best you would have ninety seconds to get out.... And what would happen if both the turret and the trapdoor were inoper-ative? What would happen is, you'd die! It takes twenty minutes for a medium tank to incinerate; and the flames burn slowly, so figure it takes ten minutes for a hearty man within to perish. You wouldn't even be able to struggle for chances are both exits would be sheeted with flame and smoke. You would sit, read *Good Housekeeping*, and die like a dog. Steel coffins indeed!"

Almost 50,000 Sherman tanks were built for Allied armies.

For a few, the ever-optimistic lads engaged in Sykewar—psychological warfare—found a fresh use: As a voice of reason.

The Talking Tank was born.

It took colossal nerve to motor into an enemy town with a blaring loudspeaker attached to your turret. Nor could the Talking Tank beat its plowshares back into swords in an emergency: to make room for the public address system's paraphernalia, the ammunition racks were removed.

But the Talking Tank turned out to be a "spectacular innovation...and outstanding success." Daniel Lerner: "A 'talking tank' could sometimes 'capture' more German soldiers than the shooting tanks could kill—thus making a greater net contribution to battle victory than any single shooting tank."

The voice of the Talking Tank had a two-mile range. It insinuated itself like a tin hallucination into cellar holes, up steeples, into firing pits dug along fir-silent ridges, over winter-hard fields to the anti-tank crews hunkered in the hedgerows.

Its tone, as required by Allied Supreme Headquarters, was "sober and factual", meant to "give the impression of Angle-American reliability, reticence, soldierly dignity and decency." Lerner: "This instruction supported the long-term aim of 'white' Sykewar: the image of the Allies to be transmitted to the German publics was that of a calm, confident, disciplined, reasonable, and responsible authority."

Lt. Arthur T. Hadley—"one of the most experienced Sykewarriors who survived the use of combat loudspeakers," according to Lerner—described a Talking Tank operation: "...just before the final stage of the fire-fight commences, the firing is stopped and a broadcast is made. Your intelligence in these cases is usually good enough for you to address the enemy unit by name. These broadcasts should be short and...the sentences should be repeated twice. The following is an example...

"'Attention, Attention, 1st Battalion, 84th Volks-Grenadier Division. A strong armored task force has taken Immenrath and Suggerdorf behind you. You are cut off. Further resistance in this bypassed position is suicidal, while to be captured means safety. Why die under artillery fire when you can live through the war in safety? You will be well treated according to the Geneva Convention.'

"Note that this broadcast contains no hint of actual surrender instructions. Nothing so increases a man's determination to fight as to be instructed how to surrender, too soon.

"If the reaction to this type of broadcast is successful, that is, if the enemy holds his fire by and large, or if white flags appear on some of the civilian buildings, then the loudspeaker and the attackers should be advanced to a point where it is practicable to issue surrender instructions to the enemy. Thus the enemy feels that he is surrendering to the force, and not to the propaganda.... Note the brevity of the broadcast. It should be forceful. The disorganized enemy is looking for a symbol around which to rally his confused mental powers. The broadcast provides this.

"'Attention, Attention, soldiers in Bad Heim! You are surrounded by a powerful armored task force. Further resistance is hopeless. Further resistance is hopeless. Take off your helmets, lay down your weapons, raise your hands. We will not shoot. We will not shoot. We see you but we will not shoot.'"

Sykewar based its appeals on what the German soldier himself already knew and deeply believed: it was a quantity, not a quality, issue. "In a battle of material, valour alone cannot offset [your numerical] inferiority in tanks, planes and artillery," printed Allied propaganda placated German frontline troops. Message: You had precious little to fight with; nothing left to fight *for*. I.e., your goddamned honor is intact.

Over and over.

You've fought hard. You've fought well. Why die unnecessarily?
Over and over.
You've fought hard. You've fought well. Why die unnecessarily?
Over and over.
You've fought hard.
You've fought well.
Why die?

Mom, for personal reasons, didn't see it that way. No Sykewar for her.

We're halfway. Let's split the hair.

On a lightly roasted Friday, 13th of July, that long-cursed day, fate of a common sort knocked on my office door.

I was 43 years old. I had frittered away my life in decade lots. I was bad second-generation material. An idle hedonist content with little: three or four puffs of weed at night; my ass drilled into a vinyl sofa; a weekly hangover; a daily shower; a few ties and white shirts for the public. I had twice the brain I needed for my job; half the ambition. I was four years into a second marriage. My weight had begun to escalate. I wore a life vest tied around my trunk: not yet fully inflated, but....

Otherwise I floated in a sea of *I don't much care.*

To my few friends and acquaintances, I was some kind of failed artist. A writer who never published to an audience larger than double digits. A lover, another abstruse writer, gave me two jobs she had a say in: "conflict of vagina" interest. When she left me, I wept like an iceberg. I raised sea level with my tears. More annoyingly, I phoned her against my will.

Please stop, she argued.

I just wanted his dick for a few nights. What have I gotten myself into?

She awarded me a handsome fellowship. It was clearly my final payoff. *Stop calling me* was her bottom line. *Fuck you very much. Thank you very much.* Was my bottom line.

I lived for several years on that award. Did nothing much. Wrote a word a day. Cheap rent left me plenty to spend on dope. *Blessings.* What I needed, I suppose, was psychiatry; what I had was ganja. And Keith and Rosmarie's Budweiser, *King of Beers.*

A Budweiser can contained alcohol, true.

King? More like 37th to the throne. An easy lay.

I obeyed the four-cans-of-beer rule: my entire ad hoc code of ethics. Three beers were too few. Four beers meant I was semi-trashed; and, yet, *could* attend work in the morning and glower down my enemies. Especially in meetings.

My salary was more than I expected or needed: Keith and Rosmarie rented me their top-floor apartment for $100 a month. They'd set the rates in 1968; saw no reason to change 15 years later.

I smoked: ten cigarettes, twelve, sixteen on a bad day. My lungs felt like locked luggage.

I drank, stealing my beer from Keith and Rosmarie's supply closet.

I toked. Reefer madness was more like: *not quite as bored as I otherwise would be.*

And I was ashamed. I fostered a Saturday hangover fifty-two weeks a year. Lucky me if it stretched till Sunday.

Here's what you learn: *How to work with a hangover*.

I didn't know then. Now I do. You have to.

Life is too hard to live sober.

Evil had a pie-dough face.

Cliff was an overweight middle-aged man—now an overweight old man—with hem-hawing eyes; come to sew the stitches in my shroud.

A lovable knucklehead, in his own opinion. And I, dumb fart; I learned in the next few minutes the extraordinary, true meaning of complacency. There's no better lesson than the real thing, served fresh. Eat your smugglies: you'll grow small.

It was almost noon. Like four hundred other toilers in our new and richly appointed corporate headquarters, I was considering lunch options. The cafeteria had a menu the equal of anything I could conveniently drive to. Fresh lettuce from the CEO's garden.

Or would it be jogging today? Jogging was a teetering bore, a sentimental nod toward the few years in high school when I had run like the wind, without hindrance, without doubt, when pain felt glorious, when my legs had more muscle than frogs'. But you could eat those. I was now in my forties. I smoked cigarettes secretly at night, while my wife slept. I was a fraud. Exercise was cheerless duty.

No, thank you. No running today. My new suit, a plaid the color of an Irish setter, still fit comfortably. I took a deep, inquiring drag of the ambient air. My office abutted the kitchen. I could usually smell the daily special through the wall, right through the concrete blocks. Friday would be some kind of fish.

Dedicated just two months earlier in an extravagant *(lots of elected officials, lots of speeches, lots of food)* ceremony, corporate headquarters was designed, not by experts, to impress and *geez we can only hope* intimidate customers, who were either geeks or mid-level bureaucrats far from home. We had an elevator. We had a three-story atrium. We had balconies. Wow.

Headquarters looked bigger than it actually was. It featured gawping vistas, dark mahogany accents, sage-green windows, just beginning to be an architectural trend-turned-cliché. A million dollars outfitted a spectacular multimedia theater and editing bay. The dining room was egalitarian. An executive chef and staff worked inside a commercial-scale kitchen.

A key company sales advantage—the industry's largest, most experienced software department—labored in clinical isolation behind glass walls, on view for tours from all over the globe.

Headquarters meant to convey technical competence, which the company had in spades; class (well, cash anyway); and market dominance. Outside, two files of double-height aluminum flagpoles led to the entrance. Far above you, at bird height, dozens of flags hard-spanked a hot blue sky, one flag for every state and country where the company did business. It looked like a replica United Nations.

Overhead you might even glimpse one of the company's two private jets.

Those jets did more for employee morale than a ten-cent raise.

I watched the sprinklers rake water across my new office window. I liked the rhythm. I liked the blur. I liked the recurring noise of the drumming drops. I liked hiding inside the rhythm.

It was another slow day for me, in six months of slow days.

My paycheck knew where to find me. Otherwise I was lost.

I'd made my little contributions toward image and reputation. I had a pampered salary and pretty title for my efforts. But I was running on a peeling reputation. The work bored me. The group I'd built from scratch worked fine without me. I knew it. They did, too. I pushed memos and meetings around like beads on an abacus, hoping they added up to something.

Plus I had a new pastime: pissing off people vital to my job security.

CHAPTER 14

LIGHT, TUNNEL, END

Two men piled up at my open door, dancing like they had to pee.

Hitting the beaches!

Cliff, my rarely encountered boss (he floated two floors above, in executive Valhalla); and Bill, a guy from human resources, HR, Aitch-Are. Are. Am. Is. HR: the dark side with a smile. Employees called them "Inhuman Resources." The company shed positions like a boa shedding pig bones out its ass. The timing was suspect. Pink slips bloomed just before Christmas; conspiracists insisted: *it meant* fewer mouths to feed at the Christmas party, which came out of the HR budget. *Hey, Bill.* I liked Bill. He played guitar in an oldies tribute band. He taught me the secrets of trapping and firing a total asshole. *(Hello, Matthew, wherever you are.) Cliff.* He sat. Bill and Cliff stared at me. I liked them both. Cliff was funny. Great delivery, fearless. He seemed nice; and females seeking nice guys fell for his lines. Always to their regret. He had a worldview of one. It rotated around his prick. Every conquest soon was yesterday's news. He enjoyed the cruelty of relationships severed. He cheated on his mates. He seduced other men's girlfriends.

We weren't a charity, after all. Layoffs were good business, leading to increased profits.

HR viewed itself as an antibody, fighting corporate tumors—waste; inactivity; obsolescent or failed positions; stale employees. Keeping the company healthy. Lean.

HR preferred an image as a social service agency, with a full trough of entitlements for its herd: all kinds of insurance, a lucrative retirement savings plan, other goodies such as tuition reimbursement. "See," they would attack your opinion, "we give you all this ... and *still* you hate us." Fair enough. For most employees, contact with HR was like sticking a hand in a terrarium in the dark, hoping the snake was fed and the scorpion in a decent mood.

Cliff styled himself "Captain Kirk."

He got things done against impossible, *interplanetary* odds.

Like the captain of the Starship Enterprise, Cliff was a sensitive warrior encountering alien worlds. We were a company of first-generation geek code-stars under frightful pressure: fuck up an online lottery and fines against the company soared into millions of dollars a day. Screaming, disemboweling disdain, were everyday experiences *down in software.*

Cliff believed the real him was a poet; born with a gift for leadership. He was practical. He was cheap. He was a soothing, take-command sort of guy, frontline material (though not to look at), calm in a crisis, always on alert, rushing *toward* trouble. He had been a volunteer firefighter for years; the role suited him. He talked a lot about rescuing naked women.

He acted harmless toward the weak. He challenged the over-confidence of the strong, and made them stronger. Over-confidence was virtually a company motto: *We've always delivered, no matter what bizarre obstacle.* Project managers pushed lotteries through jungles, under seas, into vast slums and deserts. They created electronic infrastructure where beasts of paradise still roamed. The company liked to hire from the military. Ex-fighter pilots made smooth salesmen. Saleswomen? Smart, attractive, tall; blonde was good, as a disguise for brains.

That was then. Now I'm sure it's different.

Cliff was a pinnacle species. Rara avis. Mr. Rare Bird.

In a rough and mocking corporate environment, ruled by technocrats and MBAs, where the ball-busting never throttled back, in just a few years Cliff rose from proposal writer, the next-to-lowest functionary in the sales department, presumed stupid and obedient; to marketing director, on his way to becoming a vice president; then chief of staff, the top trouble-shooter, the man who controlled direct access to the tippy-top. As Cliff rose, he amused, scandalized, honored, and seduced his staff by talking familiarly and disparagingly of "the Fat Man", the company's unjolly president.

Cliff was witty, joshing, unfrightened by a corporation; his bosses were puppets, he'd stick his hand up them any time he chose. His management style for underlings was pleasant, warm and nourishing: a mix of trust, soft tones, high expectations, and things kept in perspective. He shielded his subordinates from bullshit. He took real pride in being protective, considering it the mark of a good manager. It was easy for him. He believed in it.

Pinned inside were ulcers, the medically unfounded red badge of courage for harried executives. The condition made his father gravely ill. Cliff considered it a hereditary curse. Not that ulcers were all bad: having them meant he was doing a good job internalizing pain *and* was in control of his situation. Cliff talked freely and happily about his miseries on our behalf.

He was one of the few trained managers in our slapdash and overconfident company, and he pondered often the nature of leadership. He enjoyed outthinking the company potentates. Cliff and I had been hired by the same man, for virtually the same job. And in the five years since we'd joined the company, most of those potentates had stumbled and fallen. Cliff had risen spectacularly; I had risen well. I had received four promotions in five years, with superb performance reviews and top-of-my-range salary jumps. He was a new sun, and I was a shooting star, glowing, headed for earth. Watch where you stand. You might hit yourself.

"Can we see you for a few minutes?" Cliff asked.

"Come." I waved them in.

Cliff wore his wounded look, which I preferred it to his smug look; been seeing *way* too much of that lately. Bill closed the door, and they sat. I stared. Bill watched me intently and silently. Like me, he was in his rubber-faced early forties, with graying hair. My new office had glass walls. One of my staff walked over and peered in. When she saw who was visiting me, she grimaced and pell-melled off.

Cliff warned me: "It's bad news."

I stared, very intense, trying to stop time. My stomach

plummeted right past the sub-basement. In the back of my mind, recent incidents began to add up differently. "I'm reorganizing marketing," he continued. What can I fix in the next few seconds? I wondered. The options: I knew Cliff didn't think much of my management skills. Two months ago, he'd stuck a finger in my chest and warned me, "Your staff is demoralized." So I could be getting a new assignment. Which was fine; I needed the challenge. My face, my heart, my mind—I did a rapid check: empty, on hold, unrevealing. Ready. Set.

"I'm being forced to make cuts," he continued.

Forced? I was confused. *He wanted me to* fire *someone?*

He finished his little speech in a hurry. "And I'm forced to let you go."

It was July. Through tinted windows, the company's new lawn looked greener than it really was. My front lawn looked like biscuits. Anger suddenly surged through me.

I saw Cliff for the manipulative, self-pitying jerk he truly was. And as suddenly deflated. "Why?" I pleaded.

"You aren't the only one," he argued. He was already fading. "I'm very sorry. It has nothing to do with performance. The company's going in some new directions, and we need different kinds of people." The usual excuse. Not bad. Bill must have been nodding his mental head. *Well delivered, Cliff.*

I was about to protest—*I could be a different sort of person!*

I noticed movement. My staff, stricken faces peered in. One of them was laughing. Maybe two. Now I knew who'd betrayed me. Didn't matter. I was a moth-weakened lion skin waiting to be rolled up for disposal.

My eyes crawled back toward Cliff. He explained my severance package and said he had argued with the president to get me as much money as possible, in recognition of my past services. He pushed papers in front of me to sign. Bill spoke up to say that I was also entitled to outplacement services, to help me with my job search. He softly explained there was a "senior consultant" from the outplacement firm waiting to come in, if I'd accept the help. *Sure, Bill. Hey, thanks!* I just wanted to gather my things, remove some personal files from my computer, go home, get lavishly drunk. Bill hurried out. He was done.

Cliff stayed.

I knew the rules. I'd leapt like a deer through them: protect the company, never leave a discharged employee alone. I stared. *Not really:* I calculated what I might need to grab. This would be my last few minutes of free office supplies from a multinational!

Cliff told me what an awful night he'd had, preparing for this meeting. *Weep for my ulcers!* He had nerve: a natural-born master of the universe. He was always worse off than you. I commiserated right back. *That must be sad.* Trying to be the good employee.

I hoped, prayed, begged that counted for *something*.

Hoped, prayed, begged this was a *test*.

Hoped, prayed, begged he'd change his mind.

I asked him abjectly to tell me the real reason why I was being fired. My cells were beginning to adjust. Maybe we could argue it out.

"It's a reorg," he said.

I accepted that bland tarp. Nothing else issued from him scummy lips.

Sure, why not?

The company attempted a reorganization at least twice a year; it was growing that fast.

Bill soon returned with a tall, older man in a tired suit whose name was Bob.

Bob was what HR, in its self-congratulatory moments, called the Angel of Death.

Bob was here to ferry me across the river Styx. I was dead to these gods. Bob was their functionary. We shook hands.

Cliff and Bill evaporated. It wasn't a play. It was a formula. I didn't get to wave.

"Let's get out of here," Dead Bob hustled me up. "I'll take you to lunch. You'll feel better."

"What just happened?" I asked.

Bob had sober concern down pat. "Is there something you don't understand?"

"That's an understatement. *Fuck*." The man stood patiently. I thought, this guy has a good job: you're paid to stand patiently while another's life implodes at your feet. He was a dustpan and whisk for shattered emotions.

I was already trying his job on for size; I knew I'd need one.

The shock was settling in: I didn't have employees; I didn't have a large, successful company lending me prestige and respectability; I didn't have a position or a title except "unemployed." I was for the foreseeable future unemployed for the first time in nine years. As a labor statistic, I was a refugee: I wandered from the contributing to the non-contributing side of the ledger. My mind tapped me hard on the shoulder to whisper, "You know you're going to lose your house now."

"Where do you want to eat?" Bob prodded; he was standing a little less patiently now. The company had shaken its addiction to my presence; it was his job to ease me off the premises. *Sooner rather than later.*

I threw a few things in my briefcase, and started packing a cardboard box. He waited while I collected the remnants of my career: a notebook, some computer disks, the framed awards I'd never found time to hang. I glanced at the to-do list I'd printed out that morning: there were forty projects on it. Now they were all loose ends, and it didn't matter at all. I threw the list in the trash. So much for indispensability.

Over lunch, Bob turned into an anthropologist. He asked wonderingly, "You didn't know this was going to happen?" I said no. "Not at all?" he coaxed, laughing. He didn't believe I could be so dumb. *It was just a rough patch,* I imagined explaining. I'd done so much for the company. I was a valued employee. Please understand: this is not my fault, I am not inadequate.

Dead Bob was drifting. The desperate are much alike. My hamburger tasted like paper, sauced with delusion. He grabbed the bill and shook hands. We parted. I drove the 20 minutes home in my new pickup that wasn't paid for and drank every beer in the refrigerator. I watched the afternoon sky deepen, sprawled on the grass, smoking cigarettes. Bad for me? Who cares. Suicide was the absence of an easy weapon away. And yet ... I felt refreshed. Tomorrow held nothing I hated.

A couple of friends from the office called to console me.

Just a couple. I thought dozens were my friends. Yuri had a juicy tidbit: *Do you know who's sleeping with Cliff?*

His fucks held fading interest for me, I indicated.

She insisted, a laugh in her voice. *Go on, guess!*

"Who?"

"Nancy."

"Nancy?"

"Nancy!" My arch, cellophane-smile rival. I knew she was Cliff's protégée: he gave her high visibility assignments, spent hours in closed-door conferences with her. She was smart and caustic and ignored me most of the time. She used my staff without asking. I'd complained repeatedly to Cliff about her raids.

Well: it must have made interesting pillow talk.

The revelation was balm in a way. Better to be destroyed by a rival with an unfair advantage *(pussy? attached to brains?)* than destroyed by your own complicit foolishness. Except that wasn't true. I was a terrible employee. I knew that. I'd been promoted into management, for which I was temperamentally unsuited; I made my neurotic staff (two of the four) deeply unhappy. Three years of usefulness had faded into two years of sloth. I was the kind of employee companies *should* fire.

My wife drove up and saw me sitting on the grass, surrounded by empty beer bottles. "You're home early," Simone inquired. "Is something wrong?" Before I could tell her, though, her face exploded. She always guessed the endings of movies. "My god! You were fired!"

Oh, sweetie. That's a word you never want to hear.

CHAPTER 15

CAKED, BLOODY NAILS

M Y DIARY: *I BROUGHT NAIL CLIPPERS WITH ME TO THE HOSPITAL. Dad's fingernails were still caked with dried blood. With the nurses' help, we bathed his fingers. I trimmed his nails and, with orange sticks, cleaned out the blood. I wanted to hold his hands, just to touch him.*

It was Wednesday night, the first day of autumn, with a late, warm-flannel wind. Like rafts in a still pond, the trees rocked gently, their leaves wide, broad hands making shadow puppets under orange streetlamps.

His hands felt cool, with too much skin. The fingers were white, the skin loose. They felt clean the way desert sand feels clean; stripped, eroded, dry. For a man who smoked as much as he did, there wasn't much of a cigarette stain.

The shock of being fired wore off in a couple of days.

To be replaced by terror.

Now I was in deep, sucking psychological muck.

Have I told you about my stay in a psychiatric hospital? No, of course not. "Did you know," the Southwest Mental Health Center laments, "that many people would rather tell their employers they committed a petty crime and served

time in jail, than admit to being in a psychiatric hospital?"
Me, too.

In sum, in summer, now: I felt worthless; and ashamed;
and embarrassed I'd made myself extinct. Inside, I trembled
constantly, my stomach tobogganing over rattling ice. I
prayed for a compelling distraction. Nothing much came
along.

I lost weight rapidly. No appetite. Slept a few restless
hours each night.

I called it *The Anxiety Diet*. All rights reserved.

Trust me: it works, too. I was headed for my high school
weight, which wasn't much; being a cross-country stick on
two huge thighs.

And I was hallucinating. As each dawn lightened, I
indulged long, vivid, almost-true fantasies in which the
company president called to say a mistake had been made.

Plausible fantasies, I prayed. I, Mr. Agnostic, truly prayed.
Not to Jesus, not to Allah, not to any popular flavor deity
of the last age. To some god of common sense and righted
wrongs.

You should never have been fired! he would say.

I was too valuable. Really.

Meaning the planets would spin in reverse.

I.e., it wouldn't happen. Not in *this* three dimensions.

Company moves on. Company forgets you existed.

I encountered the president a few months later in a
grocery store aisle. As an employee I'd spoken on daily
with the man. This time, he looked right through me. I was
dead; off the payroll. No monuments for past employees.

We were ghosts. Ghosts not welcome.

I hated opening my eyes.

I hated new days.

I hated the sun and whatever it stood for.

I hated nature and the beautiful views out the expensive windows I could no longer afford. We were two years into an expensive mortgage, based on the assumption I'd have a job forever. These were my worst fears coming true, fears I'd had since I was a child: that some cold day I'd awake without a crumb. Destitute, homeless, hungry, unclean. No love left. No family. Not a friend in sight. Stung senseless by it. A victim of my own stupidity.

Even worse: that an iron constitution, inherited from my father, would keep me alive during every long second of my ugly fate.

It was a fear I'd kept deeply buried, like radioactive waste. Twenty years before, accelerated by some bad blotter acid, these fears drove me into a psychiatric hospital for a few weeks. It was an inchoate (a word Nancy wouldn't know) fear I'd toyed with many times as a morbid child. To give myself the instant willies, knowing the reckoning was still far off.

Now the day was here.

Oh, joy.

I panicked. And this was before I'd discovered prescription mood improvers.

Timing no longer mattered. I was the moon bombarded by asteroids.

The morning of my first appointment at the unemployment office, my ever-disdainful brother-in-law phoned. Bob wanted me to know that my father had broken his hip and was in the hospital, about to be transferred to a nursing home.

Except, Bob wanted me also to know, there was a problem.

The nursing home wouldn't admit Dad without a "guarantee check" of $2,200.

I promised to take care of it immediately—somehow—and hung up. My sister and her disdainful husband didn't know yet I'd "lost" my job.

I hadn't *lost* it, of course. I knew where to *find* it. Just nobody wanted me in the building.

Our house was empty. Simone was off, talking to clients.

I paced the kitchen like a tiny parade ground. Outside in the heat, the katydids chattered. Rage erupted out of me, as though my father were there and I could snatch him back from old age and frailty.

"Goddamn it," I told him and the stovetop vent, "not now! *Not now!*" It was a strange performance. I swore over and over, hammer blows. Then I wept.

And finally I felt steady enough to change my clothes.

I'd need a suit to do my father's business.

I had several—impressive, expensive, well-tailored ones—from my last job. Thanks to weight loss, I looked even better in them.

Dad's worst crisis equaled any screaming slasher film.

Only he was alone in his apartment. Which was quiet, without an audience: huddled, gray, everything dusted with cigarette ash.

His film starred his stomach pierced by ulcers.

Hemorrhage spewed from his ass.

He vomited mouthfuls of blood into his hands, painting the bathroom walls with something that darkened to steak sauce, with tiny dried bubbles and stomach contents trapped in it. His blood pressure collapsed. He passed out.

As he fell, one ankle shattered like a stage-prop bottle against the tub.

Exploded his old bones into horse splinters.

Dad was unconscious and bleeding for hours. He woke up and managed to pull the emergency cord.

The description of his apartment I recorded that night in my diary:

All that was missing was a severed head with an axe in it. He must have been very close to dying. I had tried to keep my expectations low, but this was worse than anything I'd imagined. There were pails of blood marking his trail from bed into bathroom. The toilet was solidly caked in it, and the floor completely covered. A bloody handprint marked the doorframe where he'd tried to stand up.

A few days later the housing authority called my sister. They wanted the family to come clean the place. Dad's neighbors were complaining about the smell of spoiled blood.

To fix dad's ulcer, the hospital decided to cut the nerves to his stomach.

All hell broke loose. He'd be stable for a few hours, then hemorrhage again. He was losing blood just as fast as they pumped it in.

I got a call from Dad's local surgeon, up in Plymouth.

Doctors were fleeing Massachusetts, he apologized. He blamed the exodus on fixed payments and malpractice suits run wild. I sympathized; I wasn't sure where this was headed.

Anyway, because of that, he said he couldn't find an assistant in the middle of the night, but a Boston hospital could. OK. Fine.

So Dad ambulanced an hour up the road. And at four in the morning, a Boston City Hospital surgeon called me to say the operation was finished and successful. He described the procedure to me. It sounded an awful lot like cutting the wires to a phone: the brain sends a message, but with the nerves cut, the stomach can't hear it, so it doesn't produce more acid. If acid doesn't aggravate the ulcer, the ulcer doesn't burn deeper, maybe through a major artery, which would have been lights out for good.

Funny thing was? Nerves don't cause ulcers; bacteria do.

Dad was four years too early.

In 1994 the National Institutes for Health in the U.S. endorsed antibiotics as the preferred treatment for ulcers. In 2005, the doctors who discovered the *H. pylori* bacterium, the stinking, slinking cause of ulcers, received the Nobel Prize in medicine.

In Plymouth, Massachusetts, consulting with Boston, the best they could do in 1990, with what they believed (not knew) at the time, was cut Dad's stomach nerves. The surgeons had an answer. They just didn't have a good question. Dad ended up with a dead stomach *and* bacteria. "It ain't what you don't know that gets you into trouble."

Mark Twain. "It's what you know for sure that just ain't so."

My diary, three days after the operation: *Arriving in a necktie, I'm mistaken for a doctor by Dad's nurse. She tries to explain his condition in medical terms, and I keep asking her, 'What's that mean?'*

It's a good lesson in how far a tie will take you; they're stupid things otherwise. We get that straightened out. Nurse reports that my father's never regained full consciousness since the operation. He thrashes constantly, never resting for more than a minute. He's punched someone. Sometimes, she admits, he needs to be restrained. His arms are a garden of bruises. She's convinced he's senile.

"Nope," I say.

Her second favorite theory: then he must be a heavy drinker.

"A beer a week," I tell her. *At most.*

It's all true. She doesn't believe it. His medication, she says, isn't strong enough to cause this much confusion. But he's clearly out of it. She leans over him and begins a standard battery of questions: "Do you know where you are?"

He doesn't.

"Do you know who's here?"

He doesn't.

"Do you know what day it is?"

He mentions a year, the wrong year. He starts guessing years.

"Do you know who's president?"

Dad struggles with that. He asks, "Who is it?"

She says, "I want you to tell me."

He comes up with, "Finnegan?" He means Reagan. Not a bull's eye, but at least he's in the right decade. He knows it's something Irish. "They got to get that guy out of office," he adds. A Democrat to the end.

A nurse gives me the lifted eyebrow look. I repeat: *as of four days ago, he was lucid.* My god, until a week ago he lived by himself, drove, carried on conversations just fine, and had an active social life hanging out with his buddies down by Plymouth harbor.

She asks him again, "Where are you?"

He responds, "In the clouds." She laughs. He's so right.

It's as if he's in there, trying to wake up, but he's too dreamy, too drugged, too hurt. His bed is padded to prevent injury. He has tubes in his arms, in his nose, a catheter up his prick. He tries to get up without any success. That brings the nurse back. 'What do you want?' she asks. 'Pee,' he says. 'Go ahead, it's OK, there's a catheter.' He's naked from the waist down, his legs are scabby, his toenails are still bloody from a week ago.

The nurse says she's heard he's signed himself out of the hospital several times in the past. "Once," I correct her. She disapproves on principle. But signing himself out was no more than an animal chewing off its foot to escape a trap: *anything has to be better than this.* "He hates the hospital," I shrug. "He likes to give the nurses a hard time."

At this, Dad smiles slyly.

"You know just what we're saying, don't you," the nurse leans down good-naturedly before heading off. When we're alone, he whispers to me an admission of guilt, "I'm getting old. Just getting old." The first sensible thing he's said in a week.

Wearing pajamas, bed bound, his leg in a full cast, unwieldy as a log, Dad signs a durable power of attorney agreement.

"Durable" means it has no time limit. I am now in charge of Dad's life, however long it might last.

The lawyer for the convalescent nursing home—not a disinterested third party, admittedly; they want their bills paid; but then he's seen this saddening scene a thousand times before—asks Dad a few simple questions: *Did he understand what he was signing? Did he do so freely?* Yeah. Sure. Dad was groggy. He gripped the pen put in his fingers and scratched his name in the space provided. The lawyer witnessed it and vanished. Done.

Had to be done, every expert told us.

What happens at the end of life?

I saw the answer: you step off the map.

Power of attorney gave me legal, unfettered access to Dad's bank accounts. I was authorized to pay his monthly bills. Beyond that: I could intercede on his behalf, weigh his best interests, tweak his fate. Make sure his life didn't fall apart while he was on the mend. Ironically, Dad and I shared the same low opinion of my competence and common sense. But I was what he had. There was no one else on the team.

I don't know if Dad understood the implications when he signed away power of attorney. He turned himself into a child, and me into a parent.

He could have feasibly shouted, "To hell with all of you! And your damn schemes! Screw the blood-sucking lawyers and unfaithful children who prey on the old and weak!" Dismissive—suspicious—of our good intentions. That would have been the old Dad.

But there were no shouts left in his cupboard. The old Dad was gone.

All he could manage were gargled hints, his final strategy: vague suggestions that Alice or I take him in until he was better.

He hated being in the care of strangers. "I could stay with you?" he urged. He stared at me with tender, milky eyes. I smiled a little, just to be friendly. "Not now, Dad. Now you're better off here." I tapped on his cast, to make the point.

"It's hard, Tom, to be like this." One last irresolute plea. He was in pain, embarrassed, dependent. He squinched up his face and started crying, a few dabs that tumbled over his coarse cheeks, into the drapery of his neck. "It's hard." His pillow was already soaked.

His life was changing. He was scared.

This particular episode—shattered ankle, punctured stomach—amounted to a bad few months. Dad eventually moved back to his subsidized pensioner's apartment, back into "independent living," the Shangri-La of the date-stamped, declining, and nearly decrepit.

The beginning of a rapid end. He lasted one year.

You want to look away. You can't. Among Irish and Scottish, the both sides of me, the tribe tends to the tribe, however criminal, however sick. Tended especially well? No. Sometimes. You do what you can conveniently do.

And you got what *you* deserved, when your turn came.

My sainted grandmother on my mother's side received hot home-cooked meals three times a day, the dishes she was used to, when she entered a nursing home for what would be her final two-year chapter. Her four take-charge daughters, among them my mother, delivered her meals in rotation. The sons? No, they were shiftless. I didn't see in the family ranks one strong male during my entire childhood, except my father. And I mistook him for weak.

"The thing about the Army is," Dad said, "they didn't care about the soldier. The soldier was just supposed to keep moving. Unless he got shot.

"Sometimes a guy would just lie down or stop. He couldn't take it anymore. You wonder, what ever happened to these guys? How did it turn out for them after that?

"But the good thing was, nobody bothered you. They left you alone as long as you were moving. They didn't want to be in front of you. They wanted to be behind you."

CHAPTER 16

I WISH

DAD HAD FEMALE COMPANIONSHIP AFTER MY MOTHER DIED.

He popped the occasional pud, I figure.

I've seen that pud. It wasn't much. Mine isn't much either: a thumb's worth; no foreskin. Like father, like son.

He'd show up for lunch with different women, all named Shirley as far as I remember. Typically presentable companions: perfumed skin, dyed bright hair, smiling. They were all rather nice. Faintly apologetic about dating my father, in case that distressed me. It *was* odd to see your 60-something father in the dating game. But it certainly didn't distress me. It wasn't as if were cheating on the memory of my mother. She'd abandoned him emotionally long before the suicide. I was happy for him. He had somebody.

The Shirleys always showed interest in me. I wondered about that.

Eventually, I learned that my father spoke of me proudly. Which was something I didn't expect, given my: stay in the mad house; mocking disdain; the cruel blows I hoped to inflict; contrariness; drug use; a bizarre, angry existence.

I was in my "I'm fine; please don't bother me" phase.

Two degrees from Brown University hung from my neck. I worked in a machine tool manufacturer, apprenticing. It was, by far, the best-paying job I could find. In academe, for writers, every position attracted 100 candidates. "Let *me* fire the cannon." "No, let *me* fire the cannon." I had no ambition anyway, except the subterranean kind.

I liked the machine shop. The men had families. They were serious. I was upper-body strong. My clothes smelled of metal oil, a very unpleasant odor to the dainty academic noses among my housemates. Who kept a welcome distance. They were bland and uninteresting. They could open a book. I could rip one *to pieces* with my steel-infiltrated muscles. I smoked weed three times a shift. Considered it my due. My shift—the fuckhead shift—lasted from 11 PM to seven in the morning. I drove home as the sun climbed its first few rungs and day dwellers began to stir. My closest call: I came within one casual decision of accidentally shearing off a bystander's head. Otherwise I machined above-average pieces.

But. He survived unharmed. I survived chastised. Otherwise it was bliss.

Something happened as I jettisoned my twenties and pecked at my thirties, my next decade. I'd gained some confidence. I was settling down, learning a few skills. Dad loaned me the money to buy my first car. It was a bad car, but it got me to work and back.

He and I got together for meals in "family restaurants" (big portions, low prices). He seemed grizzled. I studied his stubble; he was missing spots. He wore drug store glasses. Maybe he couldn't see. Maybe he couldn't care. The Shirleys had disappeared. I watched his mouth flex, his pink tongue slip between his false teeth, wreathed by unshaved bristles. He was losing weight, I noticed. He had been fat; now he was sack. I was in my forties. I got married a second time. He had trouble finding the wedding. Before my first marriage he prophesized to my in-laws my divorce from their cherished, expensive daughter within a year. This time, he had not a word but polite rumbling congratulations. Dad smiled mostly. He came back to the reception at our house. Circus midgets had owned it, a hundred years before. The doorknobs were still at knee level. Dad ate a few crumbs, smoked his usual lot. There were no people his age to talk to.

He journeyed back to our house maybe twice a year. It was no trip to the Grand Canyon for him; we had nothing much to say to one another. It was duty all the way.

He complained we were hard to find. One Saturday he was hours late. Not to panic. Let's be sensible. The phone finally rang. Dad was calling from a drugstore. He didn't know where it was exactly; a kindly pharmacist had loaned him a phone. *Dad, describe what you see through the windows.* He mentioned some things he could see. He was jovial enough, trying not to offend. *Dad, what's the name of the pharmacy?* OK, now I knew exactly where he was; he'd abandoned the search just a few blocks away. I hurried down to the village to retrieve him.

Now we suspected this watershed truth: Dad could no longer drive any distance. Within his town of residence, maybe; bouncing tightly between bank and drug store and diner and waterfront, where he lounged at dusk with the other retirees, listening to the lap, the gulls, the cries of the commercial fishermen.

Something started to fail in him: brain, eyesight, *something.*

"One time there we were up in Normandy, and this guy says to me...."

Chronological order meant nothing to my father. He was not a structuralist. He was a dumper. One minute we marched past a burnt-out German tank, the next we blasted targets at a rifle range in Alabama, the next we ate grass salad outside an English café. Not free association. *Anarchy.*

And I was ferociously entertained. No judgment: I couldn't get enough. He taught me history, geography, the art of war, lessons in character and proper behavior, chicanery and survival, lessons in class conflict (most officers were turds) and international relations (never met a foreigner he didn't like; strangers were surprisingly comfortable) and political science (citizen army operated under different rules than totalitarian army; better rules, rules that encouraged initiative and quick thinking, which is why we won).

And we *had* won.

The United States won World War Two. I say this because, if you were educated in U.S. public schools after 1970, you might not have learned that fact, standards being sub-optimized as they are.

I always liked World War Two. For the U.S., it was a war without blemishes. Or just the usual blemishes. And because we won, policy butt-scrambles like the incarceration of Japanese-American citizens may seem unfortunate and misguided and certainly ironic rather than evil and symbolic of evil: the ends whitewash the means.

My father's generation was the winning generation. And we were the children of the winning generation. We resented that, I bet. I did anyway.

I went to college. That was the new thing for our generation. A blade that shaved his self-esteem, too: because my father hadn't. Few men and virtually no women from his high school class went on to college.

When he graduated high school in 1929, college was, statistically speaking, mostly for other people: the toffs, the pillars, the hoi polloi maybe. You rarely met a college man. A college woman was rare as an albino. One-tenth of one percent of the U.S. population graduated each year from college back then; and there were no jobs for them, either. The Great Depression stalked the land. Life expectancy for men was 54 years. A teacher's salary was $970 a year; most were supposed to live in the same town and have verifiably impeccable moral standards (snooping neighbors welcome). It took 13 days to drive from coast to coast. There were only 387,000 miles of pavement in America.

After World War Two, different story: the G.I. Bill thanked veterans and avoided a forecast post-war recession, using college tuition and low-interest home loans. In 1948, veterans could claim $500 a year in tuition; Harvard cost $400 annually.

Dad took the home loan, but not the chance at higher education. He was old already, almost two decades out of high school. He bet against the trend. World War Two engendered the Space Race. We trailed the Soviets in the smarts department. By the 1960s college was considered a prerequisite for real success. Blue collar became a way down, not a way up. Dad labored all his post-war life in a factory, punching a time card toward a pension.

Their howling sons and daughters enrolled.

In my freshman year, I discovered booze. I gave up

every well-developed (though eminently mediocre) extra-curricular activity I'd pursued in high school. I stopped blowing the trumpet. I stopped running cross-country. In my sophomore year, I joined a fraternity and soon went on academic probation. Which meant a talk with a dean. His calm breath smelled of whiskey. I smelled of self-inflicted failure. The fraternity experience, my latest retail attempt to be *popular*, had been dismal: lots of hard, fast drinking; a 24-hour card game in the basement; blind dates who resisted my shallow advances *(I wanted to shoot my come into their lower bellies; they wanted to marry and start an adult life)*; being called asshole 20 times a day by my "brothers." *Love you!* Fraternity life was like evolution, with any chance for species improvement deleted.

College changed my point of view about my father, too: everything out of his mouth now sounded shockingly, insultingly wrong. I couldn't stand listening to him: stupid, bigoted, violent, caricatured, unreal. He obliged me by shutting up.

My mother committed suicide when I was a junior.

My father was broken-hearted. He was suddenly meek and afraid. And I was headed for a distant planet, with no return ticket.

We saw each other at Thanksgiving, Christmas, a few other times each year: unaffectionate, wary, strangers by choice, sinking from each other's sight.

It was eerie to feel that you were a stranger to your father. And your father was a stranger to you. *Who was this man?* It worried me. Did it worry him? I don't know. He'd survived German artillery. He'd survived decades in a factory, pulling a lever. He'd survived a wife who hated her life. We never talked about things like that. Our family did *not*. My father *made fun* of saying inner stuff. So I thought. I felt strangled from the inside out. But maybe he did, too. We couldn't say one honest thing to each other. It had gotten that bad. I think it started out that bad.

Dad left Europe in November, 1945, embarking at Antwerp, Belgium. He'd seen enough and was ready to go home.

My father: "We lined up at the pier. Double lines, to go up the gangway onto the boat. And right at the gangway was a big table with four Red Cross girls in back of it. They had these boxes of candy, box after box after box. And they had these little bars of candy about the length of your finger.

"This guy in front of me, a big, tall fellow, he's got a big paw on him, he reaches in, and he grabs about ten of these small bars. And when he did, the Red Cross girl taps him on the wrist. She said, 'One. There's more coming.'

"That was their standard reply in Europe. 'One. There's more coming.'

"Oh, he got so mad—I suppose he was embarrassed or something—he just took that candy, and he threw it the length of the pier. 'Keep it!' he said."

Dad forever hated the Red Cross. And with 150 service clubs operating in England for off-duty G.I.s, the Red Cross had every right to consider him an ingrate. I suspect he was right: a bureaucracy of angels. Good with a bad attitude.

CHAPTER 17

YOU'RE *REALLY* IN THE ARMY NOW

His last foxhole was in a nursing home, a bed with a plastic mattress cover. He was attended by minimum-wage angels of mercy. I couldn't bring myself to wipe the poop off his ass; I fled.

My father's great lesson: *Life is hard.*

Nothing ever whispered, among the paint cans and the thudding washing machine in the basement. LIFE IS HARD! he screamed. Even so, he said *I had no idea* how *hard*. Dad, *bless his heart*, as my southern friends taught me to say when faced with the despicable, lost his temper often. Derided incompetence. And he was easily startled. He became a critic. I learned that doing *wrong* was a hundred times easier than doing right. That a ferocious bark takes a bite.

Balanced by my mother's great lesson: there's always suicide to fall back on.

She decided it was all for the best. Like choosing furniture you'd live with for decades. That suicide, all things considered, was the best way to manage her uncertain future.

It was not how she imagined she would finish, I'm sure:

a woman who put herself through night college, managed a hospital's accounts, then a daily newspaper's booming business. It was not how she would choose to be remembered either.

But it was best, given the circumstances; she reckoned. Now that she really knew how many angels danced on the head of a pin. The answer: none.

A future that grabbed her head in its claws, like any raptor, and wouldn't let go. Shook her to death. A woman depressed, worn out, disappointed, lungs inelastic with emphysema and hard as shale (my sister's best guess).

Mother had. Parchment skin. Black hair going gray; a billboard in tatters. All that. I didn't see it. I saw my mother, a woman fifteen years younger. My ally. A woman I'd once finger-fucked as an infant. Immortal. Devoted. Content in all things me. I was desperately, depth of the ocean selfish. It felt good. All warm, me-like, and agoo.

My father said I *could* have saved her; the day she killed herself. Had I cared to. I was there in the house after all; I could have intervened.

His proposal: I could catch her in the act and stop her. Restrain her. Find some argument no one else had found. The argument of me. My grief. My pain. My shock. My transformational articulation.

Instead, that not at all special day, I stayed in bed, masturbating almost certainly, pounding the poor little circumcised thing raw. The only place I've ever put lotion of my body: there. Best way to start the day.

While she died alone in our new garage; in the family car, a small mid-sized car, light blue. Poisoned. Self-administered euthanasia. A nation of one, deceased. By carbon monoxide. Her lungs functioning perfectly well that day as an intake mechanism.

The outcome suited Dad's theory: I was hapless, lazy. And here? Fatally so. My mother died. His *wife* died. Maybe he was right. *Maybe.* He was right about a surprising number of things, I'd grant him that. As pessimists often are.

A child psychologist recommended car rides for my father, as a way to help him relax. She said the slight swaying of the car would rock his hypothalamus, inducing a restful state. It was the parent's old trick for a fussing infant: put him in the car and drive him around the neighborhood until he falls asleep. I drove a pickup truck, which bounced more than it swayed, but the psychologist's advice had given me a mission. I took Dad on drives from his nursing home.

Tanks could be relaxing, too.

Tanks may have been cramped, uncomfortable, cacophonous vaults; but, for the weary, they had their advantages: full body massage. Len Deighton quoted a German tanker: "The need to have the tank working without fault meant that the crew were always together with a vehicle. The crew became a family and the tank a home where one was secure and rested. Rested because of track vibration: aching feet, sore back, pulled muscle were all gone after half an hour on the road. And each tank had its own smell: a combination of the odours of hot oil, petrol, steel and earth." Home sweet tank. Think of a turtle's shell with more than one inside.

Still: "There is also the other side of being a crewman. I

have had to drive in freezing rain, the wind coming through the tank, and I could have cried because I was so cold. On these occasions there was only one way to thaw out—take it in turns to go outside to the back of the tank, lie flat on your back on the engine plates and let the heat come through your tank-suit. Spread-eagled, one was perfectly safe and none of us ever fell off while moving along the roads." A remarkably paradoxical invention: colder inside than out.

The tank was a "mobile dungeon," without the slightest attraction to infantry in combat. Stephen Bagnall summed up the view from the foxhole: "Tanks are different.... We didn't like them. I'm talking about the machines of course. We all liked tankmen. We admired them. [But] I would rather have been an infantryman than a tankman any day of the week. It might feel safer inside so long as nothing happens, but you couldn't hope for a pleasant death if anything did happen shut up in a blazing steel room that was rapidly becoming white-hot and filled with an infernal symphony of fireworks as your own ammunition caught fire and added to the horror."

Tankers died in bad, untidy ways, everyone agreed. Sergeant L. R. Gariepy: "In some cases the bodies were indistinguishable from one another, simply a mass of cooked flesh welded together in the great heat; we had to sift through this for identity tags. Each tank told the same story—broken legs, broken arms, open chest wounds, and so on, had trapped many, so that they had burnt alive. The screams I thought I had heard during the action had not been imaginary after all."

As a boy, I assumed—we all assumed—that our fathers

were heroes in the war, that all G.I.s were heroes-in-waiting, fighting to the last bullet if need be, then in a final combative gesture swinging their weapons like clubs, dying with their buddies ("Joe, I'm hit!"), sinking beneath the drudging weight of a massed enemy attack. Dying for what was right. It was the number one defiant military posture, the tough-guy American ethic, exemplified by Davy Crockett and his fellow Texan nose-thumbers, at the Alamo.

But the Alamo was a ten-day siege. World War II was something else again.

You were in for the duration, however long that took. Your personal heroism, your moxie, got you only so far. "An Army is a team; lives, sleeps, eats, fights as a team. This individual heroic stuff is a lot of crap." Said General George S. Patton, Jr. We were, as boys always are, vastly ill informed.

British and American psychologists soon found that combat soldiers could not fight indefinitely. Definitely not. No matter *who* they were. Heroes had no definition. Somewhere between 200 and 240 combat days, scientists realized, was the absolute, outside limit. After that the fight was gone, the soul was gone, the brain shut down; the soldier was broken and couldn't be mended. Even a Davy Crockett would end up a babbling, unresponsive mess. His ten days was a walk in the park compared to....

No one "got used to combat."

That particular transformation just wasn't possible. After three weeks of it, every day became worse than the day before, in a steady downward plod. Within six weeks the average frontline infantryman was such a basket case he was practically useless. If he was rotated out of the line, some of his resilience returned. But the fix was temporary.

John Ellis recounted the report of two psychiatrists who traveled with a U.S. combat infantry battalion through France: "In fact, very many soldiers were not evacuated until they had got beyond this point, either becoming almost catatonic or suffering a final collapse triggered off by an especially brutal incident. This was usually a very near hit or the sight of yet another buddy being killed before one's eyes. Then 'the soldier became disorientated or confused. Often he ran about wildly and aimlessly, with a total disregard for danger, rolled on the ground and cried convulsively.'

"All this," Ellis reminds, "is not the description of a handful of exceptional cases. It is what happened, in continuous combat, to almost all the soldiers of an infantry unit who were not killed or wounded. It happened to every nationality, on every front, in every company, battalion and regiment. The only reason units as a whole did not fall apart was that there was a constant flow of replacements, and at any one time most men had not yet reached this crisis point."

My father was a replacement. And trapped. He said: "One night up in Germany, see, we'd just pulled back from the front, our outfit. And course we'd been eating out of our pockets for two weeks. So this guy says, 'I'm going to have some pancakes.' I looked at him. I said, 'Where the hell are you going to get pancakes?'

"Picks up his rifle and down he goes. He finds this cook tent. He said, 'Fellows, I want pancakes.' They looked at him: 'What are you, nuts?'

"He said, 'It's either pancakes or a bullet through your

head. What do you want?' They made pancakes. And on top of that he told them, 'And keep 'em coming, too!' So he takes a load of pancakes back to the house where he was billeted. He said to the guys, 'Look, pancakes!'

"Those guys got so crazy, I'm telling you, they'd shoot their own mother."

What sets them off? You do!

Dad: "One day there we're going around a corner. Here's a building, right side of it is a German tank. Here's an officer standing up there just as straight as a die, the hatch open, he's staring right ahead. I said, 'What the hell is that?' So some of the guys got off the truck, and they walked over. They didn't go near the tank; they just walked behind it. Somebody had stuck a knife in his back. As dead as a doornail; just as stiff.

"But you never tried to get in those tanks, 'cause the Germans booby-trapped them. The Germans, they were great at that, booby-trapping everything." War Department pamphlet No. 21-23, printed in 1944: *Don't get killed by mines and booby traps...*

  - Don't be careless—Watch your step!

  - Don't be curious—Curiosity kills more than cats

  - Don't be a souvenir-grabber—Be smart—Leave 'em alone

  - Don't be foolhardy—Fools rush in, but only once

An alarming red cover illustrates what can happen when you don't pay attention: an explosion turns you inside out, and you're gone: head obliterated, dog tags unleashed, gobbets of your atomized flesh painting the air. Your shattered equipment spins away, the few thumps when it lands the last noise you ever even indirectly make. There is no you, not anymore. Welcome to your new world, richly hostile, recently redecorated to repel hordes of armed Allied tourists come to meddle: "Mines and booby traps are not placed by magic; they are placed by the enemy or our own troops...."

Now *there's* comfort.

As a ready reference to things that go bang, the pamphlet could have been improved. Among its shortcomings: a sluggish style and a vocabulary that refuses to descend. Standard readability tests unavailable in 1944 reckon the pamphlet twice as hard to understand as the average newspaper. (Though certainly not impossible: "Nearly half of all white draftees were high school graduates. One in ten had some college. These were the best-educated enlisted men of any army in history."—Perret)

Cartoons saved the day.

Even the illiterate (the Army had none that it knew of) got the picture. Throughout, a hapless G.I.—young, clean shaven, agile—is shown doing everything possible to get himself killed, pulling things, lifting things, cutting things, moving things better left alone; watched gleefully by two vile half-pint imps: a German with monocle and shaved head, a Japanese with slit eyes and buck teeth; both bearing sticks of TNT with burning fuses.

Pamphlet: "A booby trap is an explosive charge arranged so any disturbance of a seemingly harmless object sets it off. ...(B)ooby traps are used principally to scare, harass, and demoralize all our troops in captured territory. The enemy has booby trapped practically everything including their own dead and even tombstones on our dead.... The enemy preys especially on the souvenir hunter. Some ingenious booby traps include double bottom trunk, tobacco tins, parasols, ping pong balls, pistol disguised as a cane, pistol disguised as a fountain pen...." You pick up a pen, bear down to write; it shoots you in the face.

Happens all the time to writers.

Dad was spooked.

"You know, you never been in town with there was nobody in it. It gives you an awful funny feeling. The place is deserted. So we were walking in and out of houses, just to see what the hell was in there. And this house we spotted, they got a brand new twenty-two rifle up over the fireplace. The guy said, 'Look at that.' I said, 'Yeah, and it's booby-trapped, too.' He said, 'Yeah.' You could see the wires coming off it. 'Well,' he said, 'we got engineers above us.' 'Well,' I said, 'let's go up and see the engineers.' So we did and we told them what house the gun was in. They said, 'We'll get it for you.' They got the gun all right, but we never saw it."

My father was a booby trap himself. Innocent looking, rigged to explode. Pull the wrong string: boom! You were daddyfodder. A man defined by anger, I thought. Simmering, suspicious. He scared me. He loved to tell stories of guys getting punched: "Then I hauled off and popped him." When I wasn't so scared and began talking back, he prophesied, "Some day you're going to open that mouth of yours, and somebody's going to shut it for you."

You were right, Dad. It just didn't take the form you imagined. No fist smashing my teeth down my throat. I made fun of my boss in a meeting; a few months later he fired me.

We were six years old, boys playing soldiers. Bang bang.

We didn't know there were specialists like engineers. We were incompetent with artillery; no idea what that did either. OK: tanks rolled over people; so having a tank was decisive.

My personal military budget was zero. I depended on parental largesse and holiday gifts of cash from the relatives. A toy tank was expensive; our baby armies owned few. We had almost no transportation of *any* kind, in fact; though the real U.S. Army was mechanized down to its combat boots. In World War II, American infantry rode to war. Planners assigned two thousand vehicles to each division; roughly one wheel per man.

We had "guys." My guys. Your guys. My guys jammed a shoebox: a plastic tangle of cheap silhouette men, sprawling prone riflemen firing the standard M-1 self-loading rifle ("the best fighting tool ever produced," according to General Patton), carbine marksmen upright on bases, a rubber bazooka guy with a drooping tube. Our backyard battles were primitive clashes: no economics, no political imperatives, no lasting territorial ambitions, no consequences. Only sides. Action reaction. You could be the Germans or the Japs or the Americans; it didn't matter.

Actually, we were fascinated by German equipment and symbols: the swastika (easy to draw), the potato masher grenade (how silly), the Luger pistol (the souvenir of souvenirs), the coal-scuttle, box-awning helmet (knight's armor almost). Combat was exciting, a ritual, a sacrifice we made over and over, acting out death. Puny ourselves, we were fond of lost causes: the Confederates in the American Civil War and the Nazis.

Our "guys" hid behind grass stems and tumbled from

rocks. It was small unit action, just like my father's experience; verisimilitude at last. We thought combat was one-on-one, line-of-sight, my guys against your guys. We figured in a war you'd see the enemy; we argued over which of us was faster or had the better aim. Dad said no: "You know they're there, sure. But you very seldom ever see anybody. Everything is under cover. You just take potshots at them."

Nor did we fight at night, as he had. Dad: "I used to say to myself, If I ever see a streetlight again, I'm going to be the happiest guy going. You operated so much in the dark. Like one night we pulled back on a dirt road into these woods. And we were guided by a guy walking. No lights on anything, see. Black as pitch out. And he walked along the middle of the road with a cigarette in his hand. And that's all we went by, that one cigarette. And when that went out he lit another one and put it up. And we followed that cigarette for about three or four miles, and then we pulled into a forest. No lights, nothing, at night."

We never scratched out holes in the ground so our guys could escape a nightfall of terror. "I got a hole dug, because you never knew when a plane was coming over, and they'd drop what they called personnel bombs. They just made a little hole in the ground, but they scattered shrapnel everywhere." We didn't know you kept your head down: almost a third of infantry wounds were head wounds. Or that most wounds were as impersonal as a meteor strike: 75% caused by bursting shells. "I'm laying in the hole, and I got my helmet, I'm using it for a pillow. You never took your clothes off. Just your shoes, and use your helmet for a pillow. And here I am laying in a trench I had dug in the ground, and all of a sudden I hear this 'scrape, scrape' on the back of my helmet. I said to myself, What the hell is that? So I move around in the hole, and I get the helmet, and what the hell was it but a little frog. He was trying to get out of the hole, and he couldn't seem to make any headway on my helmet."

Or that it wasn't only frogs you found in holes. "You operated so much in the dark. One night there we got orders to back up the First or the Ninth division, I don't know now which one. Somebody got word that the Germans might try to break through. I think it was the Rhine river that was out in front of us. And we went up at two o'clock in the morning, and we pulled into these fields. And they said, 'You won't have to dig any holes, fellas. Plenty of holes here.' Well, this guy and myself we jumped into a hole in the ground there. And we pulled two dead Germans out of that hole. The guy with me went through their pockets to see if they had anything. All he found was a jackknife."

"A man must know his destiny ... if he does not recognize it, then he is lost. By this I mean, once, twice, or at the very most, three times, fate will reach out and tap a man on the shoulder ... if he has the imagination, he will turn around and fate will point out to him what fork in the road he should take, if he has the guts, he will take it."—General George S. Patton, Jr.

I believed, as a boy, that my true genius was as a military strategist. And that some day, when the country was in grave danger, the phone would ring (if our family's party line was open), and I would be summoned to win the battle and the war. Somehow my native war making genius would be obvious among the 200 million or so individuals then citizens of the U.S.; and I would be handed command, like a pair of driving gloves: go get 'em. The boy general.

It was a distinct shock to learn that, in fact, I had no warrior in me. Personality tests done after I was fired told the ominous truth: I had no fight. None at all. Or it was down so deep (there was always hope) standard tests could not detect it.

Add that to everything else I didn't know about my father's war.

I had no idea how horse-drawn the German army was. In 1943, awesomely powerful, the army that stunned the world with its unstoppable drives; credited with modernizing warfare, emptying the trenches, mechanizing the assault, keeping it fast, unexpected, devastating, toppling less flexible opponents: in each German infantry division more than 5,000 trudging transport horses consumed 53 tons of hay and oats each day. Commonly depicted in American war illustration: jeeps. Common in German war art: horses.

No idea that Germans were so opportunistic, relying heavily on stolen vehicles to push their military weight around. Len Deighton: "no less than one third of the German armor used against France originated in (appropriated) Czech factories," a sort of sentimental political justice since, just twenty-one months earlier, France and more particularly, English prime minister Neville Chamberlain (described by the previous officeholder—without sarcasm or irony — as a "pinhead"), had handed Czechoslovakia to Hitler on the proverbial plate. How unsuited was Neville Chamberlain to his task and era? It was written in the clouds. In his 1932 presidential bid, Hitler "flew about thirty thousand miles and spoke at about two hundred meetings. He was the first politician to use the airplane so extensively" to campaign (Modris Eksteins). When Chamberlain fluttered off to Munich in 1938 to negotiate the great Czechoslovakian give-away, it was his very first airplane ride.

Certainly didn't know that "seven-eighths of all the fighting in which the Germans engaged took place on the Eastern Front." Deighton again. "Only one-eighth of the entire German war effort was put into their campaigns in North Africa, Italy and on the Western Front." So little. What I knew was glimpsed through a pinhole: my father's tramp through France, Belgium, Germany. The Führer, fighting for the heavyweight championship of the world: for every punch he threw at Dad, Hitler slugged the Soviets seven times.

The vocabulary of a war lasts about three generations, maybe is common for two. Slang, jargon, songs hummed and an edited innocence to it all. Names of battles; accounts of combat; terrifying ordnance, legendary in its day, encountered on the road.

Dad: "You didn't travel big. You traveled by squads or companies. See, the story was: you had it in back of you. If you bumped into trouble, then you could bring up the rest. A division has fifteen thousand men. With all their own tanks and artillery and everything else. But you don't bring everything up in a line. You just send out so much in front of you. And when they bump into trouble, that's when the others come up. Our convoy was something like five miles long, just the tanks and other stuff we had with us. You can do a hell of a lot of damage. They're never too far behind.

"One day, going across France, all the convoy stopped. Somebody said, 'What's the trouble?' 'There's a big Mark

Six up at the crossroads. Ahead of us.' Somebody said, 'Get the butterflies.' That's what they called the fighters.

"So the first thing you know, one of our tanks radios. They're talking to a guy up in a plane. You can't see him, but he's up there. He's saying, 'What's the matter, fellows?' 'We got a big Mark Six up at the crossroads in front of us.'"

The Mark Six was the German Tiger tank. *The Illustrated Encyclopedia of 20th Century Weapons and Warfare*: "Judged by (modern) standards the Tiger...was a crude tank. With its vertical armor and sharp angles it had many shock traps, it was slow, maximum cross country speed being only 12 mph and the turret traversed slowly by hand (720 turns for 360°) and rather erratically under hydraulic power." It was too wide for road or railway transport unless special accommodations were made. Yet: "Despite these deficiencies the Tiger enjoyed a reputation with Allied tank crews which became legendary. Its most notable feat in the West was the single-handed attack by Oberstürmfuhrer Michel Wittman on June 13, 1944, who destroyed 25 vehicles of the British 7th Armoured Division and stopped the advance on Caen. [The] Tiger had its day and in the years 1942-44 its thick armor and powerful 8.8-cm [cannon] were universally feared." It was also, weirdly, amphibious: About one third of all Tigers were specially equipped to submerge completely—a 56-ton frog—and lurk in 13 feet of water for hours.

Dad: "The pilot said, 'I'll take care of him.' And then, all of a sudden, right out of the blue, one of these P-47s appears. He's got two five hundred pound bombs on his wings, and he's got orders, 'Don't blow that road, we got to use it.' So he drops the bomb so far from the tank, and the concussion from that bomb...here's a 60-ton tank...will blow that tank right off the road, over on its side. And when we got orders to move, there was the tank laying there, burning. Big hole over here, where that bomb hit. Five hundred pound bomb, that's a big bomb. But that's what they used to say: 'Call the butterflies.'"

The butterfly in this instance was one of several pugnacious tank-busters patrolling northwest European skies, making daytime maneuvers extremely hazardous for the Germans. The British had their pouting Hawker Typhoons, eradicating 175 tanks in one day's work. G.I.s depended on the Lockheed twin-boom P-38 Lightning and the Republic P-47D Thunderbolt, a massive fighter weighing nine hulking tons on take-off. Other fighters you wore strapped to you like a tight, awkward costume. The Thunderbolt's cockpit, said a report, was "spacious and would easily accommodate two pilots of normal girth sitting side by side. Its size, and the neat arrangement of the instruments, make it seem sparsely furnished. Clearly, the designer had the last word and the junk shop untidiness of some fighters' cockpits is pleasantly absent." Their record against ground targets was prodigious. Between D-Day and VE-Day, less than a year, low-flying Thunderbolts claimed 86,000 railway cars, 9,000 locomotives, 68,000 motor vehicles, and 6,000 armoured vehicles. If an aircraft could smile wickedly, the Thunderbolt did.

Dad: "Of course, we always had six planes over us. Fighters. There were six over us, six coming, and six alerted. At all times. Why, going through these villages in France, some of these Germans, they heard you coming, they started running. Well, these planes just mowed them down. The planes come right down the main streets and anybody that got out of town was crazy, because they were out in the open. We found German soldiers sitting on the curbing, crying. They were worn out from running."

Still, pilots paid a price for being in the thick of it. P-47 pilot Marvin Bledsoe: "I...completed 70 combat missions, almost every one amounting to a major confrontation with the enemy, in a period of just a little over a hundred days. I walked around in disbelief. My combat tour was complete and I was still alive." Half the Thunderbolts sent into combat were lost. Even sitting ducks weren't benign: many ground targets blew up into the flight path when hit, taking down the plane.

Dad had been in the Army less than a year when he was landed across Omaha Beach. He was living one of his self-images: *unshakeable tough guy, standing up for himself, freakishly durable, lasting through anything.* Maybe it was a personal dream that life could be vivid, challenging, and set in a foreign country.

This was an ordinary night in France, Belgium, and Germany, the countries he fought across. "Well, they bombarded us, and then it rained. Oh, how it rained. And there we were in holes, and you're in water. You couldn't take that in civilian life. You'd have been dead.

"But the Army had you so filled with shots you could lay in water all night, and I don't think you *could* catch cold." His immunizations included smallpox, typhoid, tetanus, and cholera. He said the Army just loved to stick needles in that hurt like hell and turned your arm to hard salami. He was nigh invulnerable, a miracle product. His immune system could spit in your eye.

Bill Mauldin, G.I. Joe's editorial cartoonist, tried to

describe what it was like, exposed for long periods to weather and enemy threats, experiencing discomfort so numbing it was an insult, if you could think at all.

He tried to give his readers an equivalent they could piece together for themselves. "Dig a hole in your back yard," he told them, "while it is raining. Sit in the hole until the water climbs up around your ankles. Pour cold mud down your shirt collar. Sit there for forty-eight hours, and, so there is no danger of your dozing off, imagine that a guy is sneaking around waiting for a chance to club you on the head or set your house on fire." That was just for starters.

"Get out of the hole, fill a suitcase full of rocks, pick it up, put a shotgun in your other hand, and walk on the muddiest road you can find. Fall flat on your face every few minutes as you imagine big meteors streaking down to sock you.

"After ten or twelve miles...start sneaking through the wet brush. Imagine that somebody has booby-trapped your route with rattlesnakes which will bite you if you step on them. Give some friend a rifle and have him blast in your direction once in a while."

The climax? Mauldin invites a homicidal bull to chase you back into your hole.

He suggests you repeat this performance every three days for several months and "you still won't understand how [an infantryman] feels when things get tough." It was a preposterous, exhausting, filthy experience that simply could not be described, even by a top-shelf describer like Mauldin. And that assumed you weren't maimed or killed.

The experience of combat so fundamentally challenged then-accepted U.S. norms that some experts seriously doubted that frontline soldiers would ever fit into civilized society again.

The weird thing was, men *were* changed; but maybe for the better, all things considered.

They came home world-beaters; filled with pride; accomplishment; ambition; supreme confidence; and bearing broader views, at least of geography. My father could as easily speak of parts of England, France, Belgium and Germany as he could his hometown. He knew little towns. He knew people in those little towns. He had eaten dirt in all those places.

Evil, the great negative, was gone, driven out—for the moment—and Americans aimed now to bring something into the world; thumb their national nose and say, "So there!"

Men came back sick of war, wanting children and home. The G.I. Bill beckoned, siren song for higher education and home ownership. A middle-class was born. A boom emerged, more and more babies, a seismic event, an episode of demographic mountain building. And the wolves of commerce yipped outside the nursery door.

Packages piled up in U.S. post offices.

Marked "Return to Sender", thousands of Christmas gifts to dead, missing or captured servicemen were undeliverable.

At the same time, three million bottles of French perfume sailed for America and the ears, necks, and bosoms left behind. G.I.s were good news for the scent industry: "This was double the number of bottles America imported annually *before* the war."

Question on the front line: in the fog of war, who's more

dangerous, us or them?

Dad almost didn't make it home to plant his next seed, thanks to trigger-happy Yanks."We see all these German soldiers running out of town, and we're taking potshots at them. Then we notice tanks. Our tanks. And the first thing we know, one of the tanks turned around and she went, 'Whoom! Whoom! Whoom!', right at the house we were in.

"Well, about nine of us went right down those cellar stairs. Why we weren't killed, I don't know. I suppose they thought it was Germans in the house. They were far enough away so I suppose we just looked like figures moving. And then one of the officers, he ran out on the street and he's waving at the troops that are coming in. Why, they opened up on him.... Yeah, they weren't taking any chances."

If your own troops didn't kill you, your officers would. "The G.I.s were just as good without their officers as they were with them. Sometimes better. The sergeants seemed to know more, you know? We were going across France, and the column was at least five miles long. And we were headquarters company, so we were up front. And all of a sudden this sergeant we got with us puts up his hand. He stops the whole column.

"The next thing we know, up comes a big tank, and the cover lifts on it. This major sticks his head out, 'What's going on, boys?' The sergeant said, 'There's German 88s up around the corner, in those woods.' 'How do you know that?' The sergeant said, 'I saw the sun hit them.' The major said, 'There's nothing up there. You go right ahead.' Sergeant said, 'I'm not moving, and my men are not moving. Why don't you call in for some artillery?' Major said, 'We don't have time for that, we've got to be traveling.' Sergeant said, 'Well, we're not moving, so you better do something.'

"So the major gets on the radio, and the first thing we know, two tanks come up. And he gives them the sign: Go ahead. They go up the road, and they just go around this big curve, and the 88s open up, and there goes two tanks and ten men. So they called in the artillery. The first big blast: right on top of the guns. When we went by up there, there was guns knocked over, dead men all around."

The German 88 anti-tank gun was voted "Most Likely to Kill or Utterly Fuck You Up" by U.S. ground troops.

In a statistically valid survey of 600 wounded G.I.s, the enemy 88 was rated more than twice as frightening and more than three times as dangerous as any other weapon, including all the usual exploding, penetrating things—machine guns, rifles, mines—things you were much more likely to encounter and that were far more likely to hurt you.

The 88 was legendary among G.I.s fighting in Europe. It fired like a no-diddle lightning bolt, straight, no arc. Its slug passed through American tanks like a cough through a hanky. Its high explosive shells were used in city fighting to tear down buildings, one floor at a time, starting at the top.

It was a Krupp product. Muzzle velocity—the speed the shot left the gun—was extremely fast, up to 3,700 feet—more than half a mile—per second. The shell headed your way in a blink "weighed over 100 pounds and," from a half mile away, "was capable of penetrating four inches of armor." It put an end to many arguments instantly.

Dad: "I was up in different places where there was nobody but Germans in front of you. And you might be there for a week, you might be there for ten days.

"Then, all of a sudden, the orders came, 'Pull back.' So you'd pull back and another outfit would go up in your place.

"We pulled back. And we're in this town, doing nothing, sitting in houses. And somebody said, 'Hey, look at these officers coming up the street.'" Officers were so rare far forward that large groups of them attracted stares. "And we looked out, and here's about twenty-five officers, and who the hell is in the middle? Eisenhower. Then we pick up the *Stars and Stripes* the following week, and they got big headlines across the paper: 'Eisenhower Tours the Front.' That was no front. Why, to us it was like being in New York City to be back there, five miles in back of the front."

Dad was proud. The front had been tough. Both sides invited divine intervention. Any gods within hearing were indifferent to weather conditions.

"One night there we were up in a pasture. And it was raining." A given, his tone suggested. "We dug holes. Even in the rain, we dug them." The army way: get below the shrapnel. "I got my hole dug deep enough, and I put blankets over the top for a roof, and I put stones all around to hold the blankets. And I climb in.

"I'm in there about fifteen or twenty minutes, and all of a sudden, *Boom!* The whole works comes right in on top of my head. The water had gathered so much on the blanket, it had made a big puddle, and then it went, *Boom!*, and I'm underneath it. Well, I wasn't the only one. The air was blue. Everybody was swearing their head off.

"Every once in a while, a German shell would come in. Nobody cared. They were so mad they didn't care. I climbed up on a halftrack. Now a halftrack has no roof on it. I climbed up on that and this guy, I don't know where he got the canvas but he got it from someplace, and we put it over the top of the windshield and the seats, and there we are huddled underneath it out of the rain. And first thing you know a shell would come in. *Whoom! Bang!* He was so mad, he said, 'I hope to hell the next one hits us!' We stayed there all night."

My father in a field at night being shelled in a soaking rain and trying to sleep in a wet steel box: all his stories lead to or from that scene.

Perret: "(Chief of Staff George C.) Marshall and (the Army's chief trainer, Leslie J.) McNair shared a common mental picture of how the enemy would be defeated. They imagined a comparative handful of (G.I.s) picking themselves up from the dirt and mud after spending hours lying on the ground; these were men who were wet, probably men shivering with cold; thirsty, hungry, tired and afraid, mentally scarred by the deaths of friends and by witnessing sights that would haunt them for the rest of their lives, they would move forward under machine gun and artillery fire. Some would fall, but the survivors would close with the enemy and kill him in a foxhole or a bunker, a building or a ditch, or die in the attempt. All the machinery the Army possessed came down in the end to that one-act drama."

CHAPTER 18

SORRY, MOM

FINALLY: I'D HEARD IT ALL A MILLION TIMES.

Knew every German POW, every ambush, every farmer. Could sing along.

I decided, he must be making most of it up.

Not really, as it turned out. Maybe a few things, but....

What I could check turned out to be accurate, down to the rivet.

HEADLINE: Why Italian brides run out on ex-GI's

The story appeared in 1954, under the subhead: "The Thrill Is Gone for Roman Wives. They're Going Home, Belly-Aching That American Husbands Make Crummy Lovers." The magazine: *Sensation*, a pocket tabloid, with a dented telegraphic style.

Get a load of this: "Along with souvenir kimonos, Samurai swords and German Lugers, the American W.W. II G.I. brought back a crop of fresh, plump, new-mown Italian war brides. Used to clammy hand-holding of U.S. sweethearts, G.I.'s fell for hungry Italian girls able to convey warmth, sex with a moist-eyed glance.

"Eight years after the war, with tempestuous early

marriage days gone, only one out of every 25 Italian war brides lives happily with her ex-G.I. husband. In typical group of 126 East Coast brides, SENSATION found 34 divorced, 18 trying for divorce, 43 separated, and 26 wanting separation but unwilling to face relatives who told them not to wed Americans. That leaves five well-adjusted marriages out of 126.

"Sad fact is that Italy's disappointed brides consider Americans to be fine husbands. 'There is no better husband than an American,' one said. 'Eager, sincere, never jealous.'

"But kindness, devotion, faithfulness are deadly sins to Italian women. 'This I could have had in a father,' a 25-year-old bride said. 'A husband must have spice. If he kicked me in the stomach once, I would have kissed him all over his body, loved him forever.'

"In not one of the 126 marriages was adultery the cause of divorce. If anything, it was *lack* of extra-marital affairs. Italian brides consider a faithful husband to be no more fascinating than a faithful dog.

"'Not once did my husband go near or touch another woman,' a shiny young Latin bride said. 'And no matter how many men I stayed with, he continued to have blind faith in me. It never occurred to him I might be unfaithful. This finally exasperated me. So I told him I didn't love him.'

"High on list of ex-G.I. sins was creating a life of comfortable monotony for their smouldering wives. After years of ducking sniper bullets, catching love on the run, Italian brides found U.S. routine unbearably dull.

"'My husband,' said a Sicilian woman, 'did everything to make me happy. He was astonished to find I was miserable. He thought of me as a machine that gives chocolate.

One puts in money, presses the button, and the chocolate is poured.'

"Tragic fact behind divorce rates is: Italian women have never ceased to be Italian. The Latin bride now realizes that the high-spirited G.I. she married is as much a stranger as the new land she came to live in."

"Imagine it: just wanting to see a streetlight." Dad again, in the Europe he knew. "You were always moving under the cover of darkness.

"We went out one night with a bunch of engineers up in Germany. There was houses that came along in a line and then they stopped. Then there was a big expanse of field. And then the houses started again. They claimed the Germans were coming through this field.

"We had to wait five nights so there wouldn't be any moon. And then there was about fifteen of us, went out with these engineers. And they mined this field. The engineers told us, 'Now lookit, if anything happens, don't run backwards. Because if you do, you're going to trip those wires and kill yourself. Run to the side.' We were all down on one knee, waiting for those engineers to run wires across with bombs on them. And we were right out in the open. Any minute we could have got it.

"Nothing happened. But what a feeling to know you're right out there in the open. 'Course, we stayed down as much as we could. But you never know."

Dad was speaking to a dumb civilian. I had no real idea what he was talking about and couldn't possibly under-stand the experience of combat, no matter how often or how vividly he tried to tell his stories. He said "See" and "You know?" every few sentences, helping me along. But I couldn't *see* or *know*. I could hear. Maybe I could listen. But I had no relevant reference points.

In *Wartime*, Paul Fussell points out — he's raging—that photos of dismemberment and worse are rare or omitted in general histories of World War II: rhetoric and discretion have remodeled the House of Horrors and left out the abattoir.

Fussell, a U.S. infantry veteran: "What was it about the war that moved the troops to constant...contempt? It was not just the danger and fear, the boredom and uncertainty and loneliness and deprivation. It was rather the conviction that optimistic publicity and euphemism had rendered their experience so falsely that it would never be readily communicable. The real war was tragic and ironic...but in unbombed America especially, the meaning of the war seemed inaccessible. As experience, thus, the suffering was wasted." Fussell estimates that only a third of the "real" story was told, the sanitized remains, the rest officially censored or self-censored out by obedient correspondents.

What *was* the real story?

Gruesome, indecent carnage. Frontline troops frequently pissing and shitting themselves in fear. In one survey of American infantrymen, a quarter admitted to "incontinence of feces" during moments of terror. Anything close to the truth would have meant a G.I. Joe® action figure that wets itself; shits its pants; and explodes without warning, tossing internal organs.

Even straight-shooter Ernie Pyle couldn't tell the *real* story. Fussell: "He too had to obey the rules, that is, reveal only about one-third of the actuality and just like the other journalists fuel all the misconceptions—that officers were admired, if not beloved; that soldiers, if frightened, were dutiful; and that everyone on the Allied side was sort of nice."

Dad on officers: "Half the time, the officers were gone. They'd take off when the going got rough and leave you holding the bag. We had a captain, he disappeared about every time we went in to take a town. And when you'd take the town and everything would be secure, all of a sudden he'd appear and they'd say, 'Where were *you*?' 'Well, I got something in my eye and I had to go back someplace and have it taken out.' He always had an excuse."

Valor, glory were more palatable than butchery. Fussell concludes: "What annoyed the troops and augmented their sardonic, contemptuous attitude toward those who viewed them from afar was in large part...public innocence about the bizarre damage suffered by the human body in modern war."

Dad arrives in bucolic Normandy: "The Germans used to go down and bomb the harbors at night, and that night, coming back from the harbor, pitch black, they dropped a bunch of personnel bombs in this field. In that field were twenty-five men and a chaplain. They were all above ground. All killed. What a mess the next morning. The chaplain...they picked parts of him out of an apple tree."

British Brigadier John Hackett, parachuting into combat: "I saw an inert mass...swinging down in a parachute harness beside me, a man from whose body the entrails hung, swaying in a reciprocal rhythm. As the body moved one way the entrails swung the other."

Friendly fire took odd forms. Fussell again: "You would expect front-line soldiers to be struck and hurt by bullets and shell fragments, but such is the popular insulation from the facts that you would not expect them to be hurt, sometimes killed, by being struck by parts of their friends' bodies violently detached."

Fussell's conclusion, published in 1989: "America has not yet understood what the Second World War was like and has thus been unable to use such understanding to re-interpret and re-define the national reality and to arrive at something like public maturity."

I suppose he's suggesting that—had the government and the news agencies candidly and widely reported the disgusting side effects, left the calamities of traumatized flesh undisguised by the syrup of sacrifice and bravery and righteousness—then the U.S. might have weighed subsequent conflicts on a more precise scale and perhaps avoided a war or two; Vietnam and a couple of Iraqs come to mind.

Maybe. I think we get the leaders we deserve. We are a selfish country. We're so rich we expect to be ever richer. Our leaders reflect that. We're collectively greedy and individually generous. Our leaders reflect that, too. I believe what Dale Carnegie said (so I'm told), "You'll have more fun and success when you stop trying to get what you want, and start helping other people get what they want." I don't have statistically valid research to back me. I just know it worked in my career. The less I cared about my income, the more useful I tried to be, the more money I made. Call it Buddhist Entrepreneurship. Call it Enlightened Capitalism. It works so much better. So much good springs from that soil.

What made the horror all too real to participants—surprisingly and suffocatingly repugnant—was impossible to convey.

It was a dimension of human experience that you could not describe in words.

Words were not the right tools. My father never mentioned it, though he must have encountered it repeatedly. The *nose* was the real witness.

Dr. Alex Shulman, an Army surgeon in Europe: "Americans have never known what war really is, no matter how much they saw it on television or pictures or magazines. Because there is one feature they never appreciated: the smell. You go through a village and ... everybody's walking around with masks on their faces, 'cause it's just intolerable. You see those bloated bodies. You see bloated horses and cows. And the smell of death: it's not discriminating. They all smell the same. Maybe if the Americans had known even that, they'd be more concerned about peace."

Maybe.

Maybe those bottles of French perfume mailed back to the States in record numbers by a-soldiering G.I.s were at least partially an attempt to deodorize the stink of death.

Anyway, horror won't keep us out of wars. The lessons of history are forgotten. The experience dies. We're too optimistic and don't fear defeat. We're awfully naive, befitting a young nation.

My father-in-law, Georges Joyaux—may there be a heaven, may it have a wine bar, may every IQ be equal: "I think Americans tend to see mostly the good in human nature. Whereas Europeans see the good and the bad, and so they are never surprised by anything someone does."

Georges was a resistance fighter in southern France during the Second World War; a member, after the Allied invasion, of the Free French Army; an author and translator; a Michigan State University professor of languages and no-nonsense department head; and for over forty years a U.S. resident, married to a Michigan woman, father of six kids.

His comment referred to Hitler's emergence, the war, and the way the Nazis treated the Jews. He didn't say it, but he felt the same as Fussell: there was something slightly gullible in the American character. Europeans had been cheated by everyone repeatedly; killed, cheated, robbed, conquered, and enslaved. By big ideas like divine ordination. Europeans knew what to expect. In Georges' view, even the Brits were naive. And they had no right to be, given their colonial record. They knew what it meant to slaughter for profit.

Europeans—at least the French; this being their primary exceptionalism—were worldly, cynical, suspicious. Starved and tight-fisted.

The off-the-rack American was casually dressed and superabundantly supplied, with gifts for everyone, care of Uncle Sam.

François Bertin: "When the GIs landed in France, they brought with them the 'American way of life', a blend of joie de vivre, mod. cons."—modern conveniences like toilets—"and luxury.

"The American soldiers were without doubt the best-equipped men in the field, but it was in their everyday life that their nation's wealth could best be measured.

"Whether on duty or enjoying rest and recuperation, the GIs had a standard of living that was unequalled anywhere else....

"There can be few people who do not remember the 'Nescafé' instant coffee, sachets of soluble lemonade, fruit pastilles, bars of vitamin-filled chocolate, sticks of chewing gum, and packets of four cigarettes that smiling GIs would toss from their G.M.C. as they drove through towns and villages.

"More than the cannons, rifles and tanks, it is this picture that was to remain in the memory of all those for whom the Liberation represented the high point of their existence. For not only did America send us its boys, it brought us jazz, coca-cola, Lucky Strikes, Nescafé...."

Liberté, fraternité, nescafé.

The Ruhr valley was the steel heart of Germany's military manufacturing capacity; home, at Essen, to Krupp, the world's preeminent arms manufacturer.

The Krupp family had been hard at work expanding their armaments empire for almost four centuries. Essen was a company town. More than a hundred street names in the city honored the Krupps in some way or form. Essen proudly built more weapons of war than any other city on earth. In the 1860s journalists crowned Alfred Krupp the "Cannon King." It was a boisterous tribute to a successful businessman, a man who made breathtakingly big guns and displayed his doom machines at international commercial fairs. The Cannon King title stuck, handed down through the generations to each succeeding patriarch, like a cherished family heirloom.

In the 1930s, the Krupps became close associates of Hitler and the Nazi party. The Nazis recognized how important Krupp would be to a German victory. Nothing was spared to keep the workshops in Essen busy. When labor grew scarce, German ministries arranged for chattel; the Cannon King became a slavemaster, the willing recipient of the Third Reich's human spoils.

By 1945, Krupp's slave labor force was immense: 100,000 bone-sore specimens wrapped in rags, Nazi political captives and POWs making weapons to uphold Deutschland Über Alles. Slaves received almost nothing to eat: the daily caloric allotment would have felt lean to a mouse. To supplement their diet, workers chewed the bark off trees.

Slaves worked day and night until they died; filthy, wretched, and anonymous, a mere number to be counted and discounted—the Nazis were always good with this kind of arithmetic—under Krupp's unweeping whip or truncheon, the preferred tool for intimidation.

By April Fool's Day, 1945, the U.S. 1st and 9th Armies had encircled the Ruhr valley.

Although Germany by now could afford to lose nothing, it could afford to lose the Ruhr least of all.

In these last weeks, the fighting was miserable and hard, the most desperate of the war. Victory in Europe would soon arrive. It was in fact a little more than a month away, putting an end to the hot war.

In the Ruhr, German remnants prepared to fight to the death. The Krupp's slave kingdom was choking on its own finished goods, the work increasingly pointless. Even without the U.S. encirclement, there were no unbombed railways left to carry the arms away.

William Manchester: "(In) Werden, directly across the Ruhr from Essen, a motley phalanx of twelve-year-old Werewolves, seventy-year-old members of the home guard,

Volks Grenadiers, *Flaktruppen* without 88's, panzer crews without tanks, Luftwaffe pilots without planes, and diehard paratroopers dug in to defend...."

While heavy artillery shells crisscrossed the night sky above his immense estate, now gloriously awakening into spring, the Cannon King played cards, awaiting arrest as a merchant of death.

Children have an instinct for perfectly acceptable truths.

So kids play war.

They know there are too many people around. They themselves are freshly baked and more coming right behind. Humans are brilliant, sure; but fungae. Killing a few (million) has social benefits, as long as you don't know them personally. Krupp understood.

Handwriting is a ghost medium.

It retains a squiggle of life long after the mind and the hand responsible lower away; into the grave, passions spent. I own nothing my mother wrote. And wish I did: something to run my thumb over, to feel the faint pressure of her thoughts staining the fibers of a page. No; not a word. She didn't add one sentiment to the book she gave me as I packed for college, my father still unwilling to drive me: a new hardbound seventh edition of *Webster's Collegiate Dictionary*; an unfathomable collection of illustrations, a clothesline of odd choices: a gig, a gimlet, a glengarry, a gnomon, things presumably that defied verbal description alone; copyright 1965, my freshman year at Brown.

It was a special gift, a bottle across my bow as I prepared to sail over the horizon toward a college education, an hour away by car, assuming my father relented and drove me, with foot locker, there. We were inside a major feud. He was utterly uncooperative.

At the time it was not at all uncommon to hear someone say they were the "first in my family to go to college." I was the third, actually: my sister Alice had headed off four years earlier; my mother had taken the bus for years into Boston to earn an accounting degree in the evenings from Bentley. Dad was the odd man out.

My sister whispered: "You know Dad's not really that bright." Which was what I wanted to hear. It explained so much, I thought.

Webster's Seventh was my mother's last gift to me. Four decades later it's still within easy reach.

I've written probably a million words with that dictionary as my primary reference. The cover long ago let go. Many vocabularies have infiltrated the language since: sublimely obsolescent, my favorite dictionary skips from "microbiology" to "microclimate", without any precognitive hint of the "microchip" now between. I sometimes look up even simple words, just for the pleasure of seeing them plain and old, like penny candy.

When she gave me the book, I was still a virgin and desperate to lose that innocence of no repute. Immediately I looked up all the dirty words I could think of: nipple, vagina, penis. I didn't know much, but somehow I knew the word *fellatio*. And there it was! A real thing! Oral stimulation of the penis! Seventh Webster's was never vulgar. There was no *cocksucker* as well. I was delighted to read that *fellatio* and *feminine* shared the same Latin root: it seemed so promising somehow.

Fact two: On the morning of January 12th, faking a happy disposition, Mom asked to use the family car. Instead of taking the bus. Errands, she said. My father agreed, and she drove him to his job at the shoe-sole factory. He didn't realize that she was now addicted to death and had her little scheme worked out. Pecking her cheek goodbye, he slid from the car, his work clothes, as always, steeped in the bouquet of rubber. His marital status was about to change.

I was in the kitchen that afternoon when he arrived home from the factory. Something bothered him immediately. He demanded, "Where's your mother?" I said I didn't know; I supposed she was at work. He ran from the house and came back immediately, reaching for the phone. "Your mother's dead in the garage," he announced while he dialed the police. He sounded disgusted.

I ran outside, thinking two things: (1) I don't want to see this; and (2) I have to see this.

I stepped inside the garage. Glanced around quickly. Her small, gray-haired body was on the concrete floor; without a coat, which seemed cruel in January. The car door was open over her, a faint tang of something wrong in the air, the bare smell of an engine run dry.

Readers: don't go all romantic on me.

I didn't kneel down and cradle her body. There were no poignant farewells. I did not want to touch her dead, heavy flesh; its heat long gone, the smile unplugged. I was afraid of her corpse. I fled and took with me one detail: she had fallen out of her shoes.

Dad fed me his lie in one quick swallow: heart attack.

But my sister sat me down with a different truth that

night: it was suicide, plain and simple. *Actually*, Alice said, her nose wrinkling with contempt, *it was Mother's second try*.

Now *that* was news.

Alice and I were raised Catholic. But we were Darwinians at heart: survival of the fittest, the survivors making mincemeat of the ones who succumbed. My mother's suicidal tendency was the last great family secret Alice owned. She handed it to me wryly, imperfectly, like the last canapé on the tray.

My *mother*, my *father*, my *sister*: a conspiracy of three. Dad held out for the cover story. I asked: Why didn't they tell me the truth earlier? Alice, supremely confident in her role as adjudicator: "We thought it was better not to. We didn't want it to interfere with your school work." Translation: "We didn't think you could handle it." Alternate translation: "We thought you'd do something wonderfully stupid."

Their conspiracy of silence had stretched a mere two months.

It began just before Thanksgiving with a curt phone call from my father.

"Your mother's in the hospital," he barked, warning me what to expect for the holiday. I had planned to come home in a couple of days, driving up from school with a friend. "She has pneumonia," Dad explained, doing his duty, but certainly not trying to shrug up a conversation with me. He didn't like me at all right then. We were in our third hard year of not getting along; the speech patterns on both ends of our calls were well established. "She's at the Phaneuf," he finished. Unspoken but obvious: *Do what you want. But with your mother sick, a real Thanksgiving is out of the question.*

The news about Phaneuf Hospital surprised me. Nobody knew Mom at the Phaneuf. While at Goddard Hospital, only a few miles away, she would be treated like royalty, in deference to her years of keeping the Goddard's books and her close professional friendship with the chief of staff.

But I was far too self-involved to play detective.

I had my own little crisis going, and my own conspiracy of silence. I'd told no one how awkwardly my adjustment to a third year of college was going. I had condemned myself to internal exile: I had stopped attending most of my classes, opting instead to read the material, copy classmates' notes, and show up only to take the tests. It worked well enough: my gradepoint average remained above 3 out of 4. But the scheme was an ominous symptom: my self-confidence was septic; I felt lost, stupid, short, ugly, poor and out-of-place much of the time. I lived off-campus because I deemed myself unworthy of living on-. The less time I spent within the painted iron spearhead fences of Brown University, the happier I felt. I drank when I had the money. I slept a lot.

I don't remember how I met Ramiro. It was freshman year. He was a junior.

Something to do with poetry probably. I wrote some, he wrote some. We were both English literature majors, though I wasn't serious about it. I just liked to read. He was calm, handsome, sincere and caustic; born in Cuba, grew up in New York City. He had a ridiculously big head on an average-height body. And he was openly homosexual, which in 1965 made him quite a find, since virtually every other U.S. gay was still in the closet. Dismissing some silly complaint I'd made, he blurted out his sexual orientation, his point being, *"If you think you've got problems...."*

Until Ramiro came along, the only gay men I'd known were the predators most boys brush against: a cousin—a young man who sold athletic equipment—chased out of town on molestation charges; and his friend—a wildly popular junior high school teacher—who "as a joke" took photos of naked boys while they showered. I was in one of those photos: fourth wiener from the left.

I didn't much care how Ramiro took his sex. I'd dragged my tongue over a dick four years earlier; not a life-changing experience. Suck a tit, suck a dick: what was the big diff? When I rhapsodized about my current girlfriend, he graciously and conspicuously took the hint. In one way, though, Ramiro was enormously attractive to me, especially as my reactions to college grew more and more freakish: he was socially adept, while I felt like a social failure. There was something I hoped he could teach me.

I hauled Ramiro like a prize up to my mother's room in obscure Phaneuf Hospital. He was a big-city guy. He had a lovely Cuban accent I thought she ought to hear. He was driving me home for Thanksgiving, then continuing on to Boston.

My mother had a private room.

Surprise again. First the wrong hospital, now the wrong sort of room. With a view. Of nothing: it was winter outside, in a small, working-class city.

I held her hand and rubbed the translucent skin. She had a few pale age spots on her skin. I was used to her as a no-nonsense business manager and the unchallenged head of our family. In the dusky November afternoon light, she seemed hazy, as fragile as a meringue doll, mechanically smiling. Her breathing, though, was fine. Apparently you could have pneumonia without symptoms.

"Are you OK? This is Ramiro." I introduced my friend enthusiastically.

He nodded her way. This was usually enough: Ramiro was gorgeous. "How are chew, Mitchus A-Hern?" Most people cheered right up when they heard his nightclub accent. People loved band leader and TV sitcom star, Desi Arnaz. Mom smiled weakly. She seemed exhausted, her hands dangling. Both wrists were wrapped in gauze, incongruous dainty white cuffs, tied tightly in place.

"What happened to your wrists?" I asked.

For the intravenous, she whispered.

To bandage the slits she'd carved in herself, like vents in a pie crust.

My father still clung to the heart failure excuse. I don't know if he was trying somehow to protect me or whether he thought a choice of explanations was his prerogative, as the next of kin. He and I never talked about the events leading up to my mother's death; one day she just disappeared from our lives, and Dad and I had one less thing to talk about. One less, *last* thing.

I decided his heart attack tale was part of a scam to defraud the life insurance company. Dad knew the undertaker and the police; the medical examiner was an old family friend. Or maybe that particular excuse was his way of deflecting criticism. You don't want a wife who commits suicide; it starts the gossips. The family motto, authored by him, was: "What will the neighbors think?"

After awhile, I wondered if he actually knew the truth himself.

He did.

My mother's death certificate—Hazel E. (McKay) Ahern's (and I have no idea what the "E." stood for; isn't *that* a shame from a loving son) —was among my father's papers. It was typed by hand, embossed with the town's seal, patted with the black rubber-stamped signature of Barbara A. Donovan, Town Clerk, a "Copy of Record of Death" certifying "that the following is a true copy of so much of said record as relates to said death." *A true copy*.

Inside was a yellow form 431, folded in thirds, and then in half again, as if to make it as small as common sense allowed. On it was the official, recorded cause of my mother's death: "Asphyxiation by Carbon Monoxide, Suicidal."

He knew. He wasn't going to share the truth with a prick like me.

We ate our usual meals in a dark, knotty-pine kitchen, crowded together by twos: Dad and Alice perched at the built-in counter, on stools; my mother and I in the pit, at the half-round table.

The menu was a daisy wheel of standards: beans and franks (to this day a favorite), fish sticks on Fridays (the Catholic obligation), pan-seared (fossilized) steak and baked freezer-burned French fries. Fish sticks, frozen peas, and French fries were our mod-cons; the fruits of World War Two in a way. My mother had a specialty, American chop suey. She tossed it together every few weeks: fried hamburger, cooked elbow macaroni, tomatoes. Dad, a man thrust far ahead of his time, made most of our suppers. His chief culinary goal: to prevent starvation.

At meals we sat, grouped by affinities, a microcosmic

two-party system.

Me, aggrieved, one party: "Dad likes you best."

Dad, proudly declaring his platform: "You never had to do a thing for Alice. She was always independent, right from the start."

Alice, disgusted, the other party: "Mother spoiled you rotten."

At one memorable supper, my mother, *beyond desperate*, silenced for once our ceaseless, three-way baiting—father, sister, and me; the three little pigs—by pleading; by screeching (something she never did) at the top of her lungs; her weakened, *emphysematous* lungs:

"I just want a family that acts like a family!"

I stopped talking. Then I started in again.

Two years later she was dead by her own hand, the echoes of that plea never fading: an eternal trumpet in a marble hall. I never stop hearing it, anyway. Poor her. Mother and wife to a family of total assholes.

My mother's final act shattered my father, branded him. Sent all the mice scampering.

Dad seldom wept.

The day of her funeral he was mush.

His face dissolved into rich suet, with a shaky mouth and gelatin eyes.

I didn't dare touch him or talk to him. You can't suddenly change a tradition of hostility into love, to suit the occasion. His wife had died; my mother had died. They were two completely different women. He'd blamed me since childhood for stealing her love. Now, somehow, surely, he blamed me for her death. I knew it; I suspected it. Was I wrong? Don't have a clue. He claimed he didn't.

But in my father's version of things, no act passed blameless. And I felt handy.

My father wept from every pore, shaking his bones loose in his meat. The brine froze to his face; and the snow that whitewashed the cemetery that morning cascaded from the shoulders of his good overcoat on each rising sob.

I was enormously proud of what my mother had done: spit in the eye of her pain. Said *fuck you* and killed herself, despite the odds against and the inconvenience.

That was good enough until, months later, I realized in a grey pitch that she was completely gone. *Then* I cried.

Dad lived alone another twenty-three years, putting flowers on Mom's grave every Memorial Day until his own ill health interrupted his annual visit. A year later he was buried beside her, a woman who had loved him once long ago, then didn't. Their skeletons can rattle together for eternity.

Her survivors were *not* one big, happy family.

My sister eventually married a man who acted as a ventriloquist's dummy: all her complaints and judgments against me tumbled out of him instead. I heard him sneer at each Thanksgiving dinner, the sole holiday we took together, re: how strange I was and useless and undependable. My sister's sentiments in a man's voice.

Odious as it was to be broadsided by an in-law who hardly knew you, his shot took an odd carom: Simone, my second wife, smelling the dry rot of old opinions unfairly prolonged, became my champion and told my sister off; and my sister, to her credit, changed her tune.

There was other progress.

My father and I arranged in a neglectful way to share a lunch every few months. He lived just an hour from me. It was a headache there and a headache back. For me. For him, too, probably.

In the wreckage of my mother's suicide I discovered one last fatality: my memories of her were poisoned. Not potable. Nothing I remembered seemed good anymore. Hindsight threw a shadow over every smile and laugh and pleasant recollection; every spin she took through the kitchen. Every devoted glimpse of her crossing the field between our house and my grandmother's house next door.

Now you knew how it would all turn out.

Which was badly. *Very* badly.

"Why did she do it?" is a question taller than Everest.

Climb it your entire life; you'll never reach the top.

My sister was sensible. She chose an explanation: mother's lifetime of accumulating disappointments; added to the ledger, depression caused by poor health.

But Alice didn't *really* know. Nor did I. The family whodunnit.

We are all tattooed, mostly on our brains. The selfish question burned across mine, in indelible ink: *What had we done so wrong that deserved such a rebuke?*

There was that plea for peace at the dinner table, but still.

I reminded myself, I still remind myself every day, a lifelong hobby: Hazel E. (McKay) Ahern killed herself to end her excruciating pain.

Pity her.

Pray for her, if you think it will do any good.

Epitaph to my mother: *I loved you so much my heart climbed my ribs whenever I saw you, and an electric wash of tender pleasure filled me. I was your son. Your spoiled son, both of us condemned. But I couldn't rescue you, not here, not in a dream. I miss you so much.*

CHAPTER 19

HOW OTHERS LIVE

M Y FATHER'S WATER WAS COLD, A BRIDGE WALKED WITH SHOES OF STEEL HULLS, WHILE ENEMY SUBMARINES THREADED A NEEDLE OF DETECTION WHOSE EYE, FINALLY, WAS IMPASSABLY SMALL. German submariners died in exorbitant numbers.

Dad's nations were England, France, Belgium, Germany and "I could have gone to Switzerland," the outing he regretted he did not make. England was an old relative. France was picturesque and grateful. Belgium was terrain to be crossed and fought over. Germany was the land of castles, fog, bristling mystery and defeat: the caldera, the ruins and remains after the vulcanism of Hitler and National Socialism. Embarrassed civilians, begging for food. Probably half the women in eastern Germany raped—then often shot—by vengeful Soviet conquerors.

The Americans made conspicuously poor haters, though.

Bill Mauldin: "Perhaps the American soldier in combat has an even tougher job than the combat soldiers of his allies. Most of his allies have lost their homes or had friends and relatives killed by the enemy.... The American has lost nothing to the Germans, so his war is being fought for more farfetched reasons. He didn't learn to hate the

Germans until he came over here. He didn't realize the immense threat that faced his nation until he saw how powerful and cruel and ruthless the German nation was.... So now he hates Germans and he fights them, but the fact still remains that his brains and not his emotions are driving him."

General Dwight D. Eisenhower, Allied Supreme Commander, recognized the problem and ordered mandatory tours of the Nazi concentration camps, to harden G.I. hearts. Toland describes Eisenhower's first camp inspection, at Ohrdruf Nord: "The stink of death was overwhelming even before the Americans passed into the stockade, where some 3,200 naked, bony corpses lay in shallow graves. Others, covered with lice, were sprawled in the streets.

"Bradley was too revolted to speak, and Patton walked off and vomited. Eisenhower, however, felt that it was his duty to visit every section of the camp." Ike insisted, "I want every American not actually in the front lines to see this place. We are told that the American soldier does not know what he is fighting for. Now, at least, he will know what he is fighting against." Disgusted Allied officials forced the town's mayor and his wife to tour the camp. That night they committed suicide. Germany was waking up.

Nazi Germany operated more than 100 major extermination facilities. Patton called them "horror camps." Most were located inside Germany, which was at that time no larger than California.

These camps had many witnesses and many neighbors. They were as characteristic as Germany's castles and housed, in conditions that were never better than brutal, the Third Reich's immense slave labor force. They were organized and operated as "money-making enterprises, feeding profits into the coffers of the SS main office in Berlin." Ohrdruf Nord—the place that made Patton heave—was not large by Nazi standards: at Poland's Auschwitz, a flagship facility, the Schutzstaffel—the SS, a linked whisper, unspeakable, keeper of secrets—eventually murdered 4 million; Treblinka processed 25,000 exterminations every day. Most were Jews.

The total number liquidated in Nazi camps isn't known (records were frequently burned as Allied forces approached); reasonable estimates climb as high as 11 million souls. Jews lead the list of victims, but in 1933 the German parliament had granted Hitler a free hand to deal with those "opposing the racial and spiritual vigor of the German people": this group included large—sometimes huge—numbers of Gypsies; the adult insane; Jehovah's Witnesses (they objected to military service on religious grounds); homosexuals (procreation was an inviolate priority); Communists, Socialists and other leftists; Poles and all other Slavs; political enemies, political hostages, resistance fighters; and used-up foreign nationals no longer worth anything as laborers. And Jews. Deformed and retarded children were starved to death in special hospital wards.

Words fail. The facts themselves sigh, exhausted. Cicadas drill away in summer grass as they would have each year outside the camp wire at Dachau, the oldest camp, constructed in southeastern Germany in 1933, liberated (finally) in 1945. Twelve years. Twelve years of irrefutable proof that authority deserves no one's trust, and that secrets are the enemy of conscience and tolerance. Twelve years of state-sanctioned torture and slaughter: applied bureaucratic and technological evil doing the bidding of hatred and will, turning "your fellow man" and woman and child into soap and fertilizer, recycling their gold teeth into your treasury, keeping their heads shaved because "human hair was especially useful for the manufacture of the special slippers worn by U-boat crews."

As Patton said: horror. There were theories that Germany was an aggressor nation at heart—a simple psychological reduction—and that, therefore, it should be limited to farming after the war; no swords, just plowshares. Political economists soon drove that notion from the door: industrial Europe must be rebuilt!

Alan Bullock: "There are Germans who...argue that what was wrong with Hitler was that he lacked the necessary skill, that he was a bungler. If only he had listened to the generals...or the career diplomats—if only he had not attacked Russia, and so on. There is some point, they feel, at which he went wrong. They refuse to see that it was the ends themselves, not simply the means, which were wrong: the pursuit of unlimited power, the scorn for justice or any restraint on power; the exaltation of will over reason and conscience; the assertion of an arrogant supremacy, the contempt for others' rights.

"The view has often been expressed that Hitler could only have come to power in Germany, and it is true—without falling into the same error of racialism as the Nazis—that there were certain features of German historical development, quite apart from the effects of the Defeat (in World War I) and the Depression, which favoured the rise of such a movement....

"Nazism was not some terrible accident which fell upon the German people out of a blue sky. It was rooted in their history, and while it is true that a majority of the German people never voted for Hitler, it is also true that thirteen millions did. Both facts need to be remembered."

Bullock is not condemning the Germans. He's warning us, putting us on alert, all of us: it can happen here, it can happen there, it can happen anywhere, anytime.

Watch out. It happens because we neglect and don't guard against the all-too-obvious—that "power tends to corrupt and absolute power corrupts absolutely" (Lord Acton, a zealous libertarian); and that hatred joined to power is a recipe for evil: "In speaking of the Nazi movement as a 'party' there is a danger of mistaking its true character. For the Nazi Party was (not) a party, in the normal democratic sense of that word...it was an organized conspiracy against the State...the sole object of the Party was to secure power by one means or another."

Hazel and Tom named their first-born, my sister, after our Aunt Alice, on my father's side.

But they didn't like her.

She was opinionated on a subject where she had no bloody, shitty, stinky experience: child rearing. Unless you generously counted her time with my adopted father, when she was already working, a career woman. Dad was just one more thing in the house to step over.

Aunt Alice carried on a lifelong affair with a married man, my sister said. Taboo and disgusting by the norms of the day. The affair made my aunt damaged goods in Mother's sharply measuring eyes.

But that was the least of it. Mom *really* hated Aunt Alice, sis confided to me over an expensive lunch one half century on, because Alice's businessman lover failed to deliver on a promise: to arrange a college scholarship for my dad. Instead, after the army, Dad worked all his life as a semi-skilled factory hand, making soles for boots. He was in a union; to the good. He was a medium fish in a small pond. He sought and won elected town office in a position so obscure it was almost a caricature: water commissioner.

My aunt's lover *did* deliver on free tickets to big league ball games. The man who dicked her regularly for years owned a sporting goods company. That was all dad got out of the deal.

I don't know if my father wanted to go to college. Mom wanted him to.

She went alone, for years riding a bus evenings into Boston to get her accounting degree.

My sister enthusiastically went.

And I went, with Mom's tiny boot shoved deeply up my ass.

Maybe that was enough for one family. Or one life. Or maybe that wasn't enough. Maybe that was the finish line for her. She had crippling sinus migraines in her last years; like a greengrocer's ax slammed into her skull and wiggled for days. Maybe *that* was enough.

Retirement.

Dad was still robust: white-haired but hale.

He had more than enough money to live. He treated himself every few years to a good used car. Never a Ford, always some General Motors nameplate: Pontiac, Chevy, Oldsmobile. Fords, he said, had "soft engines." I could only imagine.

He moved to Plymouth, Massachusetts. Where the Pilgrims landed in 1620.

In a (then) 350-year-old town, a man in his sixties seemed young.

He reduced his life to the few things he liked: a cup of coffee; a pack of cigarettes always at hand, his nicotine-yellow monkey's paw with long, hard nails and softening flesh; the occasional fried scallops and chips; joking conversation with other men: old men, too; but not as old as he. They hung out on the docks: Irishmen like my Pop, Italians, Poles, Portuguese, Jews, Palestinians, Czechs, Lebanese, whatever washed up who would talk. Pretending they were full-blooded Yankees. Sometimes giving tourists wrong directions for fun.

Plymouth, Massachusetts is an innocuous tourist trap, mostly fabricated, a micro-city with no regional mall close enough to kill the downtown.

Thousands of foreign travelers wheel in each year on guided bus tours to witness a moment in history: when English settlers debarked from a boat, the beginning of the end, the beginning of the beginning, depending on how you lean.

Off the bus: they emerge into sunshine (hopefully (it makes the water sparkle); blinking, testing the pavement, standing before one of Anglo-Saxon America's holiest spots. Everyone flings fried clams at the seagulls. The gulls are sporting. They squirt white feces, like incontinent taps; Plymouth is a town under assault from the air. It was my mother's favorite Sunday afternoon drive. I think that's why my dad landed there. It would be his next-to-last port of call.

Plymouth is amphibious. At low tide, miles of farting mudflats appear. The good replica *Mayflower II* rides the escaping flood like a *Pirates of Penzance* cork, its paint job perky. Across the harbor is a sandy neck washed by the warm effluent of a local nuclear power plant which has, I must report, no proven link to the town's elevated leukemia rate.

Waterside, under a small shrine, sits Plymouth Rock.

It is a mid-sized granite boulder with a large date, 1620, carved into it.

That was the year—on the day after Christmas—when the Pilgrims first set foot in their cold new home; on this very rock, so the story goes. It wasn't really their first step ashore: the Pilgrims picked the Plymouth site after five weeks of scouting the barren beaches of Cape Cod. Even so, they guessed wrong. The soil at Plymouth was unfertile. Massachusetts had lousy soil in general; this was among the worst.

The Pilgrims starved together, terrified that Indians would drive them into the frigid bay. Instead the nearest natives brought venison to the first harvest feast, in 1621; an event now celebrated in the U.S. as the Thanksgiving holiday.

In retrospect, Indians deeply wish they *had* drowned the interlopers. No historian is more understandably cynical than an American Indian. White folk celebrate Thanksgiving because the first colonists survived. The nearest tribes, now fragile remnant populations, commemorate Thanksgiving as a day of mourning. The natives didn't know it. They wouldn't realize it for a few decades. But the end had come. It arrived by smelly sailing ship. Bend over, thank you. And kiss your Indian ass goodbye.

I don't know why *exactly* Dad picked Plymouth.

I can guess. Plymouth, MA was likeable; what's not to? In the winter, *sans* tourists, it was small-towny. Your morning waitress might greet you, "Hello, darlin'," over thin eggs and crispy bacon. Young bucks and their old bulls manned a remnant fishing fleet; parking today's mariners next to yesterday's: a leading America tourist icon, the replica *Mayflower II,* a 17th century vessel faithfully recreated and sailed across the pond in 1957; seized temporarily in 1970 by Russell Means (actor: *Last of the Mohicans*) and other Indian protesters. A heavy-duty, must-see attraction. No brochure credible without it.

Busloads of tourists showed up. Milled around.

Foreigners were plentiful in my father's later years. How many American towns saw thousands of Japanese a year?

So.

The harbor in Plymouth, Massachusetts, U.S.A., had lots to look at; on which to comment; the exotic touch. All ingredients for a happy retirement: one focused mainly on coffee, benches, uninterrupted-except-by-sunset stretches of staring. My dad's loneliness, too. Which smelled like the mudflats.

Maybe years of family Sunday drives to Plymouth made the town special.

Dad became surprisingly widowed. Maybe in his memories he strolled again with his wife through lilac time. Sat on the same seaview park bench in Plymouth where they had stopped once, when the kids were young (i.e., cute). Ate in the same thickly varnished booth in the same favorite family (i.e, grease-indulgent) seafood restaurant. Where he recalled his Hazel's thin arms, her light summer perspiration. She was "his" Hazel for awhile. Around Christmas 1946, he'd just returned, they fucked *with issue:* I was conceived.

Maybe Mom and Dad hoped to move up in the world, to a nicer place. Where farts never existed. To Plymouth, home of the *Mayflower* elite? To happen: when they retired together and made their marriage right again.

Maybe Dad fulfilled that wish, best he could, after my mother's suicide.

By moving, he made a last gift in her—in *their*—honor.

Don't know.

Dad occupied at different times three apartments in Plymouth.

The first was a sterile, below-ground box.

The second was a floor of someone else's home.

The third was in an elderly housing complex he'd connived himself into (he had more savings than they permitted).

TO: All aging children of aging parents in the U.S. This you can expect.

His furnishings were the few things remaining from his hasty house sale. An abridged edition of my childhood home. Throughout in his final home, the elderly housing complex, the floors were linoleum. Linoleum was easy to clean after an accident such as his hemorrhage.

One idea of heaven (for combat veterans, anyway): war

without discomfort.

Real danger, but you're never hurt (be as contradictory as you want; after all, it's heaven: irony holds no sway).

"The sixty seconds I have just described, being among the most eventful of my life...." George MacDonald Fraser. "I turned to see a Jap racing across in front of the bunker, a sword flourished above his head. He was going like Jesse Owens, screaming his head off, right across my front; I just had sense enough to take a split second, traversing my aim with him before I fired; he gave a convulsive leap, and I felt that jolt of delight—I'd hit the bastard!"

No apologies, either. "It was exciting; no other word for it, and no explanation needed, for honest folk. We all have kindly impulses, fostered by two thousand years of Christian teaching, gentle Jesus, and love they neighbour, but we have the killer instinct, too, the murderous impulse of the hunter...."

Yeah.

Tough as the infantry was—and it *was* tough being cannon fodder—it was nowhere near as tough as being old and sick and fighting a losing battle for your independence.

The hemorrhaging ulcer episode: that scared him. Dad had been healthy all his life. Taken it for granted, like a birthmark.

Hospitalization doubly disoriented him. He'd rounded a corner not of his choosing, beyond his control. He knew—*and he knew* we *knew*—that he was no longer altogether sound. His brain did not work right as rain. And the enemies of his personal freedom were circling. They sharpened their pens, eager to sign his privacy away.

He'd cherished anonymity. But he'd been discovered. The puppetmasters this time? Doctors, nurses, social workers, bureaucrats. And family. Family maybe least trusted.

Still, who else was there? If you were ugly, if you were old, if you were ill, if you were purely hateful; well, your family, by Irish-American tribal fiat, still was obliged by ancient code, probably carved into a seaside stone, to care. That was never in doubt.

Dad was on stage.

Through months of slow and uncertain recovery, darkened with relapses.

His injuries were complicated, not easy to fix. He was in the hands of strangers who invaded his fleshy privacy; and were *neither* meticulous nor comforting.

The after-hours horror stories were, and are, legion. Minimum-wage workers in convalescent and nursing homes are not, understandably, faultless angels of mercy. Did you think an adult poopie-diaper was inspirational?

A quick, healthy recovery depended—of course—on Dad's cooperation, which was grudging and neglectful. He would tolerate reminders to take his medicine. Silently. But his eyes said, 'Go to fucking hell, you prick.' He smirked. He was stubborn. He cursed. And in the right pharmaco-logical frame of mind, he'd swing at his oppressors.

You had to laugh. A comment he made a thousand times in his war stories.

Yeah. It's a letdown. As your health starts to fail, this time for good, you discover you were *not* the lucky one in a trillion; you were *not* chosen to be immortal, as you'd always hoped and nine-tenths expected.

New perspective.

Everyone around you now anticipates the worst. Everyone around you will outlive you. Maybe you'll even feel like a failure, if you don't die promptly. Or a burden. That's what family is *truly* for. To make you feel like a piece of broken luggage in countless ways.

Back at his apartment, my father took up all his old privileges. They included driving.

Dad was a menace to vehicular navigation.

He rear-ended some young guy on mainstreet Plymouth, beneath the criss-crossing oaks. The other driver, eager to get home to his 2.5 kids, shrugged off the small dents; I'm guessing because my father was such a shrunken, pathetic wreck.

With the bank, Dad wasn't as lucky. After depositing a Social Security check, in a momentary lapse, he shifted into Drive when he meant Reverse. *Why is the car going forward?* He stunt-jumped a curb and pruned one fluted pillar from the four that braced the bank's portico.

The bank was not in a dismissive mood; not for a small depositor who should never have been driving in the first place. They complained to the town police. The Massachusetts Registry of Motor Vehicles suspended his license.

Dad was cagey. He was an Irish-American politician; even at the local level, thinking two steps ahead came with the job. He had his magic. Somehow, nestled in his wallet were two valid driver's licenses. Dutifully, regretfully, he turned one over to the jackbooted authorities. He gleefully slipped the other out before my eyes. He continued to slide behind the wheel, legal at least on first impressions. Who cared? The bank? In six months, his suspension would lift. He'd be on the road again. *Wheeeee.*

And look out.

CHAPTER 20

ENDIGO

THERE WAS SOMETHING QUEER AND CRUEL ABOUT THE GERMANS FROM WAY BACK.

They were always poor houseguests, with rough manners.

A fourteenth-century writer described the knights he knew: "And when they surrender to each other according to the laws of arms, they treat their prisoners well," (Jean Froissart, in his *Chronicles*), "without pressing too hard for money, behaving chivalrously to one another, which the Germans do not." *The mere thought!* Suddenly Froissart's indignant: "It would be better for a knight to be captured by infidels, out-and-out pagans or Saracens, than by the Germans."

The German problem?

"These constrain gentlefolk in doubly harsh confinements with iron or wooden fetters, chains and other prison instruments beyond all reason and moderation, by means of which they injure or weaken a man's limbs to extort more money.

"To tell the truth, the Germans are in many ways outside all reasonable laws and it is surprising that others will associate with them or allow them to practise arms beside them, as the French and English do. These..." Warming to a parting insult. "...behave chivalrously, and have always done so, but the Germans neither do nor wish to."

Jean Froissart called himself a historian. That was stretching it; he had no rigor. His account of Richard II's downfall, who was a contemporary, isn't even close to the facts. So, shrugs a standard (admiring) biography: "[Froissart] described events with brilliance and gusto ... (but his) highly partisan spirit and disregard for accuracy limit the value of his chronicle as pure history."

For Froissart, a lie was as entertaining as the truth. He commonly passed on hearsay as gospel. He was a Frenchman who hung around the English court. The Germans were outsiders there; easy targets, easy enemies. Outlanders. It didn't matter. He was right in this case: the Germans *were* shocking. They were vicious. Pitiless. They tortured for gain. It wasn't done openly in polite society.

Dad: "The Germans had a great habit, when they were pulling out of a town, of zeroing in one building so they could knock it off five miles away."

Surprise! All dead and accounted for, artillery resulting.

"We were up in France, halfway across. And we had about eight officers with us. We stopped one place, and there was this farmhouse, all by itself.

"Well, these officers go in, spread their maps out on a table, all of a sudden a volley comes in from the Germans, kills the whole eight." Instantly turns the place to bloody dust.

That's it. No more officers. "Here we are, all we got now are sergeants. So what happened? We just went along without them." In the American army, officers were optional. "We got to a crossroad. Fields on one side, woods on the other. The sergeants said, 'We'll put the machine guns in the woods. If anything comes in, they'll go for those fields, and we can blast them.' And what came in?"

Dad laughed.

"A whole German convoy, and the heaviest vehicle in it is a command car. So we opened up with those fifty-caliber machine guns. Everybody started jumping up out of the vehicles, running across the field. We started to mow them down, so they all stopped and gave up. That was fine.

"There's about fifteen hundred in that convoy. There's a chateau a couple of miles up a road there, and it was all walled in. So we marched them up there. Left a few guards with them. Went back to the crossroads, and what do you think happened?

"Forty-five thousand German soldiers came in. And what were they? Old men. They weren't thinking of fighting. They said, 'They gave us a uniform and a gun and said, *You're in the army.*' We marched *them* up to the chateau. Put them in. Went back to the crossroads.

"First thing you know a jeep shows up. With a colonel in it. He said, 'Where's your officers?' We said, 'We haven't got any.' We told him what happened. He said, 'Take any prisoners?'

"'Oh, a few.'

"'Where are they?'

"'Up in the chateau.' 'Well,' he said, 'I'll take a look.'

"Couldn't believe his eyes. There was about forty-six thousand men in there. We had about two companies: three hundred men."

"We had a lieutenant there, up in—what the hell was it: first big town taken in Germany?

"That night we slept in a cellar. This lieutenant was talking, he was showing me pictures of the girl he was going to marry and all that business. He came from New Jersey, and he'd asked to get with a front-line outfit. The next morning, about fourteen or sixteen of us, we went along with this lieutenant. We went up this hill, into this wooded section. The First Division was there."

Aachen was the town. Venerated: Charlemagne had his court there. And it was on German soil. Kraut defenders made it and the "gloomy" Hürtgen forest southeast of it specially ugly. "The advancing troops were butchered," wrote Geoffrey Perret. "The Germans filled the misty forest air with shells armed with instantaneous fuses. Hit a twig, and they'd explode, raining down shrapnel and killing and crippling anyone in the open."

Some days the Americans couldn't even fire back. They were short of ammo. The butcher's bill: one U.S. division in the Hürtgen took 4,500 casualties in just two weeks.

John Ellis: "(Aachen) was ringed with numerous inter-locking concrete bunkers. American commanders seemed to think there was something old-fashioned about such a mode of warfare, and they also underestimated the abili-ties of the garrison—middle-aged German soldiers with abdominal complaints who were contemptuously referred to as 'stomach battalions.' In such strong positions, however, the quality of the troops was of little importance. As an infantryman of the 3rd US Armoured Division remarked: 'I don't care if the guy behind that gun is a syphilitic prick who's a hundred years old—he's still sitting behind eight foot of concrete and he's still got enough fingers to press triggers and shoot bullets.'"

"The First Division was scattered along the ridge of this hill," Dad said.

"We went up there with this lieutenant. No trouble, just walking along.

"We got on top of the hill, and he said to me, 'Dig a hole over here, and we'll call this the C.P.'" Command post. "I said OK. Me and another guy started digging. I turn around to the lieutenant, and I said something. And he said, 'I'm going over here.' I said, 'You better not walk around this woods too much. There could be snipers in here.' 'Oh,' he said, 'there's nothing up here.'

"He and this sergeant we had, the pair of them walked off. The first thing you know we hear this, 'Bing...bing.' The sergeant comes running out. 'What the hell happened?' He said, 'The lieutenant just got it, right through the head.'

"It was three days before they got his body out.

"Of course, these guys in the service, they turn around and nothing means anything to them. They get hardened to everything. One guy come over to me and he said, 'I got the lieutenant out. You want his watch?' I said, 'No, I don't want it.' I couldn't take it. He said, 'Well, you were the guy next to him.' I said, 'Maybe so, but I don't want it.'"

Second lieutenants, percentage-wise, had the highest casualty rate in the Army, higher even than infantry privates. In the average U.S. division, second lieutenants amounted to less than 1% of the personnel; they accounted for almost 3% of the casualties. Statistically, a division could expect to see 100% turnover in second lieutenants, wounded or killed, every three months. Second lieutenants expected bad things to happen. Now you know.

Dad: "We were in this forest, and we weren't doing anything for about a week or so.

"We got this new lieutenant in. He was taking the place of some lieutenant who'd been wounded and was in the hospital. He came in with bags like he was coming into the Astoria; two big bags and here we are in the woods, living in holes.

"When this lieutenant found out he was with a frontline outfit, he acted just like a baby. All he did was cry. Finally, the word came down from headquarters, they wanted to see him. When he came back, oh, he's feeling beautiful, he's happy as a lark: they told him to get his stuff together, they're shipping him back to the rear. He said to the sergeant standing there, 'Gee, hate to leave you, but they're sending me back to the rear. I was wondering if you could give me a hand with the bags. They're going to take me out in a jeep.'

"The sergeant looked at him. He said, 'How'd you get them in here?'

"He said, 'I brought them in.'

"'Well,' said the sergeant, 'you take them back the same way, 'cause I'm not giving you any help.' Sergeant had no use for him. Said, 'That damn crybaby. Get rid of him.'

"Anyway, the lieutenant left four bottles of liquor, officer's rations, so that night, between twelve of us, we had four bottles: scotch, whisky, gin. Everybody was stinko the next morning."

Little-known fact—so little known that one distinguished historian, author of the "best informed study of the fighting man in our time", believed that, in World War II, "the US Army was 'dry', at least insofar as there was no free, official issue of alcohol to either officers or men.": *au contraire, professor*—officers received two free bottles of hard liquor a month, "doled out whether wanted or not."

Dad: "They took over some plant up in Germany, and it was filled with all this liquor. Thousands of bottles.

"Of course, they wouldn't give it to the G.I.s.

"They turned around and made it officer's rations. Every month, an officer got four bottles of liquor. Even when I came home: I was in this camp up in Maryland, and this officer come in this day, and he had a couple of bottles of liquor in his hand.

"We were waiting to ship home. And there's four or five just sitting in the tent, talking, and he came in with two bottles. He said, 'Here, fellows, have a drink on me.' And he left the two bottles and walked out."

"It's a hell of a thing," he spoke.

Flat on his back in a crowded ward at Boston City Hospital, during his first hospitalization, his first episode. This was the start: the road to hell. Tears rolled down his round and fork-furrowed Irish cheeks, into his white stubble. Staff had done the usual perfunctory job of shaving him.

Before he'd ended up here, I had twice seen my father cry.

Now when I visited, salt rime—evaporated tears—crusted the corners of his eyes; he'd finally found something that moved him: his own sorry state.

"It's a hell of a thing getting old," he confided to me,

bathed in antiseptic air and fluorescent light, parked in the middle of a ward, like a car left for a moment by someone running into a shop.

I thought: it's a hell of a thing to see your father's penis hanging out like a, bleached, unthriving zucchini; the zucchini rototilled back into nutritious fibers, back into the soil, unloved, unlamented.

His penis was as public as his nose. After all these years.

The inseminator. Revealed.

I began as a spurt from this flagging, flagon, flesh.

A modest, body-shy family raised me.

I hadn't seen my father's penis since it hadn't mattered. I was probably six.

In the hospital, I forced myself to look. To be clinical.

Taped to Dad's old, shaggy thigh was a thin catheter tube. Urine threaded through it.

Puke.

Incapacitation—"I *am* a sack of potatoes"—was so sad after all my father's years of fine, upstanding health—and *despite the standard dose of realism that comes to all families eventually*—a surprise.

Finally, more than four decades after the war, I could see that he was seriously wounded.

Best stinko tale from the European Theater of Operations:

A U.S. armored spearhead under Lieutenant Colonel Walter Richardson thrust over 100 miles into German territory on March 29, 1944, smashing through roadblocks untouched: an unprecedented advance for a single day. Only fog and gathering darkness slowed them down, and Richardson got out of his jeep with a flashlight, to walk ahead and guide the column.

John Toland: "The tanks, their lights shielded by blue tissue, rumbled behind, getting closer and closer. Richardson walked faster but the first tank kept gaining on him. When it nudged him in the back, he jumped aside and jogged across the road into the ditch. Like a faithful dog, the tank followed Richardson into the ditch. He scrambled back on the road and waved his flashlight frantically, but the tank continued to bear down on him. Now he could see the second and third tanks wobbling back and forth in a clumsy effort to follow the leader. Finally, in answer to his signals, the first tank stopped with a lurch. There was a loud clank as the second tank banged into the rear of the first and, a moment later, two more metallic thuds."

Angrily, Richardson climbed aboard. "What in hell is going on?"

The floor of the first tank was awash with champagne, the commander drunk, alcohol fumes chortling out of the turret. Same thing in the next tank. And the next. Units investigating Brilon, the last city they'd passed, had discovered a warehouse full of champagne. Richardson's whole fighting column was stiff on bubbly, a hundred miles inside enemy lines. Toland: "At midnight he again checked his speedometer and found that he had gone 109 miles—and his only casualties were hangovers."

It was a giddy time.

Prisoners arrived in lots of a hundred thousand.

The entire country, the world's Terror Central, cowed in

just four months.

Dad: "We were the spearhead. They had these roads. And all they had was one bar across them. We'd go right down the road and take the bar with us. *Rarrrr!* What's that to a tank? Just one pole? *Boom!* They'd take it right off its hinges. And we'd keep rolling.

"Well, we're way past the Siegfried line"—the common name for the West Wall, Germany's western frontier fortifications—"and we get a call from the outfits coming up in back of us. *'The Germans are back in the pillboxes.'* We'd gone through without any opposition. Now they said, 'You've got to give these outfits in back of you some help, because they can't get through. The Germans are in the pillboxes, and they're opening up with machine guns.'

"So we went back. And we're walking along in back of the pillboxes, putting hand grenades down the ventilators, putting them out of business.

"It was just as easy as that. They couldn't do anything. You're in back of them, and all their guns were pointed one way."

Great business parable, that. *Why did we fail? All our guns were pointed one way.*

CHAPTER 21

DON'T KNOW

T HAT'S THE THING.

The business of the world is business.

Get old? Hope you reside in a culture that reveres its elders.

When you leave the game, you're ridiculous.

The future? The future looks a lot like the past.

Strivers find the sunny spots. The rest? Wonder. Die.

Once Dad broke his hip, events moved quickly.

In July, the hospital in Plymouth discharged him into a local nursing home, which didn't want him. New cars smell like new cars; and nursing homes—almost all—smell like nursing homes: a noticeable but faint odor of mopped-up urine and disinfectant swill.

Human nostrils flare involuntarily; it's the smell of the wild.

You look like a snob. The staff resents it, just so you know.

Dad was a scribble of himself. He was in a small ward, stuck in a bed, a bare leg cooling outside the sheets, his privacy gone. I examined his bare flesh. White parchment hung from a hairless limb that had once been luxuriantly hairy. His muscles were out of work, retired, dying actually.

The man in the next bed tried to find something nice to say about my father. It wasn't much. Dad's mental abilities weren't praiseworthy anymore.

The nursing home wasn't my first stop.

I had a life ... of sorts.

Earlier I had been at the unemployment office, picking up a check—the first of twenty weeks of coverage I could pray to, at one-fifth my former salary.

It was a stifling July day. I was in a dark summer-weight wool suit; a copper plaid, nicely tailored, obviously expensive. An artifact of my old job. I drove—bounced—two hours in a pickup truck with no A/C to arrive in Plymouth, ready to battle. Presumably.

Perspiration covered me like warm onion dip.

My face was a Halloween mask; of worry, shame, hate, fear, anger, pain, hopelessness. As I drove downtown, I stretched my forehead, to loosen the hardening scowl. Dad's bank in Plymouth—the one he'd de-pillared the year before—was giving me trouble over a three-year-old power-of-attorney.

I needed a shot of self-confidence, no matter how artificial. The wool suit would do.

The world sees the suit, not what's inside. Inside I was racing laps on Panic Speedway.

The bank, it turned out, was the least of my problems; easily fixed with a phone call to a lawyer. The bigger problem was Dad's eviction.

His neighbors had ratted him out. He'd always suspected

they would; since he was a child. In a housing complex for the elderly, there was no shortage of spying eyes, prying eyes, vindictiveness. The autorité bureaucratique du jour, the Plymouth Housing Authority, wanted him gone—*for his own good,* they insisted; their facial expressions set like little barricades. They were *sure* he was no longer capable of caring for himself. That he was *dangerous* to himself and others.

My sister and I, though, used a different yardstick. We hoped to see him recover. The people sitting in judgment assumed his failings would only get worse. Dad's housekeeping and personal grooming, we dithered at them, *were never that great to begin with.* Our defense: he was always a slob.

They were right. We weren't. Dad was experiencing systemic collapse.

At first I thought I had a starring role in an archetypal struggle. I was determined not to let *someone* down. Don't know who: my mother probably, some family member looking down from heaven, where the Protestants had one side of the stadium and the Catholics had the other, maybe Aunt Doe who'd set the great example taking care of grandma and drunk, abusive Uncle Johnny. It was my turn. My turn to express the ideology: family comes first. We go to any wall for family. Blood matters; even adopted blood, like my father's.

The premise, the expectation: that those in authority cared nothing about the individual.

I expected abuse of power; an "us vs. them" attitude; the weak (him) resisting the strong (them); the statistical likelihood of his steady decline vs. a longing for just a little more happiness. But paradise had slipped from Dad's grasp, I soon saw.

The washers in his faucets had worn away: he wet his pants or defecated sometimes while he walked. The housing authority reported him arriving home more than once with a pee stain engulfing the crotch of his trousers, flooding darkly toward his knees.

His apartment, I knew, was a reeking mess. He chased away the hired housekeepers, convinced they were stealing from him. He kept decades of clothing folded in piles on his bed, up to the ceiling. The only things that went into his mouth: cigarettes, coffee, heated cans of soup. That, and the few pills he didn't forget or neglect to take.

I'd seen it coming of course.

I drove up to visit twice or three times a year. It took me months to feel guilty enough to phone and make a date.

And it was always the same. Which was exactly as we wanted it. When you're wary, predictability is good. We'd go out for fried scallops and sit through a stupefied meal, serving our sentence together. He smoked. In a nod toward rising health concerns in the media, he'd switched from unfiltered Camels to filtered Merits. He pushed a few bites of golden-fried seafood and fries into his lined, badly shaved lips. White, silver and black bristles stuck out like antennae on a Mars lander, especially at the corners of his mouth, the hardest to shave tucks, as two decades later I now know.

Dad was resigned. I was resigned. We ate. We passed ketchup.

Dad knew exactly what a retired person's responsibilities

were.

He got himself up. He was clothed when he went out the door. That was all he felt he owed the world. He was uncontrite, alone, stubborn as a thorn, and contemptuous of therapies.

Hopeless, basically.

And now he couldn't pay what he owed—he owed cleanliness, he owed competence, he owed a bright-enough mind—and world was going to do with him whatever it wanted. He was in the devil's paws, minus whatever his children could negotiate. It was like buying a prison sentence. We even shopped around.

"Do you want to go out for a smoke?" I asked him.

I had stopped at a convenience store for a pack of his cigarettes and a lighter.

"Sure," he said. It came out a croak, like a rusty chain dragged up a rusty throat.

He wore almost nothing; pajamas they'd found for him. I was his first visitor; I don't know when he'd entered the hospital.

I went looking for a wheelchair and complained to the duty nurse about the heat.

She told me they couldn't air condition the wards because the elderly go and catch pneumonia if they do. "They always say they're too cold anyway," she promised me.

An orderly hauled Dad into a wheelchair. I pushed him out of the ward. The entry was flanked by other patients, oriented toward the light and escape, if only. We were in the Speedwell Nursing Home, named for the second vessel into

Pilgrim Plymouth. The nursing home was part of a chain; it had the feeling of an absentee operation, answering to some distant bottom line, its compassion rigidly defined by state regulations.

Fox-hunting prints, powder-blue trim, plated-brass chandeliers decorated the halls and public rooms: bland, inoffensive, facile, pretend-upscale, insincere, and reassuring. Linoleum tile covered most floors. It cleaned up better than carpet, as residents leaked pee.

I read an activities schedule for residents. Nothing there would challenge a four-year-old.

I wheeled Dad outside for his smoke, into the steam heat. Stripped the cellophane off the pack of Merits and handed it to him. His fingers weren't moving properly, though. I had to help him pry out a cigarette. I lit it for him.

He smoked from memory.

He didn't seem to enjoy it much. Not the way he had when I was a kid and the Friday night fights were on TV and picking a shred of tobacco off his tongue looked like all the pleasure you needed in this world.

I wasn't nostalgic. Nor was he.

He was afraid. I was afraid; of different things.

Dad: "I don't know if it was six or seven or eight or something prisoners. The sergeant was going to march them down to a schoolhouse where they were collecting prisoners. And this guy come along, he said, 'Where you going?' 'Down the schoolhouse.' 'Ah,' he said, 'I'll take them down for you.' So the sergeant let him. And the guy shot them. The sergeant said, 'What the hell did you do that for!' 'Well,' he said, 'I didn't want to walk down there.'

"But it makes it tough for you. Cause then the Germans say, 'Oh, boy, I'll put up a good battle before they get me.' That gave our outfit a bad reputation. They wouldn't surrender to us. They'd go down below and surrender to another outfit. They knew we were up there. They'd tell you right over the radio what outfits were up there. No, if you treat them right, taking prisoners...I don't know how it gets back to their main supply, but it gets back, that you treated them half decent."

He would answer questions, but he wasn't much of a conversationalist anymore. He rambled. One suspicious doctor ran a CAT scan. The scan showed that Dad's brain had shrunk. Not to the size of a walnut. But it was clearly loose in his skull, like one olive-oiled cauliflower floret sliding around in a bowl.

We had argued a bit; me in a hard office chair, my sister in spirit (she wasn't able to come); with the housing authority, proposing a trial period back in his own apartment.

They were better informed than us about his true condition. These weren't bureaucrats; they were sensors. Roberta Hawkins, a true friend, there in an emergency, Rhode Island's top advocate for elderly rights, came with me.

She met Dad. After which she accepted the official view.

At the hearing, he sat in his wheelchair, teeth out like a drawer yanked from a bureau. His cranium was larger at every visit because his body was shrinking; he was back to his junior high school weight. He was vague: his responses ricocheted in from nowhere near the question.

I had the nursing report in my lap: "Patient is frequently

incontinent of urine." The first thing Roberta had done was bend down close to smell him: they were keeping him clean enough. "Needs supervision of all care due to disorientation. Problems with increased confusion cause him to be unable to follow directions. Frequently he attempts to walk without assistance and this is a safety problem. He is unable to maintain balance without support even for a few seconds. Decreased endurance and strength—unable to participate in treatment for more than 15 minutes. Self-care—completely dependent on another person to provide this. It is the recommendation that Mr. Ahearn," misspelled, but he wouldn't know the difference, "is not safe or physically able to live alone. He requires 24-hour assistance and even with a large home-care component he would continue to be at risk for injury. The therapists treating him cannot in our professional judgment recommend discharge to community."

Want to call it irony, go ahead.

My father became a prisoner of war at the ripe old age of 78. After all those years, captured by the enemy. Condemned to a nursing home. Among a population of people categorized by their problems, he was reduced to one alarming phrase, "incontinent of feces." *Danger! Danger! He could blow at any moment!* His bowel movements were unreliable, his bottom diapered. Walk and poop. Poop on the fly.

His age earned him nothing except contempt. "They" (the system, whatever) heaped indignities on him casually. He was, in their obvious view, a weed. About to be pulled. Forced to endure persistent humiliation, a total loss of control over what he could and could not do. His independence and privacy were nuisances, to be stripped and scrubbed away.

He ended up gaunt, shabby, poorly groomed; his face had more long white whiskers than a cat's. He no longer acted, he was acted upon: warehoused, marginalized (lovely word), living among the discarded coats, not in the human story anymore; unresponsive; fighting to reach the surface; losing touch; his body failing, his faculties unreclaimable. Useless to the species. *Dead*, if he'd just admit it.

My sister and I were somewhere around, but—spies! turncoats!—we worked for the other side. His own family had turned against him. Now what?

Like other POWs, he kept his hopes alive with the idea that rescue was on the way, that either I or my sister, Alice, would take him in. We had no intention. Yet we encouraged him. Never actually said we wouldn't. For his part, chief of Old Age Strategic Command, Dad dropped unmistakable hints. "If I could just stay with you, Tom...," he would speculate.

We couldn't. He couldn't. He needed serious medical attention and chronic care. He needed cleaning. You couldn't hold a coherent conversation with him. He ate from cans, like a cat. He was an untrimmed specimen with false teeth. In his coffin, at his wake, he'd want a last cigarette: "My only pleasure," he assured everyone. He *loved* smoking. And some day he'd burn the house down around him. He was a fire hazard. And he shat bowling pins. The last time Dad had visited, his typical prodigious bowel movement caused the first floor toilet, our most capacious, to overflow.

I could deal with that once; not on a daily basis.

Frankly, honestly, ultimately: we didn't want him.

The ride to his first nursing home sucked. It took for *fucking* ever. Round trip: six hours if my sister did it, four hours for me.

The Speedwell nursing home was a chicken coop anyway. It was shelter for people who had no choice. It wasn't even a chicken coop: no one here laid eggs. Nice enough, in a Motel 6 sort of way. But my sister and I wanted him someplace nicer. And a whole lot closer.

We moved him from the Speedwell.

He sat in a chair by the nurses' station. My diary: "He is weary, bored, scared, and depressed."

The station was the town square. Besides Dad, the nurses and aides, there were five others: all women, all in wheelchairs. One of them had legs that ended a few inches below her crotch. She was—most of the women were—tied to the wheelchair with a sash. There were state laws, I soon learned, restricting how and with what you could tie a person to a wheelchair; presumably because at some point such laws became necessary.

One by one staff departed. They pushed the other chairs off to supper. They left to feed a hundred people with assorted dementias, incontinence, blindness, amputations, arthritis, and adamantine likes and dislikes.

The station emptied, became an empty stage, with my father and I, sitting side by side in chairs, watching, pushing the conversational rock back and forth. A woman wandered through, chased at a distance by an aide. "Emma," the aide called, directing, "go right." Emma immediately veered left. The aide caught up and took Emma's arm and led her back on course.

Dad smiled. *Maybe this was a joke. Maybe Emma went left on purpose.* My father liked to fool people. We debated more than once whether his mental fog was some kind of daddy joke; or a defense; or an attempt to control things when things were no longer quite inside his reach.

None of those things.

It was plain, old-fashioned, let's-admit-it intellectual collapse. The tool in his head was worn and feeble. He forgot the names of simple things like "fork" or "car" or "scallops," the only seafood he tolerated. He stuttered. He substituted words freely. It was a sort of universal language: everything was a synonym for everything else: "I went to see the...the...the thing, you know...the...restaurant. Not the restaurant, but the...the.... What's the word?"

"Ballgame?"

"Ballgame. Right."

Tonight, as dinner murmurs down the linoleum hall, he knows he's not returning to his apartment. He knows why: because a circle of social workers and family got together and declared him physically and mentally incapable of living by himself.

He's surrounded. Cut off. Behind enemy lines.

My sister and I are part of that enemy now, cruel because we're lazy, stupid because we're ineffective and can't restore his freedom. Light in his eyes? We gave him up without a fight. At least that's how I feel in my darker moments. Dad has no doubt. He's the victim. But then he never expected much of family; orphans don't.

"And that's what waiting for all of us," I say.

I have two clients whose business is elder care. I see what happens to people.

"Unless we die first," my wife comments.

"Amen."

We've had the discussion many times: *pull the fucking plug*. My wife's perspective: her father had the largest personality on the planet; fierce, untamed. Declared healthy and fit at his annual checkup, he left for his native France at age 58 to visit family and old friends. And died three months later of so much never-detected cancer that nothing inside him worked anymore.

I believe in the right to die when you please. I do not believe in the eternal verity of any governmental policy. The first presidential candidate in America who declares she or he would rather die (painlessly, ecstatically) at the time and place of their own choosing, will (1) not win; and (2) go down in history. We have 310 million people in the U.S. in 2010. We expect to have 420 million in 2050, four decades later. Surely, that's enough. Some few thousand right-to-diers won't be missed.

I expect the abortion-rights battles in my lifetime to be eclipsed by the suicide-rights battles. Consumers will demand new and improved termination experiences. And corporate Christianity, which has made a fortune on prolonged suffering, will have another huge fight on its hands.

Dad called them, "Dee pees." A bird chirp: deepee, deepee, deepee. Years later, in college, I learned that D.P.s were Displaced Persons, official shorthand for the uprooted millions wandering middle Europe immediately after the war.

Dad: "You should see the trains coming in. They're hanging off the sides of even the locomotive. They're going from one town to another, trying to get something to eat. Jumping a train no matter where it went. And stay on it, pull into a town, get off and rummage around, trying to get food from the G.I.s. It was a mess.

"One day there, there was bunch of G.I.s in a room, in this college, and they were playing poker. And this German came in, a German civilian.

"Course, they were all civilians then; if they had a uniform, they hid it. But he came in, and pulled a German pistol out of his pocket. And he wants to sell it.

"These guys are sitting at a table. One guy put up his hand: 'Let me look at it.' So the German gave it to him. The guy looked at it, said, 'Pretty good.' And he shoved it in his pocket. And the German started...."

Dad made a loud complaining noise, a rapid bark-and-quack.

"He wants to get paid for it! And the G.I. looked at him: 'Get the hell out of here before I knock your head off.'

"He didn't know what to do. He got the hell out of there. But he lost the gun."

Dad: "We were up in a town called Charleroi, up in Belgium. I used to have charge of a warehouse. They had a couple of thousand German prisoners there, and every morning I'd get about fifteen prisoners, and they go up to the warehouse with me.

"It was a big yard, and there was a lot of scrap lumber in the place. So one of these officers, he got the German prisoners together one day. They were sleeping on straw on the floor of a warehouse, see.

"He said, 'Any of you fellows are carpenters, and you want to build yourself a bunkbed instead of laying on this straw,' he said, 'there's plenty of lumber out there, and we'll give you all the nails you want.' He said, 'Go ahead and build it. It's alright with us.'

"Well, I got one of these prisoners, see, one morning there, and he could talk a little English. And he come over to me and he's telling me how he just built a bunkbed, how nice he built it and all, with this scrap lumber. I said, 'What do you want from me?' He said, 'I was wondering if you could get me some pin-up pictures.' Well, honest ... I started to laugh."

By the time I got to Dad's apartment, my sister had finished sorting and packing his things. Getting rid of what she could: where he was headed, he wouldn't need a braided rug or a sofa or a dining room table or a recliner or his own bed or a coffee table or a cabinet filled with knick-knacks or a desk where he could pay his bills. The Salvation Army had been by with a truck. Why not? Dad thought Salvation Army was OK.

Alice was watching TV. She sat on a folding chair, pretty much the only furniture left, smoking a cigarette, an ashtray in her lap. I recognized it from my childhood. It was Dad's kitchen ashtray, the one that got the heaviest use.

"This is it?" I asked her.

By the door was his suitcase and a plastic trash bag, both stuffed with clothes. The suitcase was small, inexpensive, covered in russet leather. He'd had his initials—T.F.A.—stamped in gold beneath the handle.

The apartment looked larger and impersonal again, ready to close in around the next life. The blinds, always drawn, today were open on an insipid *(bad mood)* September sky, cool robin's egg blue, torn cotton dabs of cloud, the trees out back still fleshed with leaves. That happened near the ocean. Tempered the frosts. Leaves hung on.

His exhaust had redecorated the place: the bare walls were lion-tawny with a decade of Dad's unceasing cigarette smoke. There were a few patches of lighter-colored wall where something had hung, like his framed map of Irish family names.

Why did *that* interest him? Had he finally adopted his adoptive family? Or did he really, secretly, press a finger against the glass, searching out the Scanlon clan, the surname of his biological parents, wondering *what if?* Or both.

He was bi-familial. A bi-breed. A tri-breed, really: his adoptive family had been close (in their way); the family he'd married into, the McKays, had been close (in their ways, some not recommended; chasing each other for money got ugly more than once, in a high school stage farce sort of way).

"I left the stuff in the closet for you," Alice said. Her temperature never varied more than a degree. She had two moods: disgust, and the rest of the time. She hadn't acted disgusted with me for a decade, since Simone (wife and super-hero) set my sister straight on a few misunderstandings lingering from childhood that were no longer true nor relevant. I went to the closet to peek: a hand vacuum, a broom, a box of tissues. Dad's tool chest.

"These, too."

She handed me two of my high school yearbooks.

An emotional tornado cut through me. I'd hated high school. Dad had held onto my yearbooks for twenty-five years. The yearbooks – inside a few photos of me as an athlete, as a trumpet player of slightly better than average caliber, with a list of activities – portrayed me as a lad of promise and substance, always young and on his way.

Dad didn't keep all that much as he moved around after my mother's suicide. But he kept these. My estimation of him melted like a pat of butter on hot corn. "He's more sentimental about the past than I am," I told her.

"You're right. He was very sentimental," Alice said, shocking the shit out of me. A thing I completely did *not* know about him. I hadn't read the signs well, of course: Why tell stories over and over *if you're not sentimental?*

I never tried to learn about him. I owed him that, I think. Regrets are the truths we finally tell ourselves. I never tried very much with him; being a selfish son came more easily, almost from the start. I would always be younger than him. My mother, his bride, liked me better. By a furlong. He would always be verging on irrelevance to me, unless I needed a little cash. What's wrong with sentimental, anyway? Sentimental gets a lot of good done. I merely wish I were worthy. And now he's in my hands.

I opened his toolbox, expecting it to be a diary of sorts.

A man's tool box? What does that tell you about him? It tells you about the chores he attempted. About the projects he wanted to do. About the kinds of emergencies he antic-ipated in his life. There was an unopened roll of plumb-er's tape. Dad expected his plumbing might spring a leak apparently. Cheap trope: *It just wasn't the house that gave way, that blew gaskets, that flooded the floors: it was his mind.*

There was a three-prong conversion plug. There were dozens of screws unscrewed, heads frosted hard-shut with old paint, stored in a jar; someday to return to rightful holes. A good children's book in that idea? Children's books, turns out, are easy to write – when you don't have to actually pick up a pen, found a sheet of paper, and write one of the little buggers. In his 70s, Dad wrote a children's book in his head; he wanted me to put it on the page. A raccoon starred; Ricky, I believe. Helpful but mischievous animal. The story? Gee, I don't know.

In the bottom of the tool chest was a replica antique fire plate I remembered from my childhood. When fire departments were private and belonged to insurance companies, these plates identified the houses that could be saved by a particular fire crew. He'd sold the house and took that plate with him. I think Dad saw it as a vestige of the ways, the bad ways, things used to be. Before the Democrats. When you had to pay for your safety and your place. Before unions came along and organized labor to fight back.

He didn't hang the plate again. Why bother? It was a memento of my mother; something they'd bought together somewhere inside a long married life, and in the same confined house. She loved antiques. A low-grade form of snobbery, by one lame measure. Indulged by him. Casual racism was his snobbery.

It didn't extend far. Dad was racist-lite. Short. An orphan. Irish when the Irish were as hated as weeds. He never attended college, which had become the new standard for achievement in America by the time I came along (1947). The G.I. Bill went and upped the bar.

Am I critical?

I am a consultant. At my current billing rate, I earn a full year's minimum-wage salary every eight days. Frankly, I have so many people to thank, I don't know where to start.

Never again. The toolbox had been a promise to *do* things, to *right* domestic wrongs. Now: just a small steel box rattling with regrets. Dad, though technically alive at this moment, would never see this apartment (his life as a Plymouth dock-rat) again. He would never again rummage among his accumulated tools and nostrums; planning, coping, improvising, looking for something *that would do.* He would never again own anything that required fixing, except himself; and *he couldn't be fixed!* That therefore thankless chore would go to strangers who would maintain him in exchange for money, mostly at minimum-wage. His life as a simple commodity was about to begin.

We loaded the television into my car. I planned to set it up for him when he'd settled into his final nursing home. He had a surprise for us, though.

My father had seen a slice of the world while he was away fighting World War II.

"Anybody in uniform could travel free. You could jump on any train or any subway, and it didn't cost you anything."

I'm here in a strange land. Most people act as if we're demi-gods just because we're Americans. I theoretically could get shot any day. And I am making a considerable personal sacrifice.

Hit the road. "I had got a furlough, and I was in Belgium. And I took the express from London to Glasgow. That damn thing goes about a hundred miles an hour. And I was sleeping. There was only myself and another G.I. in one of the compartments. So he was sleeping on one seat, and I was sleeping on the other. Three o'clock in the morning the conductor came through to wake us up, tell us Roosevelt died.

"Boy, that man was liked, now I'm telling you.

"And they're saying," the Brits, "'What are you going to do now? What are you going to do with your president dead?'

"I said, 'Well, we're lucky, we always have a good man to take his place.' And Truman took his place. Truman will go down in history in my estimation as one of your best presidents. He dropped the bomb, but as Truman said, 'I'd do it again to save ten thousand men.'" My father, of course, never knew a President George W. Bush or a Vice President Dick Cheney. Those two would have ruined my father's "always a good man to take his place" theory. Truman and Roosevelt set a high standard. *We like Ike.* The Kennedys. Bobby never had his chance. Reagan. Clinton? Clever, when humility would have worked better. A preening stud with a gifted mind. History's a comedy when it's not a disaster.

John McDonough, fifty years later: "Was the (dropping of the atomic) bomb an act of vengeance, as the revisionists insist? ...(Here) the revisionists may have something. Vengeance was a perfectly appropriate response in World War II. In fact, if a country doesn't hate its enemy in wartime, it is probably fighting the wrong war. Of all the signs warning us away from Vietnam, maybe the most fundamental was an absence of visceral hatred for the North. A war is no better than its villain.

"Vengeance, like it or not, is also part of the emotional process of closure. World War I ended before a shot was fired on German soil. So the allies took their vengeance at the peace table and set the stage for World War II. The final surrender of Japan, like that of Germany, handed history a rare luxury: an opportunity to rebuild on a clean slate."

Twenty years on, Alice sold a small manila envelope she'd picked up that valedictory day. The envelope contained Dad's gold fillings. Around the age of 50, he'd had all his teeth removed and dentures installed; he was tired of the pain. The envelope held the valuable leftovers: the gold, some still attached to teeth. "They grossed me out," Alice said. When the gold market went crazy in 2008, she sold the envelope and sent me a check for half the proceeds, $65. She took half, she gave me half. Alice is a straight shooter. The realized sum at that moment was maybe worth one tank of gas for my Honda hybrid. It was the principle of the thing. And Dad was grossing her out.

War works. Some, anyway.

Despite President Franklin Delano Roosevelt's mild taps to the general morale, his demonstrations that Washington really *did* care, the Great Depression was alive and quite well in 1934. And for years after. In 1938, many Americans were near starvation. More than half the states had laws by then to keep out other unemployed workers: you couldn't travel if you didn't have a job.

It was the war that finally got the engine revving again.

CHAPTER 22

BETRAYAL

Here's a story for you.

In a corner of our living room, growing up, was a small table.

It was round and red-dark; with two dainty, polished shelves.

A milk-glass candy dish sat on the smaller, top shelf. Over the Christmas season the dish rustled with butterscotch hard candy in bug-light-yellow cellophane. You could hear fingers herding candy from the other room.

This was our "Don't touch!" table.

Each tender, mahogany toe wore a little brass shoe. The second, mostly ignored shelf, displayed my parents' few treasures: glass paperweights; figurines; fancy never-used ashtrays; and one photo, on the table's bottom shelf. I don't remember whose likeness it was: some relative, probably Uncle Johnny, who lived next door. If so, it was a reminder that he had once been a handsome, happy-go-lucky fellow and not just an out-of-control drunk.

My sister Alice beckoned me over. She slid the hard easel backing out of the bright brass frame. There was another, smaller photo hidden inside, a snapshot, which she handled gingerly. And revealed to me in her palm. It captured a bursting white man in his late twenties; smiling, prosperous, confident, and wearing a suit and tie back when ties meant something.

"That's the man Mom could have married," Alice confided, giggling; like this was a great practical joke on our Dad. OK: I was thrilled she was trusting me. The face in the photo meant zero. He was a coulda, not a did. He must have meant something to my mother, though; she kept him nearby for years, hidden in the living room, eavesdropping on every family conversation, a secret lover-to-be, her better option, *if only*. The photo seemed to sigh: *Here is the man I should have married, if only I'd known.* Who knows: *If only I'd put out.* Maybe that. My mom had narrow, nutcracker thighs. And she was on fire.

Alice reassembled the photo frame, slipping Mr. Right once again into hiding. She carefully propped Uncle Johnny back on the shelf, in exactly the same spot in the dust. More precise than Einstein. Putting things back undisturbed was an important survival skill for kids.

"Don't tell," my sister turned and solemnly warned me.

Don't touch, don't tell. We all now shared a family secret: Dad was a disappointment to Mom. Childhood went into reverse.

On February 23, 1945, Dad wrote a postcard to my mother.

The European war was in its final weeks—not a walk yet, and certainly not a run; but seven American Army corps, at least 300,000 U.S. combat soldiers, could say with all honesty that they stood on German soil, an armed intrusion indescribably heinous and bitter to a people who regarded their destiny, their sovereignty, their racial purity with mystical awe. I question whether the Germans have ever gotten over this, but I've done no research.

The postcard shows a Parisian street, with the characteristic plane trees and Second Empire stone apartment buildings. And the scrawl says:

Honey Honey; This is where all the expensive shops are. Maybe we could see it together some day.

Tell me *that* message doesn't shrink your perineum. *Never to be!* Knowing what you *now* know, dear reader. The printed legend on the back of the postcard says: PARIS ET SES MERVEILLES, La Rue de Rivoli. *Paris and its marvels.*

The closest my parents got to Paris was Canada.

We drove one summer to Quebec. A family car trip that long was a lesson in practical physics, demonstrating forcefully, with every repetitive mile, the concept of eternity without parole.

I wore my boredom like a shroud.

At my mother's insistence, we visited, as we did wherever my family traveled, the major religious attractions, including the shrine of Ste Anne de Beaupré.

I experienced my own spiritual crisis this trip. My first panic attack (of eventually many). A gullible and sensitive child, I reeled in hallucinating horror out of Quebec's wax museum and stood gasping in the historic gutters while Dad tried to comfort me.

Modris Eksteins: "A common feeling among soldiers

was that their experience at the front had created an insurmountable barrier between them and civilians. Communication with home was no longer possible. People simply could not understand what the soldiers had been through, and the soldiers themselves could not articulate their experience appropriately."

He's talking World War One, but no matter. Things only improved a bit with the Second World War. The journalists were more honest about the combat experience. Less government-sanctioned propaganda, maybe; more reporting. America was proud of its citizen soldiers. Cartoonist Bill Mauldin was with the 45th Division: "I'm convinced that the infantry is the group in the army which gives more and gets less than anybody else. I draw pictures for and about the dogfaces because I know what their life is like and I understand their gripes." He died for that opinion. Ernie Pyle, "the first correspondent to make the common soldier his subject," may he rest in honor, was killed by Japanese machine-gun fire. This was embedded before there was a term *embedded*; foxhole-embedded. He died for that particular story; a national treasure. "I can't be funny about the war," he said. "The only way I can try to be a little funny is to make something out of the humorous situations which come up even when you don't think life could be any more miserable." Nursing homes must have been different back then; just saying.

My father spent a lifetime trying to describe the war; was always willing to answer. He was inspired by it, by all of it. It had elevated him: he was a G.I., along with 7.5 million others. He stood, therefore, on a pedestal; which got shorter as fewer and fewer people knew or heard or learned the history. It got shorter in his grass shack because he did not go to college on the G.I. Bill, as my mother would have wished.

The pedestal had a half-life in the next generation; and no life at all in the one after that, because granddads don't look like warriors and grandkids consider all old wars the same: a question they will flunk on an exam.

A moment of pity, therefore. Feel free to light a candle. *We* do, wherever we happen to be in France. Every village chapel has a box of matches and a coin slot. There's almost always a candle burning. It's a pious, mystical country, much visited by saints.

My personal saint?

Dad, now in the dual clutches of a health care bureaucracy (at the strategic level) and a profit-seeking nursing home (at the tactical level).

He had helped save the world from fascist enslavement, outfought old Europe, been one of 7.5 million beacons of hope. This would be the largest hero class, after the Soviets, ever created. Much good it did him.

I had several girlfriends whose poop holes smelled of cigarette smoke. My favorite girlfriends. Their back ends smelled familiar.

I grew up in a smokers' home. My father was a chimney all his life. My mother quit late. We were raised in a smoky den. I don't know if that explains anything. Smoke made my asthmatic lungs seize. I saw it as an enemy. But coming out a young woman's asshole? Different. Exotic. Romantic. Feral. *Yum.* A lot of things were yum where sex was involved.

My father never saw a concentration camp like Auschwitz,

which was in Poland far beyond where the American line stopped.

After all, things got a little hectic toward the end. Sixty-one days after U.S. forces crossed the Rhine—Germany's most formidable natural defense in the west and its last significant psychological barrier—the war was over. Total defeat. Total surrender. A ferocious government wiped from the earth.

It is ironic, though hardly uncommon, that he landed in a concentration camp himself at the end of his life. Fate has nothing good in store for any of us, I suspect; prove me wrong.

You never know.

When you're 78.

A home away from home.

Consider the semantics. In a confidential whisper that begs for understanding, you—the adult caregiver, a son or daughter now being exchanged for professional, 24-hour care—are told—gently, come closer—to realign your preconceptions: "Here we call them residents."

Or "guests." Guests is good. An attempt to reverse polarity, to empower the failing. To give them a home where the buffalo roam. Noble.

Or whatever euphemism offers some distance from the probability that most patients will stay in this new location, this concentration camp; i.e., a place where we concentrate certain types of people, out of the general population; to better serve them it goes without saying, but alas very much against their will, until they die.

One progressive facility insists that it really *is* a home, and that the *staff* are "guests" in that home. You want to insist back, "It's OK. We know. It's hard for you, too."

To call residents "patients"—I conspire to agree; whispering, too—draws undue, unfair, unseemly attention to their chronic ill-health and suggests, perhaps, that healing will follow. Which would be misleading.

Roberta Hawkins, founder of the Alliance for Better Nursing Home Care, gave up her Saturday to guide me around. She was staunch. She wanted this to end as well as could be expected. Dad couldn't remember Roberta's name from visit to visit. But he listened comfortably when she bent down beside his wheelchair and pinched his arm. She spoke close to his ear in a rich, smoke-riddled voice; and he laughed when she made a joke.

Roberta learned her standards for care at home, practiced on loved ones: her husband, with the serious degenerative disability; her ill and elderly mother, fed, changed and bathed by Roberta for years. The woman died at home, in her own bed. Roberta was proud she had given her mother that.

At hellholes, a visit from Roberta Hawkins sent the human roaches scuttling. Occasionally, someone would try to keep her out. Roberta weighed well past two hundred pounds. She was loud, unafraid, dismissive, and right. A choir of angels roosted on her bull-proud shoulders. She made a lasting impression—like a truck bumper—on people who presented themselves as obstacles. She championed residents' rights, and one of those was the right to unrestricted visits from friends. Every nursing home resident in the state was, by definition, Roberta's friend.

My father could see that.

He had no reason to trust me. He could, though, trust Roberta.

We spent one Saturday looking at nursing homes.

The only names on the hit list were good, honest, true, in Roberta's opinion. None were absentee-managed. None were too remote. One place was run by nuns. Dad had shown no interest in religion in forty years, but he needed comfort and care. Why not nuns? He'd know how to act, at least.

The other most important criteria: near the water, with a view.

My father stood sentinel on Plymouth's town dock most days, for nearly 20 years. Taking it all in with a bunch of other retired guys. He was an unambitious, bit player in a quaint scene; watching mother tide fill the basin and lick the barnacles open each day.

I don't know what water meant to him. He didn't swim; he didn't even wade. After World War Two, he had boarded only one boat, a popular steamer named the Mt. Washington. Which fiddled around Lake Winnipesaukee on a five-town route, a toy in New Hampshire's biggest bathtub. Still, somehow, obviously, water meant something to him. "People your father's age get disoriented easily," Roberta warned. *Put him next to water!* I panicked. I wanted to make good decisions. Any straw that promised a happier ending.

Roberta and I visited three nursing waterside homes. "Arrive unannounced," Roberta instructed me. So we strolled in. We talked to residents. Or she did. I stuck a coathanger in my mouth and smiled and smiled, then pulled away in a hurry, easily overwhelmed. "All set," I'd urge her. "Seen enough." Why? Because there was *always* some bedlam happening, in the best places. Screaming dementia; an incoherent argument: somebody didn't want to get dressed, didn't want to take her pills, didn't want to have sizzling thoughts and excelsior hair and who knows what else. Mental weeds invading mental gardens.

At the end of the day, we sat in a shore restaurant, picking at seafood. Roberta smoked a cigarette (no wonder she and Dad got along), awaiting my decision; whichever I chose, she'd already promised to make a personal appeal for the next available bed.

"Call the first one," I said. *End of game; done.*

The first one we had visited that morning was small; built out in flat, modern wings around a tall Victorian home, looking like a square ten-gallon hat. This nursing home easily passed the scenery test. It perched on a bluff overlooking a large marina, and wide and busy Greenwich Bay. The place was well-kept, brightly lighted; it smelled noticeably better than others we toured. Roberta thought the owners compassionate, with high standards for the staff; framed in the office were many "zero deficiency" ratings from state inspectors. The Boston-New York train zippered past the back door, a few moments of scheduled thunder fifty yards away.

The train seemed evocative of something nice: romance, travel, adventure, excitement. Activity. Something to wonder at. A star Dad could wish on several times a day.

That's what I had to give him.

That. *And* a demented roommate three feet away in a hardshell room painted institutional green, an odd green, one of the few without hope or life.

That. *And* he didn't have to do anything ever again except draw breath. Everything else provided. *Except privacy:* that was gone. *Secrecy?* That was gone. Dad *hated* anyone knowing anything about him he didn't want them to know. Yet here he was, turned inside out for any stranger with a probe or a towel or a mean look. So that. *And* a little inconvenience; and maybe, who knew, some pain. That. *And* it was strange. He had arrived. Now for sure he could say: *I have arrived.* That. *And* we had together learned the last secret, that life at the end in our country right now is *not* for the weak, the powerless, those in need of mercy. Tending the old is filthy, thankless, boring work. Don't expect poorly paid laborers to be angels of mercy; angels don't have their own problems.

Instead: expect the worst; hope for little. You won't be disappointed, I promise.

The surprise he had for us?

Dad wanted nothing.

He didn't want his TV. He didn't want a radio. He didn't care about pictures on the walls. Visits were unimportant. "Don't feel you have to come, Tom," he insisted every time I managed to show up. Much of what he said was incoherent, but this message? This he always stated with perfect clarity: he wanted me to know. *Don't bother.* This was policy. He knew death when he saw it, smelled it, heard it. And he was ready to die. He had been ready forever. The Irish, his Irish anyway, were always ready to die. It was their principal national virtue; much appreciated during the American Civil War, the First World War, and other times when a willingness to die was the point. You can't blame the British for all that, either. The Irish always thought death was a good party.

I drove Dad out to our house from the nursing home once, as a test, to see how strong he was; what was left. Give him a shot.

He collapsed in the living room, on the first seat he came to.

Sat heavy as a basket of clothes, smoking untidily, stunned, quiet. He tried to tell stories; his tales leaked. Start, stop. He took no apparent pleasure in our company. He had to pee and couldn't climb to the second floor, where we had a guest bedroom. The floor beneath his feet was dangerous: shining oak throughout, slick as bowling alleys. Dad couldn't walk across a room without my arm to lean on.

He flunked the visit.

I'd help him move a few feet. But I wasn't going to shave him or change him or feed him or clean the pudding-like shit from his butt. Talking with him was out of the question: he just moved his mouth. Used any old words he could find. Nonsense. He had no interest left, and I had no interest left.

My wife shook her head: *He can't stay here.*

I *know.* I didn't think he could. You try, within limits. Mine were stingy. I was unemployed or starting a new business, depending on the day; and monstrously self-absorbed, anxiety ravens chewing away my midriff.

Let's pretend I could have seen the future. Let's pretend I knew he would die inside a year. Would that have made a difference? No. My first adopted child was not going to be an 80-year-old father with multiple medical crises.

Dad: "This guy—I was chumming more or less with him—he was the biggest and the ugliest-looking guy you'd ever want to look at, and they used to say to me, 'How the hell do you put up with him?' I said, 'He's a hell of a good guy. I don't do anything. He makes everything. If we move into some field, the first thing I know, he's got a big hole dug, he's got pegs in the wall, he's got a tent over the top, he's got hay on the bottom, he puts down blankets.' I said, 'He makes a home no matter where we go!'

"And what the hell was he? He was a scrap iron dealer from Maine, beard on him down to here. All he had to do was look at you, and they'd start backing off, he was that ugly-looking. I don't why he liked me, but he did. We got along fine. I let him do anything he wanted to do. We got along beautiful."

Back then, you faced death, and you could beat it. Now, everything was stacked against you. A German anthem popular in both World Wars:

> *If one of us grows tired,*
> *the other stands watch;*
> *if one of us should doubt,*
> *the other faithfully laughs.*
> *If one of us should fall,*
> *the other stands for two,*
> *for to every fighter God gave*
> *a comrade-in-arms!*

In this fight, though, God had turned up dead. I wasn't going to be Dad's comrade-in-arms. His mind was no longer in charge. His body was detritus, a collection of failed and failing systems: a hip as fragile as a toothpick tower, pustular diabetes, missing dentures. He was pre-cadaverous, now stuck in a nursing home, without a single friend who knew where he was, ashamed of his own wrecked condition.

Sometimes I'd hold his hand. I was shocked, pleasantly. He didn't pull away.

The old days? Everyone remarked on Dad's stout constitution. He *never* got sick. Super-ish human. But fathers aren't trees. Trees aren't stones. And even stones aren't infinity. We're each a tent pegged to the ground, then blown away. The storm was up. His pegs were loose.

CHAPTER 23

YEAH

DAD DIED IN KENT COUNTY HOSPITAL, LOCATED IN THE STATE OF RHODE ISLAND AND PROVIDENCE PLANTATIONS, ON AUGUST 9. He was a few months shy of 80 years old.

He died of pneumonia, the attending physician wrote, a case that lasted "weeks." Dad's warranty expired. His body wore out. The germs won or the lungs lost. Pneumonia is the leading cause of death among the elderly. His parents had died of the leading cause in the year 1919, then Spanish influenza. Now he too had died of something all the rage.

A dove flapped up into the reaches of St. Joseph's church in Holbrook, Massachusetts; its flight a fact, not much of a symbol. This particular dove *lifespan three years?* might have noted below *who knows what dove's minds track* a few unfamiliar heads. Mostly the familiar, though; the faithful who attended mass every day; any mass, every mass. A funeral was ketchup squirted over the hour, but nothing much changed. They were all women. They were all under kerchiefs. Lonely sticks; long dead from the waist down. Yes, I am an asshole; a *total* asshole, in fact. They were the realists.

St. Joseph's was the same church where, as a boy, I would faint each Sunday, knocked unconscious by a ground fog of human-manufactured carbon dioxide. Though: my mind was freshly sown with witness. Eyes laid gratefully on bra straps and slips detected first-hand beneath translucent white blouses; and of *all*, the tangible all, that those particular straps contained. Not just contained on top; on the bottom, too. When I masturbated (all the time), I masturbated to those straps stretched across perspiring female backs.

The white-strap sex jungle.

Loitering at their stations around the edges, smelling of cigarettes, stood the professional attendants, dressed in wretched, stain-hiding black.

They were in their work clothes, trousers too short by an ankle. Canted posture: stomachs out, shoulders fallen. Haircuts overdue, wings of grey hair tucked behind flaring, cartilaginous ears. Except for the heads of the younger pall bearers, which were shaven prole.

The real mourners numbered less than a dozen, sweating lightly in the August heat. Powerful fans pushed the air around the altar.

Essayist Richard Rodriguez stood, in his pressed white shirt and black trousers, listening to the priest. The priest wore his cassock, butcher's apron of the Lord; he would change for the burial.

The family of the dead child embarked in limousines.

The priest confided: "It's not as sad as you may think." Rodriquez pursed his lips. As an essayist, he was used to betraying confidences; he would betray this one; everything ended up in a book. "There is at least spectacle in the death of the young," the priest insisted. "Come to the funeral of an old lady sometime if you want to feel an empty church."

Or an old man.

Today.

The only memorial I have at hand to give him is a paragraph break.

There was almost no one in a pew except his family: my sister, me, a few outlier cousins and aunts. The family who faithfully visited graves once a year to lay flowers and uproot the crabgrass. Very few friends, very few neighbors. My two business partners came, out of respect; rightfully crossed with enlightened self-interest. We did marketing for a living; my skills would float the company for the next few years. Let's call it even. I was glad to have them there. My future, not my Dad's. I liked having a *tribe* (marketing term). I had *two* tribes. Simone was there; she was/is my wife. She protected me from my family, including my father. She was my future, too.

I knew Dad was dead because he didn't squirm in his casket, hating the fuss and the cost. Him. Though, in truth, there wasn't much of either. Undertaker: what lovely potential in a job title—"someone who takes the dead under." Boo hoo: it doesn't mean that. Undertakers *undertake.* That's all. Slap on some somber ceremony. Be done with it. Dad half-filled the cheapest deal we'd found in our undertaker's showroom. It was a presentable crate; nothing more.

At the wake, I didn't recognize the human remains cupcaked in the puckered satin.

I moved a few feet. Try a new angle. Squinted. *No.* No

one I knew.

My own dead father. Yet, if I'd encountered him on the street *resurrected*, had walked right past him without a nod. Today. in this church, he was "Dad in disguise." Somewhere he had fully slipped away and left a stand-in; a no-resemblance stand-in. No one said: "He looks so real. He looks like he could sit right up and ask for seconds." People drawn by the obituary trickled in, to kneel and cross themselves; murmur a prayer on his behalf. His few old friends who could still get around. A handful of dutiful relatives, those who were not involved in feuds.

Relatives, gathered outside for a fag, bragged about their kids; all rich geniuses. A Catholic lay pastor arrived to lead us in prayer. My brother-in-law, Bob, lapsed Lutheran and know-it-all nonpareil, took umbrage, questioning the volunteer's sincerity and loudly insulting him. Everyone ignored the outrage. The man scooted away as soon as *Amens* fell silent.

Sure, this faith-volunteer was potentially a dick, Bob. But *today* you had to press the issue? Though, honestly, it was kind of cute. We were all tense. You did something wonderfully stupid. Thank you. Broke the tension. *Good man:* Lutheran Bob at an Irish Catholic wake,

As wakes went, my father's wasn't much; not even close to mythic.

Aunt Doe's wake: now *that* was theater. Her eyes closed from exhaustion on her small, bald, maple darning ball of a head. And yet she still wore glasses, as if some menu were on its way. Was there a reading lamp in the lid of the coffin? you wondered. Aunt Doe (pronounced *Dough-ey*) was a McKay, given to acts of charity that soured. She was headed for a Presbyterian heaven run by Scots, almost certainly; waste not, want not, that bunch. In Catholic heaven they just gave you a new set of perfect eyes. Of course, the Catholics could afford the extravagance.

My father's funeral was unhaunted.

The imposter didn't look asleep, just arranged. He wore his Harris tweed jacket, and a McKay plaid tie; familiar touches supplied by my sister. His artificial teeth were gone, so his lips tucked in. You know, vanity wasn't playing a starring role.

Around his lug's hands a rosary twined. Without personality, he looked weightless; like a deflated dummy placed in inventory. There was no need for sentimental gestures. I took a picture; the Polaroid ground out a mechanical prayer as it ejected.

Dad opened one eye.

No, he didn't. Wouldn't that have been lovely for Polaroid's sinking stock.

My father smoked cigarettes for, oh, about sixty-five years.

He was an impassioned consumer. When I objected to the smell of smoke at dinner, he rattled his chains. "This is the one pleasure I have left in my life!" No argument. The man was almost 80, sagging under his own vanished weight; a dull-sighted shuffler, toothless, diabetic, with explosive blood pressure; negligent of his health, disinterested, a widower living alone in subsidized housing; a lifeform slowly eroding toward death. He had been a handsome young man. Now there wasn't one unravaged square inch on his head.

"Sorry," I sniffed. Which summarized poorly the many apologies I felt I owed him. For my cheap, snotty, steel-jacketed contempt, delivered from a distance I easily assumed thanks to my education and my opinion that Dad was rather stupid. So my mother had often implied. Common opinion in our little nest. My sister confided, "Father's not that bright." She was working out a bit of family history. "I think that may be the real reason he never went to college." It sounded almost like a sturdy virtue: *"My dad's not smart at all. How's yours?"*

My father loved cigarettes. Cherished the little buggers.

Chemically-incited tobacco fragments tubed inside chemically-saturated-to-burn-better paper. Cherished them I think finally more than wife (suicide) or offspring (fled in disdain). Nicotine was dependable, comforting, nonjudgmental, easily purchased at a good price; always the same number, tapped from a pack. A friend indeed. Best friend he had. The tidal caress of smoke inside lungs? Sublime. An internal hug. Health is for the weak.

G.I.s in the field got free cigarettes with their food. Enemy fire, weeks of discomfort, paralyzing boredom, meals tasted like shit anyway: all great incentives to smoke.

Lots of U.S. men loved their cigarettes, until about 1965; then the number who smoked fell below 50 percent for the first time in four decades. The Great Depression, the War Years, and the Fifties all went up in deeply savored smoke. Women, too; though not as much. For them, 1960 was the peak; still, the number lighting up was under 40 percent. Something held them back. Womb? Tobacco? Unsure.

Dad smoked unfiltered Camels. Two packs, forty times a

day, he screwed a tube of tobacco between his lips and lit up. The pack in his shirt pocket was his pet. His finger-stroked it. Cigarettes were continuity. He'd smoked before the war. The war ingrained the habit in millions of new lungs. Hundreds of thousands of workers contributed a dollar each week to buy cigarettes—pacifiers—for the fighting boys overseas. For G.I.s, smokes were free and plentiful; coin of the realm—"Ja! Zigaretten!"—in occupied Germany, a transitional economy based primarily on good American tobacco. Getting laid demanded food, nylons, zigaretten.

For three decades, Dad lovingly applied from his lips tiny brushstrokes of amber patina—a puff at a time—to the knotty pine cabinets in our kitchen. The softest things out of his mouth. Smoke rings wobbled off at our insistence— "Do it, Dad!"—settling like quoits around an upheld finger. Smoking was a craft he'd mastered. Yellow stained his white hair, marking his membership in the zigaretten guild; like a machinist missing the tip of a finger. Without a cigarette planted in my father's face, life had no meaning. He veiled himself in smoke, hiding there.

The nursing home took away his matches and lighters because he wouldn't obey the rules. He'd light up in his room, forgetting (ignoring) that smoking was forbidden except in the lounge.

He told me repeatedly that the staff were stealing his cigarettes and lighters, another sad dilemma. He was right. Maybe not in all the details, but right enough. Stealing from people with diminished capacity is the law of the jungle in nursing homes. On one visit to the wretched joint in Plymouth, I found Dad's good watch gone from his hairy wrist; and a cheap broken Timex strapped in its place. Another mark against him: his time was done and gone. A shame. Shame on preying thieves. True, he couldn't tell time any more. But Dad took pride in his watch. You minimum-wage fuckers. Yeah yeah, the system made you do it. Thieves are thieves. If you're old and helpless, welcome to the thieves' den.

Victory in Europe—VE day—didn't signal the end of Dad's war. The Japanese Empire was still fighting, with delusional and suicidal determination. Judging from the bitter defense of Iwo Jima and Okinawa, Allied planners now estimated that a full-scale invasion of the Japanese home islands could cost up to a million extra U.S. casualties. On Okinawa, 7,400 Japanese troops surrendered. But 110,000 fought to their deaths with a tenaciousness that left little doubt about Japanese willingness to continue. American divisions on Okinawa suffered 35 percent casualties. The math horrified decision-makers finished with Europe and wary of further sacrifice. The first of many landings on Japanese home soil would alone yield over a quarter million casualties, "or about as many battle deaths as the United States had suffered throughout the world on all fronts so far," military authority John Keegan figured.

From May to August, 1945, it was a cliffhanger for G.I.s in Europe. Men like my father expected to ship out for the Pacific. And die.

Meantime, he and a pal hung around Paris for a few weeks; then Frankfurt. "So we're in Frankfurt, and this guy wanted to go somewhere, and I'm standing on a street corner. I said, 'You coming right back?' 'Yeah, I'm coming right back.' So while I'm standing there, this German civilian—a man—walks right up to me, and he kept saying,

'Japanese kaput! Japanese kaput!' Pretty soon this guy comes back. I said, 'Have you heard anything about the Japanese surrendering?' He said no. He said, 'Let's go up the Red Cross.' So we went up the Red Cross, and there it was, coming over the radio. They had dropped the atom bomb the day before. And the next day Japan surrendered."

The wounded often suppose, "I must reconcile with my father or mother before he/she dies. Say my piece. Make peace. Speak my heart. Put it all behind us, the garbage: a lifetime of anger and grievance and self-imposed exile and sulking and hurt feelings and erratic temper. To say: Mom or Dad, I love you. The simple truth. Why wouldn't I/ shouldn't I? You're the flesh that brought my flesh into the world...."

Sure. Und so weiter. I don't know how the speech should end. It ends differently for each of us. You understand, it's an emotional fantasy; almost (not quite) a sexual fantasy: it expresses our desire for a pleasing outcome, a release of tension in a controlled situation; it's a safe exploration of an environment where the forbidden—unguarded talk with a parent—is permitted. It has something to do with a need to express love.

I tried; I couldn't. Most people can't, I imagine. *Fuck:* you're either out of the nest, or you're not. You don't suddenly become open and honest after decades of just the opposite. Plus, takes two to tango: I'm certainly not going to open up if you won't/haven't/didn't. What to say? *Let's review my sordid past.* I'm sorry I acted like such an idiot? *(Your turn.)* I've thought about how we've thrown away a life together, out of spite. *(You?)* I'm sorry I failed you, *if* I did *(yes, yes; of course I did)*. Hint, hint: forgive me, I'll forgive you. Can we *please* move on now?

Well, no. The Irish don't move on. Each mark against, graven; sins against, graven; a knife in the chest, a souvenir. Thank you. Each betrayal tattooed into the DNA. The Irish have no common truck with science. Science is for the god-arse-fucking English. You do me. I do you. Question is: *Clubs or stones?*

Yet here we are: the day of reconciliation.

I sit in Dad's tightly sealed apartment.

Smoke from his cigarette tumbles out the top of the lampshade, riding the only draft in the room. A cone of stage light dramatizes a familiar deeply woven green and formerly white tablecloth on which my plate had rested for a decade anyway, until I left home for college. And on the tablecloth: two sets of tapping fingers; his, mine I guess. Otherwise his apartment's dark; its corners obscure; shelves cluttered with dusty keepsakes.

The apartment is, I see, a shorthand version of my childhood home.

I recognize everything. Just a lot less of it.

He's saved the pictures. And trophies. I was something in high school, using objective measures; lots of local achievements: team captain twice, record holder, selected for the statewide band, honor society, things I don't remember. I was also eyes-rolling-around-in-my-forehead mental. Terrified. Monumentally egoistic. Playing with myself like I had a windmill attached to my groin.

Today would be the day: I'd reached that inflexible decision.

If I did not speak the truth today—about you, me, us—I couldn't go on. Really. Rite of passage. I'd learned, *Do this if you are any kind of (1), adult, (2) man, (3) son, (4) honest person.* That thought for how long? Five years? At least. Twenty-five years? Probably. Of course you want to be speak freely with your father. He's your guide. He's your foil. He's your cautionary tale. You evolve together. So. "Today *is* the day!" I'd promised my car's dashboard as I drove up see him. I saw him—what?—maybe four times a year? I released the breath I'd grabbed and clung to. Reporting ready to jump off the seawall. Rocks below? Sharks? Who cared; a little emotional truth would not kill me. Or him. I was going to say it. I was sick of feeling angry. Anger might have helped some people; it wasn't helping me. Of course, the first words would be hard. Finally uttering the *very words* after years of rewrites. Like trying to give birth through your mouth. How would Gilbert and Sullivan proceed (the light opera approach)? Bernard Shaw (a theatre of ideas)? How would a screenwriter set it up? Did something follow or was this the climax? Was I in act two or act three?

"So," I offered, "how are the Red Sox doing?"

I didn't know baseball teams or players or standings. The only things I liked about the game were the food, the beer, and the glorious burst of green when you first stepped into a stadium. After that it was a clinical study in tedium. For me; though beer could dull the ennui.

I assumed Dad was a fan. He had played a lot of ball when he was a kid and talked about the town teams and the semi-professional circuit. Surely the Red Sox, the most distressing team in baseball fandom, could tinder up a little conversational fire.

"Enh," he dismissed them atop a buckle of phlegm. He pulled out a handkerchief. Wouldn't want to speculate on when that was last cleaned. "To tell you the truth, Tom, I don't follow it that much."

OK.

Let's just start, then.

Dad was in his seventieth year, his body a demonstration of the effects of gravity on loose flesh in the absence of countervailing forces such as good diet and upperbody exercise. Not today; but other days, I took pictures of him to have a record of how he was changing. He looks skeptical in the photos. He walked maybe 50 yards daily, and drove the rest without remorse. He'd earned a rest in the 1930s, the 1940s, the 1950s, and the 1960s. The Great Depression, World War Two, the factory, his wife's suicide. He'd earned his fucking rest; *he talked like* that *behind my back*. And he was taking it; The rest.

"Dad," I said. His eyes slid toward me.

"Dad, do you remember when...?" I lost my insertion point. *Which when?*

Was I about to apologize for all those regrettable things I'd said to him? Hurtful remarks that hung by the hundreds, like fishhooks, from my heart's wall? Complaining at thirteen in a bitter rage: "Why are we so poor!" Because my family wouldn't buy the one thing I needed to keep my head above an engulfing sense of worthlessness: a new car; instead they were saving for my college education, as if that mattered.

Or long years after, erupting in derision: "Dad, you can't live in a tin can!" Because he wanted to move near his friends up in New Hampshire, and a nice mobile home was all he could afford. I could not envision a father so fallen in his circumstances that his residence would be a trailer park, alongside all the other plaster gnomes.

"Tom, please don't laugh at where I live," he admonished me quietly that time. Let's be authentic. He'd dodged bullets fighting Nazis. I was a preppie snob. This I wanted to say, "I love you despite everything we got wrong about each other." Who cared anymore?

Yet.

I didn't dare. *I couldn't push the words off my tongue*. In my mind, Dad was a man who didn't *believe* in love. Who *ridiculed* words like love. Who thought that love was like Santa: something *for kids!* One other thing I knew for sure: any lousy deficiency I suspected of someone else was true of me as well. I was the one who didn't believe in love. *But I did!* My eyes thickened, about to overflow. A grimace ached to round out a smile. I tried to start again. Couldn't.

He said to me, "It's OK."

Smiled like a Buddha because his head looked like a Buddha.

We lived an hour apart. Unmetaphorically speaking. A year when I felt guilty, I'd see him five or six times, including Christmas, the Christian holiday of choice and certainly the family favorite. By this time I thought Christ was no more than a baseball-card figure of his time. Soapy Irish Catholics and the Protestants agreed: Christmas foremost. Loving it for secular reasons: plentiful if not delicious food; seeing the family once and be done; gifts each side could lampoon later. Across the divide. My mother downsized her immediate family. Who wanted to face the relatives? Or acknowledge their co-existence? Christmas was now always at my sister's house. Total annual face time: no more than 16 hours. Add phone calls, and what did our companionship amount to? Maybe 20 hours of uneasy conversation over twelve months. A relationship never fully, irreparably snapped. Tenuous as a weed.

Dad and I stared at each other. To make sure we were still alive.

I was from the Moon; him, too.

I stayed mute. In fact, by now I needed a psychiatrist's care, complete with a plunging needle dripping oblivion. My palm bounced against the plastic steering wheel. I was obsessed *slash* petrified of explaining my feelings to him. I knew, like sunrise, that derision would toast his words.

Furthermore, I knew that what I had on *my* mind—the little rudder kicks and absolutions—were wrong to begin with; an hysterical defense. He expected the world to be a shit. He expected me to be a shit. I *was* a shit. *Was there something else you wished to discuss?*

How did I really feel about him and me? I couldn't find a thing to say that didn't seem like an obvious lie; or devious, self-serving, disappointing, stupid. I was in suspended emotional animation. Been there *really* since the second grade? Prejudged, locked in a trance I renewed with each visit. And how did he feel about me? Not a clue. Which mattered ... (sigh) very little. Until. Until it became my responsibility to make arrangements for his care and comfort.

And his world plunged screaming into mine, blasting custard everywhere. I had a secret mission: to save him from his decline, make him whole and immortal. Pump some sense back into him. End the confusion. Allay his suspicions. Make it all add up.

But he was no longer a co-conspirator. I desperately needed a window into his heart. He admitted nothing. If he tried too hard to converse, gibberish fluttered out. "How are you feeling?" His first question at every visit.

"I'm OK." All purpose.

He didn't have another question. He didn't want to make a mistake.

I scrutinized his upkeep: a military buzzcut, leaving tiny filaments sparkling on the sides of his scabby dome; a careful shave, not too many bristles untrimmed around the brown lips; clean clothes.

He looked up from his hospital bed: "Tom, you don't have to come."

Just saying. My father saw duty in my face. Worn like a mask.

As always now I smiled down. A pre-emptive strike.

"How's work?" His next question.

They came in a sequence. The bones of his values poking through. It never went far. He didn't know and never asked really what I did for a living. I could have been a stranger. However I paid the mortgage, however I earned the pecuniary respect of my spouse, it never happened in his world. Not an endangered species: a *fabulist* species.

I worked for somebody. I had a paycheck.

Then I was *fired* by that somebody. Clear evidence of a character flaw *in me*. I had no paycheck. Dad was union. No one was fired. Anyone fired *in management* deserved it, ipso facto. I had some kind of business going now, after the fact.

The few inches of sky out his window were as blue as a paint chip.

I made a living somehow. Nothing he knew. Understood. Respected. "Fine," I answered. I'm doing fine. *Me-jet-ly*. Delivered in an impeccably chipper voice. *Really*. Not exactly the truth. I wanted to advance past a square on the gameboard as Dad knew it, circa this year. I didn't want him or any other human in my immediate family to worry (translation: *judge*).

And there was his WIIFM: *what's in it for me*. The practical side. *You will Dad be cared for*, I wanted my answer to convey: *whatever it took*. **I might look like a putz. I am all you have. I understand that.** The chapel in my heart wasn't big.

At least I had made that vow. Sincerely.

I added a kicker, delivered with stage presence: "Business is good."

Now.

True?

My stomach churned like a washing machine 24 hours seven days.

I was what robots became, before new models arrived. *Human obsoletes.*

My teensy sub-chapter-S corporation had a couple of skeptical clients. One of my two partners was an Olympics-grade incompetent, angling for a divorce. It was perverse fun to watch him fall 3,000 feet down El Capitan. To a point. My paycheck was one-fifth what it had been 12 months before; though my and our expensive lifestyle continued full strength and without question.

For lunch money, I stirred coin jars with a stick. And my wife carried our hefty mortgage alone, like a pregnancy. Without complaining, mind you. She = brick. But I saw a monster in the mirror no one else could see: a panicked face loosely rolling on my neck. A placard hung off me labeled by the World Court and my disposition: *Failure. Yes! Of course!* I treated my father, the invalid, like a child: *Don't you worry your little bald head about it honey.*

I am now 60. As I travel and flee and write. The waitress at the U.S.S. Chowder Pot in Connecticut calls me "hon," concluding her every inquiry: "Was that delicious, hon?" *I know I look old to you; but do you mind?*

And yet here I am, same attitude: **Everything will work out just fine; nothing you can do; end of story OK?** I thought back one hundred years, to when I'd entered second grade. Dad saw something then he didn't like at all: that *I was not happy*.

Which offended him.

He knelt to eye level, to scrutinize my face. "What is *wrong* with you?" Dad asked.

I had his brown eyes. Sometimes backed by plaids, all to myself. I liked that.

"Look at you," he said perplexed. He was in charge. I rolled my lips up like an awning; at age seven you're all false starts. "Why do you worry all the time?" he laughed softly, soothingly. *Did I?* I didn't know. He reached over and stroked my head. Confided man to man: "You're *too young* to worry."

OK. *Man*, I'd love to stop. Jumping the gun I guessed.

Nervous in the service; Dad said that all the time. Sure; covered everything from bug bites to anal intrusion. Something you weren't supposed to be: *Nervous in the service*. "OK?" I answered. I liked having his eyes on me.

He didn't stand up.

Still on his knees, in our tiny living room.

He studied himself some more in whatever miniature mirror I was to him.

He made me a promise there and then that *the world will keep*.

"There'll be plenty to worry about when you get older." With a goldsmith's precision, Dad accurately weighed my soul in the scale of his experience. I was fragile. Probably doomed. As a good pragmatic Irish father, the best he could do that day was swaddle me in hopeless platitudes. The chilling message, passed down *this day* this moment father to son: *If you think* this *is bad, just wait. No one escapes*.

Almost four decades later, looking at him: hard to argue.

CHAPTER 28

EULOGY

I GREW UP DURING THE TELEVISION DUSK OF THE 1950S AND '60S, BEFORE THESE THINGS WERE PERFECTLY CLEAR. But I never believed women were less capable than men. Certainly not in my household.

My sister marched around like a one-girl "capability pride" parade. From the moment she could talk about how self-assured she was, she did. She actually crowed. She knew.

And my mother made money. She put herself through business school, riding a bus into Boston and back for years at night.

In my waist-high opinion, my mother was a ton more capable than my father—better educated, more ambitious, smarter, wiser, stronger in everything except maybe lifting capacity.

Until she committed suicide.

But maybe that was even more proof, who knows.

My dad told war stories.

ABOUT THE AUTHOR

Tom Ahern's literary career peaked abruptly in 1984 when the New York Times said a few nice things about his first full book of short stories.

A half-dozen years later, another Ahern story collection came out — this time, the reinvented writings of an unforgiveable early-1800s French horror author, Petrus Borel; slit throats, cannibalism, voodoo, that sort of thing. Ahern was trying to learn to plot.

Then nothing ... until now. Ahern remained a "word artist." He wrote prolifically. But he stopped trying to publish.

Tom Ahern graduated from Brown University with a MA in Creative Writing. That program's first head, Keith Waldrop, was a sublime teacher and model and mentor; in 2009, Keith won the National Book Award in Poetry, capping a rich and mesmerizing career. Rosmarie Waldrop, Keith's just-as-celebrated wife/poet/translator, was also an irreplaceable mentor/model/teacher for Tom Ahern. "Honest tribute. As any kind of writer, I don't exist without them. I would have disappeared into the daily gravel when I was 22 without their years of help and belief and support."

That was Act One.

In Act Two, Ahern learned the craft of pleasing general (rather than literary) audiences. For more than three decades now, he's paid his bills (including the mortgage on that second home in France) as a successful commercial copywriter.

And then the nonprofit sector opened its arms. Tom Ahern began writing fundraising appeals. They worked. He began teaching. People responded to his plain-spoken, common-sense, zero-jargon approach. He began writing "how-to-improve" books that became industry standards: his 7th fundraising book will appear in 2019.

In 2016, the New York Times mentioned Ahern again. "Tom Ahern … is one of the country's most sought-after creators of fund-raising messages."

112 Harvard Ave #65
Claremont, CA 91711 USA

pelekinesis@gmail.com
www.pelekinesis.com
Pelekinesis titles are available through Small
Press Distribution, Baker & Taylor, Ingram,
Bertrams, and directly from the publisher's
website.